Norman Hardy.

THE KLONDIKERS

Norman Handy

novum pro

www.novum-publishing.co.uk

All rights of distribution, including via film, radio, and television, photomechanical reproduction, audio storage media, electronic data storage media, and the reprinting of portions of text, are reserved

Printed in the European Union on environmentally friendly, chlorine- and acid-free paper.

© 2017 novum publishing

ISBN 978-3-99048-714-3
Editing: Nicola Ratcliff, BA
Cover photos: minnystock, Dmitryzubarev | Dreamstime.com
Cover design, layout & typesetting: novum publishing

www.novum-publishing.co.uk

CONTENTS

Chapter 1: The Klondike Gold Rush   7
Chapter 2: Gold 19
Chapter 3: The Rocky Mountaineer 37
Chapter 4: Vancouver and Victoria 49
Chapter 5: Voyageur canoe and Victoria 61
Chapter 6: Juneau 77
Chapter 7: Skagway 87
Chapter 8: WP&YR over the White Pass 103
Chapter 9: Whitehorse 113
Chapter 10: The Golden Stairs 125
Chapter 11: Canoe to Carmacks 143
Chapter 12: Bear Encounter 165
Chapter 13: Five Finger Rapids 177
Chapter 14: Below Fort Selkirk 189
Chapter 15: Dawson City 205
Chapter 16: Gold Panning 219
Chapter 17: Sourtoe cocktails 227
Chapter 18: What happened to …? 231
Author's note 237
Anecdotes 239

CHAPTER 1

The Klondike Gold Rush

It was not until July 1897 that the ships, Excelsior docked in San Francisco and a few days later, the Portland docked in Seattle and what had happened up in the Yukon the previous summer, leaked beyond the Yukon to the outside world. The Yukon lies in the far north west of Canada, named after the great Yukon River that flows through it and turns west across the border into neighbouring Alaska. The state covers an area of nearly half a million square kilometres, or put another way, twice the area of the whole of the United Kingdom. It became a state in 1898, when the increase in population allowed it to be a state in its own right and split away from the Northwest Territories.

Less than half way up the state is Dawson City, which sits on the confluence of the Yukon and a tributary called the Klondike River. Here was the scene of an extraordinary gold rush, following a discovery in 1896, that propelled a small village into the most populous city in Canada, only for it to shrink again and now has a population of just 1,300. This is the story about the lure of gold, and the journey that a prospector may have taken from the Prairies east of the Rockies to the gold fields.

The tallest mountain in the state is Mount Logan 5,959m which is also Canada's tallest peak and the second highest on the continent, situated in the Kluane National Park, in the south west of the state. Despite its huge area, the state's current population is about 33,000, with two thirds living in or around the state capital, Whitehorse, located on the Yukon River, towards the southern edge of the state. In short, it is a large area, extensively covered with forest in the south, thinning to tundra in the far north, with a very low population density of 0.07 people per sqkm (that compares to 255.6 per sqkm for the United Kingdom).

In summer, the weather is dry and sunny. In winter, it is very cold, with snow starting to fall as early as September, and the rivers freeze over in October. The ground can freeze to a depth of three metres and the long cold winter can last through till May, before any sign of the first frost free days. Thunderstorms can have lightning strikes that ignite the dry forests. The resulting fires can burn for days and spread over hundreds of hectares.

The First Nation peoples (the politically correct reference for the local native Indians of the area) have lived and hunted here for centuries, eking out a living in these harsh conditions. The first Europeans to show an interest in the region, were fur trappers followed by traders, largely represented by the Hudson's Bay Company. The area had been explored by the Hudson's Bay Company, and by the Russians (who ruled Alaska until 1867 when they sold it to the U.S. for the knock down price of just $7.2m) but fur trapping was the main aim and they over looked rumours of gold.

Travel was painstakingly slow over land, as there were few trails and the First Nations made extensive use of the rivers. There are now some major roads in the area, such as the Alaskan Highway, built during the Second World War, to ensure that there was a secure land route into Alaska and the Klondike Highway, linking Skagway in Alaska through Whitehorse and north to Dawson City. The Dempster Highway runs north, from Dawson to the Beaufort Sea in the Arctic and is unpaved, but all the roads were only recently constructed. Until the end of the 19th century, over land travel through the state was difficult and slow, particularly through the forest, as there were no roads. But this didn't put off prospectors, who were used to challenging conditions. Gold had been found in some areas over the border in Alaska, in the gold mining town of Circle City, with a population of 1,200 people, which was established in 1893. Gold had been found in small quantities near Dawson, but not in sufficiently large quantities, for claims to be staked out.

Robert Henderson, born in Nova Scotia in 1857, prospected in Colorado for 14 years up to 1894, when he set out for Alaska, landing at Dyea. From there, he portered his equipment and supplies across the Chilkoot Pass. Once over the pass, he built a boat on the shores of Lake Lindeman and paddled down the Yukon River. He was prospecting along the river and climbed a dome shaped mountain, looking out across the Yukon forest with the mountains in the distance, when he came across George Carmacks' camp.

George Carmack was born 24 September 1860, in California. In 1885, he had prospected the upper Yukon River without success. He joined William Ogilvie's survey party, to guide them across the Chilkoot Pass. He then spent many years throughout the Yukon, logging, hunting, fur trapping, fishing and prospecting.

By August 1896, George Carmack and his extended family, consisting of his native wife Kate, their daughter Graphie, her brother, 'Skookum' Jim Mason and nephew, 'Dawson' Charlie, had set up a fishing camp on the Thron-diuck river. This was reputed to be the best river for catching salmon in the area. The native name, Thron-diuck was too complicated for Europeans to pronounce so it became bastardised over a period into Klondike.

There were several conversations between George Carmack and Robert Henderson, but at one point, Robert Henderson disclosed that he had found some gold flakes or 'colours' up Hunter Creek but didn't want the natives to stake a claim there. He also had tobacco that George Carmack's party had run out of, but he refused to trade with the locals. One of Robert Henderson's parting comments to George Carmack was the suggestion to prospect up Rabbit Creek (now called Bonanza Creek), a small tributary. He asked them to let him know if they found anything and he moved on.

The Carmack party went up Rabbit Creek and found gold on 16 August 1896, although their first haul was barely enough flakes of gold to fill a spent Winchester cartridge case. But, the potential promised considerable quantities. The group agreed that George Carmack would stake the claim as his, as they were wary of the mining authorities, recognising the claim of a native Indian. George Carmack, duly staked out four claims, two for himself and one each for Dawson Charlie and Skookum Jim. He registered them at the local police station, over a hundred kilometres down the Yukon, on Forty Mile River. Not surprisingly, they didn't tell Robert Henderson, having refused to trade his tobacco with them.

News travelled along the river quickly and other claims were staked out on Rabbit Creek. Another prospector found more gold, up what was to become, Eldorado Creek and yet more claims were staked out. News reached the 'over wintering' prospectors and miners, at Circle City. Despite the harsh winter conditions, several set off to stake their claims, so as not to lose out. Robert Henderson did not hear about the finds and the staking of claims, until the best claims had already been staked, including the most productive claims staked out by Antoine Stander and several of his colleagues.

News of the new finds did not reach the world outside of the Yukon for quite a while, due to the bad weather of winter and the frozen river. About a year later, in July 1897, a few days after the ships, Excelsior, docked in San Francisco and the Portland, docked in Seattle, the news finally leaked beyond Yukon and reached the outside world. The Portland arrived in Seattle with more than a ton of gold on board. Returning prospectors, sometimes with hundreds of ounces of gold, each worth over a million dollars (this is over a billion dollars in today's prices) told their stories, which were printed in newspapers. The news about the gold find, soon spread far and wide.

The public's imagination was gripped by gold fever. People left their jobs and homes to journey to the goldfields, in search of fortune and adventure. Other newspapers, reprinted stories and carried human interest stories that kept the gold news fresh. Even some of those that didn't actually go, still made money from the 'gold find' news, advertising and selling goods for the prospectors, allegedly, specially designed for the Yukon. Other more cerebral entrepreneurs published guidebooks on the routes to take and how to mine for gold.

The prospectors were joined relatively quickly by others, who could see they could make a living out of the miners. Writers, photographers, traders, carpenters, gamblers, casino operators, entertainers, barmen, pimps, prostitutes and con men, decided they also had a nose for adventure and wanted to try a bit of gold mining on the side.

Shipping companies made money out of the prospectors as well. Ticket prices for the sea voyage north, went up almost daily, encouraging other boat owners to join the race, to carry people and provisions northwards. Some boats were not seaworthy or suitable and several of the over loaded or unseaworthy boats sank.

The quickest route to reach the gold fields was by ship to Alaska, to the sheltered port of St Michael, a short distance up the coast from the mouth of the Yukon River. Travellers could transfer to a river boat that could take them up river, to Dawson. Boats could actually navigate further upstream, all the way to Whitehorse. This route had the advantage of speed, the ability to take as much equipment that a prospector might need and avoided the difficulty of travelling overland, in the inhospitable terrain.

This route had two major drawbacks. Firstly, it was expensive, even before the shipping companies took advantage of the prospectors and started inflating the prices, secondly, it was only feasible when the river was ice free. For seven months of the year, the river was impassable as it was frozen or as the ice broke up there were large chunks of ice being carried along by the river, making navigation difficult and dangerous. If you hadn't made it to Dawson before the freeze started you could be marooned on the river's edge for the winter, for several months until the river was ice free again.

The route by river boat wasn't even danger free in summer, as the boats were typically built of wood and used wood as a fuel for the boilers, so there was the ever present danger of fire on board. Navigation wasn't always safe either, as although the river boats had shallow drafts, there was always a risk of grounding, even for experienced navigators of the river, due to the constantly shifting sandbanks, hidden beneath the river's surface. Of the 1,800 people who attempted this route, in the first autumn, after news of gold leaked out from the Yukon, only 43 reached their destination, before the river froze. Many were stranded along the river and had to wait all winter, until the spring thaw, to continue their journey.

There were all Canadian routes overland that could be followed. The shortest at 1,600kms started in Ashcroft, in British Colombia, 330kms up the major modern artery of the Trans-Canada Highway, 90kms west of Kamloops. It runs north parallel to the coast, through the Rockies. The route heads through swamps, over mountains and across gorges, until it reaches Glenora. Here, it is joined by another route, taken by some prospectors, who had travelled up the coast to Wrangell on the Alaskan shoreline, up the Stikine River, then across the Rockies and down to Glenora.

The route continues from Glenora, over the state line, between British Columbia and Yukon, towards Teslin Lake. Finally, it reaches the Yukon River, to follow it down to Dawson. Fifteen hundred people travelled the Ashcroft route and 5,000 took the part sea and part overland option, via Wrangell. The route was too gruelling for some of the pack animals, who struggled with the cold, the soft ground and the mountainous terrain. Some prospectors, found the route too hard in winter, so they set up camp and waited till spring came. Many animals died en route, leaving prospectors with piles of equipment and no means to carry it any further.

Three other routes started from Edmonton. One route headed north west, crossing the Peace River and Liard River to Dawson, the other two routes were a combination of overland and river. One route followed the Pelly River to Dawson and the other, had a lot of easier river and shorter overland travelling, but the big drawback was reaching the Yukon River 600kms downstream of Dawson, requiring a tiring struggle to get upstream or a long overland trip. Nearly 2,000 chose these routes but only 685 eventually made it.

Some prospectors attempted to avoid Canadian customs by sailing to Valdez, further up the coast from Skagway. This proposed route crossed a glacier that proved very difficult to negotiate and only a few managed to climb it successfully. The wilderness beyond also proved too difficult to negotiate and those that got this far turned around.

The most popular route was a route up the coast, a short overland trek and then a long river journey down to Dawson. Prospectors would take a boat up the coast from wherever they started from, to arrive in Skagway or the nearby town of Dyea, 20kms further up the coast by road. Skagway was located at the head of the Lynn Canal, on the Alaskan coast, 125kms up the coast from Juneau, the state capital since 1906.

After landing in Skagway, the next part of the route was over the White Pass, named not for the thick covering of snow found in the winter, but after Sir Thomas White, the Canadian Minister of the Interior. From here, the trail headed down to Lindeman Lake and onto Bennett Lake.

The route traverses several mountains, but the paths in places were narrow, very steep with large boulders and sharp rocks. Horses were worked to death, giving the pass the alternative name of Dead Horse Trail, a term coined by the writer, Jack London, who was one of the prospectors that took the trail. The numbers using the pass wore away the trail and created increasingly difficult conditions. Therefore, local authorities closed the pass in late 1897, stranding 5,000 prospectors in Skagway who had hoped to cross the pass.

There was a toll road that had been constructed and had recently opened, which reduced the pressure on the pass. This was a 19km long road, built by former Northern Pacific Railroad construction engineer, George Brackett. Prospectors ignored the toll gates and the venture was a commercial failure. The colder weather, which froze the ground, reduced the wear and tear on the pass and it was re-opened by the authorities.

An alternative to the White Pass was the Chilkoot Trail which was higher and steeper than the White Pass. This was a more popular route for some people, who used it to reach Lake Bennett, as the route was shorter than the White Pass. It was a gentle gradient until the last section, which was too steep for pack animals. This was called the Golden Stairs, named from the steps, cut into the snow and ice that would lead people to riches.

The cold, the steepness of the trail and the quantity of people using it made for slow progress up the last 300m slope. Prospectors and animals would stand in line for hours, due to blockages, but no one wanted to step out of line, as they may not be able to re-join the line. This was the route that I was going to explore, to reach Bennett Lake and then follow the river downstream to Dawson.

Prospectors carried their wares up the slope themselves and had to undertake the journey several times, to get all of their goods across the border. At the base of this steep slope were The Scales, where the North West Mounted Police would weigh the prospectors' gear, to check they had the one ton of supplies required by the authorities, to ensure they could survive the first year in Yukon. The gold rush was vividly recorded by several early photographers, for instance, by Eric Hegg, whose stark black and white iconic images of the Golden Stairs on the Chilkoot Pass, became iconic images that were widely distributed.

An alternative to carrying the goods up the slope in several trips, was employing a porter. This also gave employment to those that needed the income, such as other struggling prospectors and the local First Nations peoples. Activity carried on throughout the winter, when the weather allowed, although avalanches were a constant danger. One particularly deadly event in April 1898, killed 60 people.

Entrepreneurs saw opportunities and other methods were developed, to get goods to the summit where animals could not venture. Aerial ropeways were built and at a significant cost, goods could be transported to the summit, thus cutting the time to cross the Chilkoot Pass. This was only if prospectors could afford the rather steep charges.

After 1867 and the American purchase of Alaska, the boundaries between America and Canada were still not defined and were open to dispute. Both countries claimed Dyea and Skagway, but the issue was not pressing until the numbers of prospectors brought matters back into sharp focus. Diplomacy would have to wait, as the immediate matter was not, where the border was, but enforcing the rules on the thousands of people making their way across the border.

The North West Mounted Police was established in 1873 and was a fore runner of the police force that would eventually evolve into the Royal Canadian Mounted Police. They were the enforcement arm of the various requirements, set out by the Canadian authorities. They enforced custom duties on those crossing and confiscated illegal firearms on the border, wherever it may be and set up police check points on the White Pass and the Chilkoot Trail. These were proper functioning border controls and hence, some people's preference to travel to Valdez, to try to avoid those duties.

One regulation that was strictly enforced, was the requirement that prospectors had a year's supply of food, to tide them over, as they attempted to satisfy their gold acquisition aspirations, whether or not they had money, or were successful in striking gold. The authorities didn't want a massive influx of people or to be responsible for their deaths, if things went wrong. The Yukon could be a harsh environment and individuals had to be self-reliant.

This also had the effect, that if you were planning to carry your goods yourself over the pass, to save on employing porters, or paying for the aerial ropeways, several journeys would have to be made, to get it all over the passes. This had the unfortunate effect of increasing the wear and tear and congestion on the pass, which explains why it had so much usage and had to be shut.

After negotiating the passes, whichever one was chosen, the trails converged and the next challenge that had to be faced, was at Lake Lindeman, or a bit further down the valley on Lake Bennett. The next part of the journey for the original prospectors was to build a boat and follow the river 800kms to Dawson. The modern road route is only 600kms, but it takes a much more direct route, but was not built at the time of the gold rush.

Many of the trees immediately around the lake were cut down and various rafts and boats were built to carry their occupants down the river. The river is generally relatively easy to navigate but there is a dangerous set of rapids just upstream of Whitehorse, called Miles Canyon, the White Horse Rapids and Squaw Rapids. Miles Canyon was originally called the Grand Canyon but Schwatka renamed it Miles Canyon, after Brigadier General Nelson A Miles.

Frederick Schwatka, from 29th September 1849–2nd November 1892, was an army lieutenant, with a law and a medical degree. He had led an earlier expedition to King William Island, high in the Canadian arctic, to search for Franklin's lost expedition of HMS Erebus and HMS Terror, prompted partly by Franklin's fame and the offer of a finder's reward. The first relics were found off the east coast of Beechey Island.

They went by ship up the Hudson Bay and then using dogs and sledges, the expedition travelled across vast stretches of the north. They found a skeleton but no papers. In 1883 he travelled over the Chilkoot Pass, built a boat and travelled the length of the river to its mouth, renaming Canadian landmarks after people he admired, without any regard to local place names or sensitivities.

Several boats carrying prospectors, during the gold rush, capsized during the descent of the Miles Canyon rapids and people drowned; partly because the prospectors were not used to building boats or shooting rapids. The NWMP took action and introduced safety rules. Boats were vetted for their robustness and weight carrying ability. Women and children were not allowed to travel on boats through the rapids, so had to disembark and walk around them. Boats carrying passengers had to have a licenced pilot. This cost money and some decided to unload their boat and let it drift down the rapids empty, hoping to collect it undamaged, at the bottom of the rapids.

Then from Whitehorse to Dawson, it was just a matter of travelling down the river. After Miles Canyon, the rest of the river is relatively easy to navigate. There are no waterfalls or strong rapids, except a couple of places that are more challenging. There is Lake Laberge which is 50kms long and with its unpredictable weather, boats have to rely on either sail or oars, to get back into the flowing waters of the river at the end of the lake, to carry them downstream. The other hazard is Five Finger Rapids where four hard rocky islands divide the river into five channels and only the most easterly channel is navigable.

Finally, people arrived in Dawson, after a long and sometimes, dangerous voyage. Of the more than 100,000 who started out, fewer than 40,000 reached Dawson and of these, less than half would become prospectors and find gold. The majority were men, but it is thought that eight per cent were women, mostly travelling with their husbands, but some arrived alone, perhaps in the hope of marrying a wealthy miner.

Few women actually worked as miners but had plenty of domestic chores cutting wood, thawing snow for water and collecting wild food from the forest. Some took in washing, worked as waitresses or opened roadhouses and worked as cooks. Plus of course, with the great gender imbalance, actresses, courtesans and prostitutes were in great demand.

By the time the majority of people arrived in the gold fields, the best claims had been staked by locals and the first arrivals, such as those who had braved the winter and travelled up the river from Circle City. The winters here are cold but the river is frozen and provides an easy gradient and tree free space for travelling, especially by dog sled.

The original feeling was that gold in placer deposits would be found along the stream beds, but the distribution of gold was uneven. Ancient riverbeds had been left on the tops of hills, as rivers had eroded the land unevenly, so gold was found, both in the river valleys and on the tops of surrounding hills. The only way to be sure, using best Time Team terminology, was to put in a trench and see what you could find.

There was a ready market for buying and selling claims, although new arrivals would have to have money in order to buy a claim. These might be cheap, if they were unproven or could be worth ten times as much if it was a proven mine. Swiftwater Bill Gates was one who made it good. He traded in mines, but hired labourers to do the mining, rather than do it himself. In 1896 he was working in a saloon in Circle City when news of the Klondike gold finds reached Circle City and he, along with six others, leased claim no. 13 on Eldorado Creek. Shaft after shaft was sunk, but they found no gold and he found himself alone on his claim until his last shaft reached pay dirt and he became the wealthiest man in Dawson.

He was ostensibly extravagant, a gambler, with a fondness for the ladies. In particular, one lady had caught his eye, Gussie Lamore. She was a 19 year old entertainer in Circle City, who Gates had first met there and had also moved to Dawson.

Gates wanted her so much, that on one occasion, he offered her weight in gold, if she married him. In the winter of 1897, Gates saw her with another man and he was so jealous that he wanted revenge. He knew that Gussie loved eggs, so he took his revenge and bought the town's whole supply to deny her eggs. She was so desperate for her favourite food that she went home that day with Gates.

Gold has always been with mankind and has always exerted a strong influence on individuals. It has defined civilisations and shaped history. Before continuing the narrative, on the journey retracing the route, that some of the miners had taken to get to the Klondike, it is worth taking a look at the lure of this yellow metal and the story of gold and man's constant bewitchment by the metal.

CHAPTER 2

Gold

This is a story centred on gold and its magnetic pull for men and civilisations throughout history to search it out and the lengths that they go to get it. The Klondikers are just one group of miners who struggled to get their hands on the yellow metal but history is full of stories of men seeking gold, some of which the Klondikers would have been aware.

Gold has adored rulers, kings, emperors and noblemen, throughout history and made up a substantial part of the wealth in their treasuries. It is universally valued for its shiny, bright nature as it does not tarnish. It can be easily worked into fine jewellery and ornaments and it is recognised as a good store of value. In small quantities, is easy to transport. Part of its value is that it is a rare metal, in short supply, so its value is unlikely to suddenly plummet or vanish.

Every civilisation values gold and seems to want more of it. Most people can conjure up images of the pharaoh's death goods in their pyramids, stacks of gold bars in Fort Knox and stories of the fabulous wealth of the Aztecs and Incas, to name just a few.

Gold is immortalised in films such as the James Bond films, Goldfinger, released in 1964, starring Sean Connery or The Man with the Golden Gun, released in 1974, starring Roger Moore. On the stock exchanges of the world, the prices of shares in companies, changes as traders' demand and supply, establish the prices of shares, which also interacts with the demand for gold and consequently, the price that investors are prepared to accept for gold also varies.

The willingness to trade gold at a certain price charges upwards, with any sniff of major international tension that increases the likelihood of conflict, as gold is seen as superior to paper based storages of wealth. As a consequence of those fears, share values fall and the price of gold increases, as tensions increase. However, gold doesn't produce any income. When there is peace and companies are making good profits, investors will buy shares and the price of gold may go down.

India has historically been the largest buyer of gold, with a deep tradition of buying gold for jewellery and dowries. It buys around 800 tons annually. China is the second largest buyer, both by the state and the public, but buys half that of India, but its purchases are growing as the economy continues to expand and are expected to overtake India. There is constant demand all over the world for the metal. In Western countries for example, there is big demand for gold wedding rings, let alone all the other items of jewellery.

Despite the well-known numerous and deep gold mining companies in South Africa, China has overtaken it as the world's largest producer of gold. The world's largest single gold producing mine is Freeport McMoRan's giant Grasberg mine in Papua New Guinea (PNG). Its main product is copper but also as a by-product, it produced nearly 30 tons of gold in 2012 although just a year earlier the figure was 40 tons of gold. Despite this huge production from a single mine, the PNG as a producing country, is not even in the top ten of gold producing countries (it is 13th).

There is gold everywhere, if you know where to look and how to get to it. The Romans mined gold in Wales at Dolaucoth, using slave labour. The technology used was said to be relatively advanced for the times, but conditions for the slaves were probably not so good. In Scotland, a gold bearing vein of quartz was discovered by Ennex in 1984, near Tyndrum, 70kms northwest of Glasgow and is now owned by Scotsgold Resources, who are patiently waiting for permission to start mining. Permissions are required from the Crown Estate, who own all rights to gold in the UK and from the Loch Lomond National Park where Tyndrum lies, near the north west border of the Park.

This would be a small mine and originally, would have been expensive to exploit, but now the price of gold has soared in recent years, the economics may be such, that it has become economical to exploit. There are pros and cons of course, more jobs for the local area with increasing industrial development against the potential to spoil an area of outstanding natural beauty in a national park, so the politics may be difficult and commercial production is not imminent.

Contrast these two small deposits and the small scale of the operations to get at the gold, with the world's deepest mines in South Africa. The title of the deepest is in dispute, as different sources give different depths, but given that both mines are actively digging deeper every day, the accolade will swing between the two over time. My personal choice on the deepest at the time of writing, is Tau Tona, which is adjacent to Mponeng mine, which is the second deepest, both west of Johannesburg. However, Mponeng has reserves of over 13 million ounces and has plans to dig deeper.

Tau Tona is about 3.9kms deep with over 800kms of underground roads and tunnels. Annual production levels vary, but the recent lowest was 2012 at 189,000 ounces. At 32,000 ounces to a ton, that is nearly six tons of gold. Production has been three times that level, in some years, but even at the lowest level of production that is over 5 tons, but is miniscule compared to the annual Indian purchase of 800 tons.

South Africa is the fifth largest producer at 170 tons, against China in the number one slot at 370 tons. China is the world's largest producer, but not because it has some big mines like Freeport McMoRan's Grasberg mine in PNG. It is the largest producer, because it has a lot of mines that range from the large commercial operations to some that are relatively small family operations.

The gold production figures from South Africa are unreliable, as there are suggestions that up to 10 % of the gold production in South Africa is from illegal operations. These are the ghost miners, so called, as they spend long periods underground. The lack of sunlight and therefore vitamin D, discolours their skin to a grey colour. Miners dig into abandoned mines and abandoned areas of operating mines, to dig out ore.

Commercial underground mining extract ore but in order to support the roof and continue mining deeper into the ore body pillars of ore are left to support the roof. Responsible commercial mines take out as much as they can but must strike a balance between commercial economic exploitation and safety. Ghost miners can dig away at these pillars and remove more ore, despite the dangers of collapse. And there are many desperate people ready to risk their lives for gold.

Since some ghost miners work in abandoned areas of operating mines, they may find access to active working areas underground. Given half a chance, they steal ore and spirit it away through abandoned workings. Details and statistics of fatalities and illegal ore production are by their nature, non-existent, so there is plenty of scope for speculation, but it is a known factor in gold mine security.

Underground mining is dangerous and unpleasant. The Tau Tona mine takes safety very seriously but on average, there are still five fatalities a year (but it does employ over 5,000 miners so it is no worse or better than other mines). This statistic doesn't show the conditions that men have to work in. Besides the obvious dangers of heavy moving equipment, the dangers of gas, and travelling in a cage or a lift down hundreds of metres, there is another hazard. Due to the geothermal gradient, temperatures rise as the mine gets deeper towards the centre of the earth where there is a molten core.

The temperature at the bottom of the mine is around 60°C. Air conditioning, in the form of air blown over ice is constantly pumped down to the deepest sections, reducing the temperatures to the high 20°Cs, which is still high if you are undertaking hard physical labour.

Collapse and cave-ins are a constant danger. Due to the pressures on the rock, after boring a tunnel and the removal of support, the rock naturally wants to equalise the pressure and close the gap. This can result in sudden and catastrophic collapse. In order to counter this hazard, bolts are drilled and grouted into the surrounding faces and a mixture of bars, netting and concrete are used to support the tunnel.

Collapses are usually fatal but there are lucky escape stories. On 5th August 2010, in Chile, at the Copiapo copper and gold mine in the Atacama Desert, there were a series of collapses in an access tunnel, trapping 33 miners. The mine had been in operation for over 121 years and the miners were 700 metres underground and over 5kms of underground spiralling service roads from the surface.

The country had suffered a tsunami, following a massive earthquake measuring 8.8 on the Richter Scale, just six months before, on 27th February 2010. There was a national feeling of, facing disaster together and pulling together, to overcome adversity so public opinion was quite strong and demanded action to rescue the trapped miners. With the help of the national miner, Codelco, several boreholes were drilled, to where it was thought the miners could have had access to, if they had survived the initial collapses.

On the 22nd August 2010, one of the drill bits was withdrawn from a borehole. Attached to the drill bit was a piece of paper with the words 'Estamos bien en el refugio, los 33' or in English 'we are well in the shelter, the 33'. It was more than two weeks since their entrapment, but they were still alive. More boreholes were drilled with international help from around the world. Food, water and medical supplies were lowered through wider boreholes until an even wider borehole was able to reach the area where the men were sheltering.

This larger borehole was able to take one man at a time in a special cocoon to be winched to the surface. The operation to winch the trapped miners to the surface lasted 24 hours and finally, after 69 days underground, the last of the 'Los 33' reached the surface on 13th October 2010. 'Los 33' as they became known worldwide, were lucky, as they were only 700m underground, not 3.9kms where the miners at the bottom of the Tau Tona mine work.

Broadly speaking, there are two types of gold ore, gold that you can see and gold in ore that is so fine, it is invisible. The easiest gold to get at, is that which you can see, such as in placer deposits. Placer being Latin for loose. These form where weathering has weakened and eroded the rock holding the gold and the subsequent erosion, has washed the weathered material into streams and rivers.

The gold, being much heavier than the surrounding debris, gets deposited in gravel bars, where the flow of the river and thus its energy to carry heavy gold, is reduced and the gold is dropped. Therefore, by excavating the gravels and rinsing away the lighter rock debris by a process of panning or its industrial equivalent, gold flakes and nuggets can be recovered from the otherwise worthless gravel and sand.

One of the oldest and well known such deposits, is on the Pactolus River which is a tributary of the Gediz River in Turkey, which has been used as a source of gold for thousands of years. It is speculated that it may have been the place that is referred to in the Greek story of Jason and the Argonauts and the story of the Golden Fleece.

Travellers in Georgia, that borders the eastern end of the Black Sea, are told with the certainty of the converted, that this is where Jason found his Golden Fleece. The fleece story holds a modicum of credibility as, although the location is uncertain, there is a history of putting sheep fleeces in rivers to collect gold.

If a fleece is anchored to the bottom of a gold bearing stream, over time, as the water washes sediment over the fleece, the heavier particles, being the gold, are washed over the fleece which are captured within the fleece. Meanwhile, the comparatively lighter unwanted fragments are carried over the fleece. The fleece can be removed after a while and dried. The gold can then be combed out or the fleece burnt and in the ashes, there will be a residue of gold flakes. It is not a very efficient method of gold recovery but given its low technology and minimal input of labour, it might look attractive to a poor subsistence farmer.

An alternative to the simple fleece process of obtaining gold, is panning for it, which is ever so simple and requires no sophisticated equipment. Gravel is scooped into the pan which is then gently agitated, making the denser material sink to the bottom and the lighter materials are allowed to spill out over the edge of the pan. The resultant sandy muddy deposit left in the crease of the pan can be inspected and the shiny gold flakes removed.

A more advanced method, is to use sluices or rocker boxes which utilise the same physics, but on a larger scale. Panning is a useful method for finding gold placer deposits or for extracting the larger nuggets and flakes (or colours) of gold but is inefficient, as some gold is often missed. Rocker boxes and sluices and modern equivalents are simple technologies but can capture a lot more gold on an industrial scale.

The alternative to panning and a method used for non-placer gold deposits, is to mine for it in the solid rock. Gold commonly is associated with quartz and where there is a quartz vein, there may be some visible gold. This is a vein that can be mined and by eye miners can chip out the rock and separate the bits that hold gold and separate it from the host rock, at a later date.

Heating gold ore and melting the gold out of the ore, is used as an assay process that can assess the quantity of gold in a given weight of ore, which may be only a few grams per ton. This is fine to predict the volume of gold but as a production method, it uses a lot of energy and is expensive. An ore body is only worth exploiting if the costs of extraction are less than the price of the final gold metal that the miner can obtain in the market.

After the traditional methods, used by ancient gold miners, come the more technical exploration and extraction methods of gold mining, that require an increasing amount of science, technology and chemistry. Ancient gold miners had already discovered that gold sticks to mercury, so gold bearing ores could be processed by crushing the ore and mixing it with mercury to pull out even unseen gold particles from a crushed rock. Further processing of the ore and mercury mixture can achieve recovery of the gold. Therefore, more gold rich deposits, which were not so obvious to the naked eye could be mined and the gold extracted.

Much later, the chlorination process had been discovered. Crushed ore that is moist has chlorine passed through it, which forms gold chloride which is leached out in the liquid run off. The gold is then precipitated out with ferrous sulphate and the miner can obtain his gold. But using chlorine is far from a safe or ecologically friendly way to extract gold.

Then, in 1887 the cyanide process was discovered to extract gold. Just by the name, any chemistry student would recognise that this is not exactly an eco-friendly way to extract gold, either. Crushed ore is mixed with water to create a slurry. Then, cyanide is added to the slurry that pulls the gold from its previous host rock to create a gold cyanide, then, using a process called carbon in pulp or CIP, carbon pellets are introduced to the mixture and they attract all the gold cyanide, as if it was blotting paper.

The gold rich pellets are screened off the mixture and are subjected to an acid bath, which strips off the gold. The carbon is recycled, the cyanide goes to the tailings ponds and the gold rich solution undergoes an electrolysis process that extracts the gold and the miner has his gold. He can then heat the fine grains up and cast ingots for easier handling, transportation and trading on the international market. But the process does leave large tailings dams, holding a large amount of poisonous liquid.

A cheaper method of gold extraction was developed, called the heap leaching process. A big mound of gold ore is built above an impervious membrane and the cyanide solution dribbled over its surface, to percolate through the heap. The cyanide strips out the gold from the ore and is collected at the base for further processing. This ability to process low grade ore, that may have previously been uneconomic to recover, can significantly increase the economics of marginal gold mines and increases a mine's economic potential and ability to produce gold at an affordable price, for the shareholders. The major drawback is that it too produces large ponds of toxic liquid waste.

One of Europe's worst environmental disasters, since the Chernobyl disaster, occurred on the night of 30th January 2000 at Baia Mare in Romania. There was a gold mine, jointly owned by the

Australian company, Esmaralda Exploration and the Romanian government, operated by Auril Gold that had used the cyanide process to extract gold that had left large ponds of poisonous cyanide, laced with other heavy metals and dangerous chemicals. The company had claimed that it had the technology to process the poisonous tailings. After a heavy snowfall, the dam burst and 100,000 cubic metres of toxic waste, containing 100 tons of cyanide, split into the Somes River.

The Somes River, flows over the border, into Hungary's second largest river, the Tisla, which forms a short border with Ukraine, before flowing on through Hungary and subsequently, into the Danube. It is a major water source for millions of Hungarians. Thousands of fish and birds were killed and volunteers pulled the dead animals from the rivers, to prevent the carcasses causing more damage, further along the food chain.

Where the Tisla joined the Danube, the concentrations of the toxic waste were diluted, but it still caused a lot of problems for wildlife. Fishing was banned, environmental groups such as, Greenpeace and Friends of the Earth, tried to get cyanide extraction banned and three attempts were made in the Romanian Parliament to ban this method of gold extraction, but all to no avail.

Gold is not only produced from just gold mines. Gold occurs as an associate mineral with deposits of nickel, copper, zinc, lead and silver. Therefore, mines which were established for one of these other minerals may also produce gold almost as a by-product, but which also enhance the economics of the original reason to establish the mine. Many of the giant copper producing mines, high in the mountains of the Andes in Chile, produce millions of tons of copper, but also produce significant quantities of other precious metals, including gold and silver.

Peru is currently South America's largest gold producer, producing 165 tons in 2011. Its southern neighbour, Chile, is the world's largest copper producer, at six million tons which is over three times larger than the next biggest, China, but Chile also produced 50 tons of gold, largely as a by-product of copper mining.

Chile is ranked 17th in terms of world production gold charts, but that is likely to jump with new developments. Gold mines are not unknown in Chile, for instance, the El Indio gold mine opened in 1982 and gold production peaked at 16 tons a year, before reserves were exhausted and the mine closed in 2002.

Barrick Gold Corporation plans some big developments in Chile, to boost gold production. Its Pascua Lama exploration site, 600kms north of Santiago, on the Argentine border, has reserves estimated at 470 tons of gold and 21,000 tons of silver. Annual gold production, is planned at 39 tons of gold, but it is remote and at altitudes of between 3,800m and 5,200m, so development is proving difficult.

Another development is at Cerro Casale, not far from Pascua Lama, also in northern Chile and jointly owned by Barrick and Kinross Gold Corporation. This ore body is rich in gold and copper with reserves of 720 tons of gold 2,600,000 tons of copper.

There are other ways of acquiring gold, other than mining for it, you can steal it. On 26th November 1983, a gang broke into the Brinks MAT high security warehouse, at Heathrow. They had assistance from one of the security guards, Anthony Black, the brother in law of gang member, Brian Robinson. They poured petrol over the guards and threatened to set them alight, unless the guards revealed the security codes to the vaults. They had expected to steal £3m in cash, but were faced with 3 tons of gold. They finally left with £26m (over £75m in current values) of cash, gold and diamonds.

Brian Robinson, was arrested the following month, after a tip off from Anthony Black to investigating officers. Anthony Black got six years and another gang member, Micky McAvoy got 25 years. Micky McAvoy had entrusted part of his haul of gold to George Francis and Brian Perry, who employed Kenneth Noye, to fence the gold. Noye melted it down and mixed it with copper, to disguise the origin of the gold. The Bank of England, got suspicious of large bullion movements and the police placed Noye under surveillance.

He discovered and killed a police officer in his garden and whilst a jury found him not guilty of murder, due to self-defence, another jury found him guilty of conspiracy to handling stolen property and he was sentenced to 14 years. George Francis, was subsequently murdered and suspicion fell on Kenneth Noye, but it was not substantiated. He served 7 years of his sentence and was released in 1994, but in a road rage incident on 19th May 1996, he stabbed and killed Stephen Cameron on the M25, near Swanley and immediately fled the country. He was extradited from Spain and on conviction, was handed down a life time sentence in 2000.

In the early 1990s, there were five shootings, connected to the Brinks MAT robbery and the laundering of the proceeds, of the crime. Some of the participants were never charged, due to a lack of reliable evidence. The bulk of the gold was never recovered, but it is widely suspected that it had made its way back into the legitimate gold market. There was a widely held urban myth, but may it be true, anyone buying gold jewellery after 1983, could well have been wearing gold that had originally been part of the haul from the Brinks MAT robbery.

That theft pales into insignificance, compared with the Spanish plunder of South America. The Moors had invaded southern Spain from Africa and started the conquest of Granada, in 711AD and had widened their sphere of influence, so that by 790AD at its full extent, it covered a large proportion of the peninsula. They had ruled parts of the Iberian Peninsula for nearly 800 years, expanding their influence over the peninsula and for a while, over the Pyrenes into Aquitaine in France. In later years, their area of influence had been shrinking. By the mid-12th century, the Moors only controlled the southern half of the peninsula.

The Reconquista was the name given to the slow attritional skirmishes and wars that gradually won back the land from the Moors. The end of the Reconquista, was the Spanish monarch's King Ferdinand and Queen Isabella's triumph over the Moors, with the capture of the Alhambra fortress and palace, which was the capital of the kingdom of Granada. This impressive fortress was formally handed over on 2nd January 1492. Following this, was the expulsion of the Moors, from the Iberian Peninsula and the incorporation of what is now modern day Andalusia into the Spanish kingdom.

Shortly, following this achievement, and full of new found confidence, and in part, as a celebration of the re-unification of the Spanish realm, under full Spanish control, King Ferdinand and Queen Isabella, funded an expedition led by Christopher Columbus. In his pitch to the king and queen, he promised to convert the heathens to Christianity and bring back gold. There was plenty of mentions of conversion to Christianity, to give the expedition a cloak of respectability but there was much more mention of gold and riches, than religion.

It was this expedition that is accredited with the discovery of the Americas, and for claiming it for the Spanish crown. However, the first European to set foot in America, is actually thought to be Leifur Eiriksson 970AD–1020AD, also known as Eric the Red, a Viking who according to Viking sagas, found America nearly five hundred years before Christopher Columbus. But, this fact is over looked in most history syllabuses and every schoolboy will tell you that Christopher Columbus discovered America in 1492. Indeed, this urban myth is perpetuated in the United States, as well as several Latin American countries, where Columbus Day is celebrated on October 12th every year.

Other expeditions followed the initial discovery by Columbus, led by a host of other adventurers. One such expedition, was led by Hernan Cortes, born sometime in 1485 and accompanying Diego Velazquez on the capture of Cuba. He was made a clerk to the treasury, to ensure that the crown obtained its 'quinto real'. This was the requirement that a fifth of every expedition's profits, was due to the crown.

In February 1519, he set out with 11 ships, 13 horses and 500 men and reached the Yucatan peninsula, in present day Mexico. He claimed it for the Spanish crown and after picking up more troops and horses in Trinadad, continued back to Mexico, to land at present day Veracruz. He had asked for a meeting with Moctezuma, who ruled the area from the Aztec capital Tenochtitlan. The capital was located on an island, in a large lake, which is now largely drained and forms part of the sprawling metropolis of Mexico City. He was continually declined an audience, but was not put off.

From Veracruz, he headed into the mountains, to the Aztec capital with 600 men, 15 horsemen and 15 cannon, plus loads of local porters and soldiers. He gained several allies on his journey, such as the Nuhuas and Tlaxcaltec. At Cholula, the Aztecs' second largest city, he massacred a great number of the nobility, partly in order to instil fear and partly to prevent treachery, amongst the local population.

He was finally received by Moctezuma in Tenochtitlan, on 8th November 1519 and was lavished with gold gifts from Moctezuma. It is thought that this was to buy them off, but it only whetted the adventurer's appetite for more gold and plunder.

By 1st July 1520, Moctezuma was dead. Sources are contradictory, some say the Spanish killed him and others, that his subjects stoned him to death. The populace were hostile and Cortes had to retreat, losing much of his treasure, his artillery and his rearguard, who were massacred. This was a major setback, but with the help of his Tlaxcala allies and reinforcements from Cuba, he besieged Tenochtitlan, cutting their supplies and gradually conquered large swathes of present day Mexico and established several cities and developed farming and mining, during his rule, over the next four years.

Hernan Cortes had several further expeditions to Honduras, Baja California and Algiers, but returned to Spain in 1541 and died in debt, in Castilleja de la Cuesta, in the province of Seville on 2nd December 1547, aged 62.

Hernan Cortes' initial setback in 1520, did not stop other Conquistadors' intent on fame and fortune and more importantly, gold. Francisco Pizarro, born in the 1470s, (records are contradictory as to whether it was 1471 or 1476 or any other date early in that decade) and a distant cousin of Hernan Cortes, had sailed to the Americas, on 10th November 1509. He arrested Vasco Nunez de Balboa, on orders of the new governor on charges of treason.

Vasco Nunez de Balboa, was famed for crossing the Panama isthmus and discovering the Pacific Ocean. He led subsequent expeditions up and down the coast, including naming Puerto Pinas, after the profusion of pineapples found there. He sailed up the Balsas River, from where the well-known modern light weight modelling wood, called balsa wood, originates.

His fame and discoveries counted for little. He was found guilty of trying to usurp power and despite his protestations of innocence, which could well have been true, he was executed on 15th January 1519. Francisco Pizarro was rewarded for his role in arresting Vasco Nunez de Balboa, as mayor and magistrate of Panama City from 1519, a post that he held until 1523.

Francisco Pizarro had heard of the riches of the Inca Empire and set out on two expeditions in 1524 and 1526, both of which were unsuccessful, due to hostile natives, poor provisioning and bad weather. On his second expedition, the governor of Panama, Pedro de los Rios recalled Pizarro, but he ignored the orders and continued his exploration.

In April 1528, Pizarro finally reached northern Peru and encountered Indians with large quantities of precious metals and gems. He was determined to undertake a third expedition but Pedro de los Rios refused his pleas for authorisation for a third expedition. Undeterred, he returned to Spain and appealed directly to King Charles. Pizarro gained the permission he needed and in addition, considerable authority over any lands that he conquered.

In 1532, Pizarro landed and established a colony and then marched inland to Cajamarca, with 106 soldiers and 62 horsemen. The current ruler of the Inca Empire, was Atahualpa, who would not tolerate a colony on his lands. The Inca Empire was established nearly a hundred years before, by Pachacuti Yupanqui, an Inca ruler, who was a great leader. He defeated their traditional enemies and incorporated them into his kingdom. That was the first of several successes that expanded the empire until it stretched for thousands of miles, through the Andes, bordered by the Pacific to the west, the Amazon jungle to the east and deserts to the south. He is thought to be responsible for the construction of Macchu Pichu.

The Inca's didn't have money, as we now understand it. Wealth was in the form of animals and land. But they had lots of gold, which was valued for the artefacts that could be made from it, not for the gold itself, or for its usefulness, as a store of value, as understood by Europeans.

There was not an established rigid system of succession, within the Inca Empire which often led to court intrigue and plotting. On the death of Atahualpa's father, he became the Inca ruler and his brother, Huascar, controlled the army but civil war broke out. At the time of Pizarro's arrival, one of Atahualpa's armies, was fighting Huascar at Cusco, but he was not yet aware of the outcome of the battle.

Atahualpa, had 80,000 troops with him and knew that Pizarro was coming and also knew that he had just a small force. Pizarro, meanwhile, was planning to get Atahualpa to submit to the Spanish crown or to capture him, so had deployed his troops and kept them hidden. At the meeting on 16th November 1532, Atahualpa demanded the gifts he had sent earlier to Pizarro, be returned.

A priest who was negotiating on behalf of Pizarro, handed Atahualpa a breviary, which was thrown to the floor. The significance of this was that Conquistadors' (term used to refer to the soldiers and explorers of the Spanish Empire or the Portuguese Empire) primary aim was meant to try to convert the locals to Catholicism, before enriching themselves (and the Crown) which was a secondary aim. The priest ran back to Pizarro, who gave the order to attack and the Battle of Cajamarca begun. The attack was such a surprise with cavalry and guns that thousands of lightly armed Incas were massacred and Atahualpa captured.

Pizarro's men sacked the Inca's camp and found loads of gems, silver and gold. Atahualpa, noticed the invaders' desire for gold and promised to fill a room 5.2m by 6.7m with gold and twice with silver, presumably for his release, or to avoid death, but this is not recorded in any of the surviving records. This was agreed and orders went out to bring gold and silver from all over the empire, to fill the room. And because the Inca was treated like a god, this order was fulfilled and soon the room was full.

Huascar had been defeated by Atahualpa's forces and there were still tens of thousands of native soldiers, but Pizarro went on to conquer Cuzco, establish Jauja as the provincial capital and claimed the former Inca Empire on behalf of the Spanish monarch. Atahualpa was subsequently found guilty of killing his brother and plotting against Pizarro and was strangled and his body burnt on 26th July 1533.

Jauja was too high in the mountains and a long way from the sea and later Pizarro established Lima, which he felt was one of his outstanding achievements. He continued to establish cities and consolidate power. He survived until 26th June 1541, when he was assassinated by conspirators, again proving that gold and wealth does not bring happiness; and just nine years after obtaining fabulous and unbelievable wealth.

The wealth of the Incas, from across South America and Mexico, in the form of both gold and silver, flowed to Spain, not that it helped them, either. English and French ships regularly attacked the Spanish galleons that took the precious metals back to Spain, in an effort to curb the wealth that might fund Spanish aggression against them. It caused a huge increase in the money supply and inflation. It had one benefit, in that it expanded banking, and prompted the introduction of paper money, so that huge and heavy amounts of metal, no longer had to be carried around, as the metal backed paper money, was freely convertible.

This only brought more problems, as in times of crisis, there would be runs on banks, as people chose to exchange their paper money, backed by metal for physical metal. Ultimately, all countries left the gold standard and the formal link between paper money and gold, is now broken and paper is no longer freely exchangeable for gold, other than using paper to buy the metal.

The Bretton Woods agreement, was negotiated towards the end of the Second World War and signed on 22nd July 1944. It established various procedures, to regulate the international monetary system, rules to guard against competitive devaluation, established the International Monetary Fund and the International Bank for Reconstruction and Development.

Importantly, for the story of gold, signatory countries had an obligation to develop a monetary policy that maintained their exchange rate, by tying its currency to the US dollar and the US dollar, was freely convertible into gold which instantly made the dollar the world's reserve currency. It was Richard Nixon, who on 15th August 1971, ended the link between the dollar and gold convertibility, that finally cut the link between paper and metal, in order, he claimed at the time, to protect the dollar.

Gold has a hold over men's minds and attracted the adventurous and the greedy, as it seems to excite the idea of acquiring wealth quickly and easily, although there does seem to be a lot of danger, associated with its acquisition.

Gold discovery and the gold rushes that followed, was not always bad news. It is true to say that the increase in money supply, was an international problem, but on a local scale, it could be good news. The then empty western seaboard of the United States and other young colonies, which were under populated, welcomed the economic development that accompanied a gold rush and the attraction that it offered, in encouraging new settlers.

There would always be the professional pan handler, who came to exploit the gold and would move on, after extracting as much gold as he could, before the supply dwindled. There were those that lived nearby the discovery, who would take a chance and leave home, to try to make their fortunes.

But, there were just as many gold seekers from much further afield, who were attracted by the gold rush and the chance to make it big, who having dug and sweated, trying to make their fortunes, eventually settled down in the country, to become farmers or labourers, thus adding to the local economy.

There are countless gold rush fevers that attracted people from all over the world, with the potential of making their fortune. There was a gold rush to Coloma, in the Sierra Nevada mountains, in California, when gold was discovered there in 1848. The gold rush, lasted for several years and attracted 300,000 people to

California, from elsewhere in the United States and abroad. These prospectors were called Forty-niners and the local area was subjected to a mass of artisan miners, hard mountain men panning remote streams for gold. It is likely that some of the Klondikers had grandfathers who were Forty-niners

San Francisco grew from a population of just 200 to 36,000, in just eight years. Other towns sprung up, roads were built and merchants came to supply these new towns. The increase in population was also an influence in the development of local government and ultimately led to California becoming a state in 1850.

There were other gold rushes elsewhere in the world, such as to Victoria, Australia in 1851, to Gabriel's Gully, near Dunedin, on the south island of New Zealand, in 1861 and the Witwatersrand gold rush in South Africa, in 1886, to name just a few, that all drew people from outside of the host country.

Many of these prospectors, subsequently settled in the countries that they had arrived in and helped to develop the local economies and ultimately, their chosen country's influence, on the world stage. At the end of late 19th century, the discovery of gold in the Yukon, led to many hopeful prospectors, heading to the remote north west of Canada, to try their hand at panning for gold.

CHAPTER 3

The Rocky Mountaineer

I started my re-creation of a Klondike prospector's journey that he may have taken in Calgary. I did not fly into somewhere on the coast, to start the journey up the coast, such as Seattle or Vancouver, which was where many of the prospectors had departed on their sea journey north, to reach the gold fields. Instead, I elected to start in Calgary, located to the east of the Rockies, on the Canadian prairies which was an established wheat growing area and already widely settled.

Some years previously, I was white water rafting down the Fraser River and after leaving Boston Bar, we shot the rapids at Hell's Gate, which has a huge drop and then continued down the river to ride the standing waves at Sailors Bar.

All along the trip down the Fraser River gorge, there are two single train tracks, clinging to the steep cliffs, high above the raging river. There's one on each side of the gorge, one built by the Canadian Pacific Railway and the other built later by the Canadian National Railway. Every few minutes, there was a train slowly making its way up or down the gorge. The tracks are reversible, so sometimes, there is a break in the traffic until the last train reaches the next switch over and then more trains follow each other along the track, in the opposite direction. Although there are two tracks, the direction of travel is alternated, both for operational reasons and to allow even wear on the rails.

The river valley is a bottle neck for trains, as they negotiate the route through the mountains that link the ports on the coast, to the vast interior of Canada. These goods trains are not like the trains I am used to seeing back home. These are monsters with multiple locomotives, with two, three or four locomotives at the front and hauling over a hundred wagons. As they went past, I counted wagons to see how many there were, in the longest train. There were so many trains that after a while, if the train didn't look very long, I didn't bother to count.

The longest train I counted, was 156 wagons, pulled by three locomotives. That is a train over two and a half kilometres long. With that much weight, they don't go very fast either. Therefore, if you get stopped at a level crossing as a train is approaching, you have plenty of time to kill before resuming your journey. You can turn off the engine and read another chapter of a book, or do a cross word, as you wait for it to pass.

Some of the trains carry bulk goods, such as coal, ore and timber. Others, were long trains of grain, in special wagons, heading for the coast and for export markets. The container trains, taking goods into the Canadian interior, were big, even staring up from the small inflatable, being tossed around in the quick flowing river. Containers come in various sizes, but there is a constant movement towards standardisation. Shippers talk about TEUs being twenty foot equivalent units and most European containers are 40 feet long and eight and a half feet high.

The containers on the trains, travelling along the gorge, are larger at 48 feet long and nine and a half feet high. Plus, they were double stacked, one on top of another. I was having a wonderful time, rafting down the river and gazing up, as the trains went past. There are few passenger trains, but one did come past. This was a tour train, with the top and upper sides made solely of glass, to give a panoramic view. The name was painted down the side, 'Rocky Mountaineer'.

It took a while to get back to Canada, for a trip that incorporated that ride on the train, but taking the Rocky Mountaineer was a little extension to retracing the journey, that the Klondikers would have followed, more than a hundred years earlier. And since the CPR was building its tracks through the mountains, around 1881–1885, it is quite possible, that some of those prospectors would have travelled by train, to reach the coast at Vancouver, so I felt that it was perfectly legitimate to start my Klondike journey in Calgary.

Calgary is the largest city in Alberta, with over a million people but only slightly ahead of Edmonton, which is the state capital. The city is located in an area of low rolling hills where the land begins to change from the expansive granary basket of the prairies to the mountains of the Rockies. Driving from the airport into the centre of town, the landscape was open rolling countryside, not many trees but a huge blue cloudless sky above with a bright sun shining down.

As I approached the city centre, I could see on the horizon the skyscrapers of the central business district, led by the iconic and distinctive Calgary Tower. My hotel was a short walk away and I was surprised that I had two king sized double beds, plus a large reception area, a table with chairs, a fridge and a small kitchen area, plus a large bathroom and shower. It was more than I had expected, more like a flat than a hotel room. I was just expecting a bed and a shower. Perhaps I had been given a complimentary upgrade.

I spent a while walking around the city. Rather than walk directly to where I want to go, I like to take diversionary walks, to get to see more of the city and some sights that you might otherwise miss, so I was really tired when I went to bed. I had forgotten to set the alarm and after a long night's rest, to recover from the flight and the change in time zones, I woke up very late in the morning. I had hoped to visit the Heritage Park Historical Village, which is one of Calgary's top visitor attractions.

This is a large site, over fifty hectares, displaying railway steam locomotives and wagons, collections of cars and lorries, traditional ways of life, museum exhibits, amusements, traditional wooden architecture, a steamboat, horses plus everything associated with the way of life in Canada from 1860's to 1930's and some mining equipment. There is so much to see, that by the time I had worked out how to get there and travelled there, I would not have enough time to see everything.

As it happened, it was only a few kilometres away from the centre of town, but I would rather have a whole day to visit, to see everything at leisure, rather than rush it and miss bits. So, I decided to leave it for another trip and do something else. I had to come back anyway, as I also wanted to see the famous Calgary Stampede. This is a festival of chuck wagon races, rodeos, stalls, fun fairs and amusements that lasts 10 days in July but I was visiting at the wrong time of year. This was even closer than the Heritage Park Historical Village and hosts other events, throughout the year but the day I walked past, it was shut and there was not much to see from the perimeter fence.

I walked along the banks of the Bow River that flows slowly through the centre of the city and wandered around the Core Shopping Centre, before reaching the Calgary Tower. This is a 191m high tower started in 1967 and finished the following year to celebrate Canada's centennial anniversary and was planned to be the highest building in North America. The developers kept the true height of the tower a secret, claiming it to be only 187m. When the developers of the Tower of the Americas in San Antonio, Texas, which was being built at the same time, tried to claim the record, the true height of 191m was revealed and it was confirmed as the tallest building.

It has since lost this accolade, with another building in Calgary being higher. The Calgary Tower has slipped down the rankings in international terms, to be dwarfed by more modern buildings built by aspiring architects and promoters. The Burj Kalifa in Dubai is currently the tallest building at 830m. The Petronas Towers in Kula Lumpur, a little way down the list, but worthy of a mention, as it is widely recognised due to its appearance in several films, which at 452m, is over double the height of the Calgary Tower. The Kingdom Tower, under construction in Saudi Arabia and due for completion in 2019 will be over 1,000m high.

Having said all that, however high you may be, if you are out of your comfort zone, then that is too high for you. I felt comfortable on the observation platform, looking out of the window, at the city, spread out below. I could make out the river, some of the parks along its banks, a host of buildings laid out in a grid pattern, plus major roads following the larger grid lines and sometimes, cutting across blocks diagonally. The buildings are well spread and there is plenty of green areas and trees, but some of the view is obscured by the increasing number of tall office blocks, clustered around the central area and others that are under construction nearby will further limit the view.

Beyond the central area, the buildings were all low rise and I could see buildings spreading out as far as the eye could see and no agricultural areas, even from this height. This gives a good indication of one of the current issues for the city which is urban sprawl. The metropolitan area is encroaching on neighbouring areas as urban development continues. More offices are being built and Calgary boasts that it is the second most popular location, for the head offices of many of Canada's large companies and all those workers need somewhere to live.

The tower itself is a concrete column, with the functional bits, such as the observation platform, a restaurant and a souvenir shop at the top on several stories that jut out beyond the sides of the column. This gave the designers, the ability to have a glass floor on which you can stand and see the pavements and traffic on the roads, a long way below, between your feet. I didn't want to lean against the glass let along stand for too long on the glass floor.

I am not relaxed with heights but will always give it a go. Sometimes you can get a greater adrenalin rush from being outside of your comfort zone. I felt alright, until two large men wearing check shirts, standing next to me decided to dare each other and test the strength of that glass. They started jumping up and down, first alternately and then adding pressure, by jumping together. This was a bit too much for my nerves and I moved off the glass, back onto solid concrete.

I didn't need a map for the next day, as from my vantage point I could see my hotel and the route to the railway station. I took a winding route back to the hotel, enjoying the late afternoon sun. On my wanderings I found a Mountain Equipment Co-Operative shop, or MEC as it is also affectionately known. Nothing unusual you may think, but it is like a mecca for me and is my favourite chain of shops in Canada.

It stocks clothes, equipment and gadgets for everything you could ever want for trekking, camping, walking and a host of other outdoor activities. The quality is great and the prices are ever better. I love to wander in and see what latest gear and gadgets there is on offer. I find it hard to resist getting the latest thing that I haven't yet tried and invariably, buy something. However, I was able to hold onto my money and resist temptation before returning to the hotel. I had a rather tasteless and overly cold beer at the bar in the hotel and decided to call it a day, making sure that this time, I set the alarm.

At an ungodly hour in the morning, before the restaurant was open for breakfast, the alarm went off and I caught a pre-ordered taxi. I knew the route to the station, but thinking of the baggage and the early morning cold before dawn, I had decided to take the expensive option of a taxi, to take me from the hotel to the station. The receptionist offered me a coffee which I happily accepted. I was grateful the taxi was late and I was able to warm my hands on the cup, as well as savour the taste.

I had wondered whether the traffic would slow our progress and I would be late, but my concerns were baseless about missing the train, as the taxi driver was a reincarnation of Michael Schumacher or Lewis Hamilton and except for the one speed camera en route, for which he braked sharply and slowed to the speed limit, he almost relished racing through the deserted streets of downtown Calgary. The streets this early were empty of both pedestrians and vehicles and I was delivered to the train station in what must have been record time.

Together with my fellow passengers, we sat around in the station foyer, well past the time that we had been told to arrive and wondered what was happening. Eventually, we queued up to have our tickets checked and were directed to our reserved seats on specific carriages. You can take a small day pack or handbag with you if it can squeeze it under the seat but big bags were placed into a baggage carriage.

I had chosen to travel upmarket in first class equivalent, despite the extra cost so I was on a Red Maple Leaf Train. We had specific seats allocated and I had chosen and paid extra for a window seat. I need not have worried, as the carriage had a glass dome roof, to give a panoramic view of the scenery wherever you sat. The seats were large and had an abundance of upholstery stuffing so were very comfortable.

The carriage was on two levels, with meals taken on the lower level included in the price and reserved seating on the upper level, with glass domed carriages. There were opportunities for sightseeing to be taken, on the upper level with complimentary drinks brought to your seat. There was a small viewing platform, at each end of each carriage, if you wanted to stand and get some fresh air.

Right on time, we slowly pulled out of the station, almost without noticing that we were moving as the start was so smooth. We slowly picked up speed, to move steadily through the suburbs of Calgary on our journey towards Vancouver through the mountains of the Rockies under a clear blue sky.

I took a moment to reflect on my journey, on the Rocky Mountaineer through what promised to be spectacular mountains. This was not part of the original idea of retracing a Klondiker's journey, to the gold fields but some may have taken the train to Vancouver so I felt that it was legitimate to include this part of the trip in the telling of the story. However, I doubted whether they had the same level of comfort that I was enjoying. We passed through rolling countryside with few trees as we climbed towards the foothills of the Rockies.

I walked along the train for a while to get my bearings and stretch my legs. At the end of each carriage were the steps to gain access between the upper and lower levels of the coach. Outside either end was a modest viewing platform that connected one coach with another. It was large enough to take several people and passengers could get some fresh air and views of the countryside and take photos without the interference and the glare of glass. Several other of my fellow passengers were also exploring the coach when we were called to breakfast.

I joined a couple that I had been speaking to on the viewing platform. They were English, Gordon, a former engineer and his wife Sarah, both from Swindon, both retired and as they said, spending the children's inheritance. They had heard about this particular rail journey and had always wanted to do it and now they were fulfilling their dream.

Breakfast consisted of cereal, a full English cooked breakfast, croissants and a choice of fruit juice, tea or coffee. I have to say, that it may not be very healthy, but I do love a cooked breakfast and devoured the lot. Outside the window, the hills were getting higher as we passed through forests of pine and we were definitely approaching the mountains. We crossed rivers, travelled alongside lakes and had lovely views of craggy peaks, as we climbed inexorably up into the mountains.

We passed sidings where freight trains waited, before following each other along the track, after we had passed and the way ahead was clear. We went through Banff and shortly afterwards Lake Louise, both well-known and large ski resorts. There were lakes where the water was crystal clear and submerged trees that had become waterlogged and too heavy to float, had sunk to the bottom of the lake, but could still be clearly seen. It was eerie, to see these trunks with their branches like arms raised heavenward, lurking below the surface.

Then we reached the Kicking Horse River, the Kicking Horse Pass and the spiral tunnels at Rogers Pass. Kicking Horse was given its name by the Palliser Expedition, led by Captain John Palliser, who was leading an exploratory expedition to survey various passes through the Rockies, in 1857–1860, on behalf of the CPR. The story goes that a member of the expedition, a naturist, geologist and surgeon, called James Hector, was kicked by his horse, hence the name given and it has stuck ever since. The track was finally built through the pass in the 1880's, instead of the original proposal to build a track through the more northerly Yellowhead Pass.

The spiral tunnels came later. The original rail route over the pass was a steep 4.5 % gradient that heavy trains couldn't manage on their own and a separate pusher locomotive was required on constant standby to help get trains up the slope (or to add braking power for trains descending the gradient to maintain control). There were numerous incidents and several disasters, so an alternative solution was sought.

The solution, was to reduce the grade to 2.2 % by tunnelling a three quarters of a circle tunnel, anticlockwise through the mountain, then run the track downwards across the face of the incline, followed by another three quarters of a circle clockwise tunnel to achieve a reduced grade. It may have lengthened the distance, but crucially, it reduced the grade to make it manageable for all trains, ultimately to get safely through the Rogers Pass, under their own power without the need for an additional locomotive on permanent standby.

All the way down the valley we caught glimpses of the Trans Canadian Highway, as it made its way, along the same valley through the Selkirk Mountains and occasionally, crossed the river and the railway. As we made our way over the watershed, we travelled alongside smaller rivers that had been damned by beavers with great piles of logs flooding the upstream sections of the river and causing small deltas to form where the rivers dropped its sediment as it entered the dammed lake. We were also lucky enough to see several beavers swimming in the lakes or traversing the open stretches of ground, as we slowly passed by.

In the afternoon, we passed through Revelstoke, a small town with a ski resort and an airstrip that extends into the local lake. It had had several names in its short life but finally renamed to its present name by the CPR in appreciation of Lord Revelstoke, chairman of Baring Brothers, a UK investment bank which bought all the railway's unsold bonds in 1885 thus saving it from bankruptcy and allowing it to finish the building of the railway through the Rockies that we were following.

We travelled along the southern shores of Shuswap Lake, through Salmon Arm. The lake has a unique outline that is in the shape of an H, and it is a very popular destination with water sports enthusiasts and mountain loving holiday makers. From the train, several boats could be seen on the lake and on the far side, several holiday cabins and resorts were clearly visible.

As we approached our evening destination in Kamloops, there was a spectacular sunset with the sun setting, throwing vivid yellow, orange and red colours off the lower sections of the scattered grey clouds overhead. The train pulled into a siding and we all piled out onto waiting coaches. We were to be taken the short distance to The Thompson, a local hotel. It was dusk darkening to night by the time we reached the hotel and dinner was ready so there was no time for a walk to see anything of Kamloops.

I was up before breakfast and took the opportunity to go for a walk in the twilight of dawn. It was a lot colder than I expected and I returned to the hotel, to get my waterproof, not because it was raining but as my top layer, to keep the heat in. I hadn't checked the map and wasn't sure which direction was the centre of town so I just walked. There were a few shops, a Tim Hortons which is a large chain of coffee shops throughout Canada, next to the Lansdowne shopping centre, with a few cars parked here and there, at the edge of wide roads.

The Thompson River was to the north, on the other side of the railway tracks and the station. There was no pedestrians about and only a few cars passed by. The town's buildings were largely low rise buildings with only one that I saw higher than three storeys. All around the near horizon I could see barren hills rising above the rooflines of Kamloops.

After breakfast we got back on the coaches for the short ride along Victoria Street, over the railway tracks and back to our train. The train pulled out of the sidings and crossed a bridge, over the river through the outskirts of Kamloops, taking a sharp left hand bend across a tributary river. Soon we had left the outskirts of the town and we were rolling along the north shore of Lake Kamloops.

This is a long finger lake, less than 2kms wide and 29kms long. The water level fluctuates by up to 9m when the spring thaw increases water flow into the lake. Consequently there are broad beaches on the lake sides, scattered with logs washed down by the floods left high and dry, after the lake levels drop in the summer.

There were few trees growing here and the vegetation is best described as scrubland with patches of bare rock. Across the lake, long goods trains could be seen with their locomotives pulling their wagons east as we headed west. There were several sightings of eagles flying and roosting. Due to the shortage of trees, their nests were easy to spot, including one large untidy nest built on top of one of the railway bridges.

At the end of the lake, the sides of the valley close in and the Thompson River enters a gorge with railway tracks on each side continuing to follow the river. In some places, the track bed was hacked out of sheer cliffs with avalanche protection above and tunnels through promontories. We passed through Ashcroft which was the start point for prospectors on one of the overland routes north to the goldfields.

The Ashcroft trail is an all Canadian land route running parallel to the coast. It traverses the length of British Columbia on the east side of the Rockies and runs for nearly two thousand kilometres just to reach Whitehorse. After this, prospectors could either continue over land or more likely, take the river to reach Dawson City.

At Lytton, the Thompson River joins the Fraser River and the valley turns southwards. We crossed the river and headed southwards on the east bank of the Fraser River. The scrubland has receded and there are more trees on the valley sides. About 45kms from Lytton, we passed Boston Bar. Shortly afterwards the train slows right down and crawls past Hell's Gate which is a sudden narrowing of the river, with its rapids and a cable car for tourists to access the far bank of the river. We glimpsed the cable car, the associated buildings of the tourist venue and a foot bridge, over the river through the trees.

Standing on the viewing platform at the end of the carriage you can hear the water cascading over the rocks and plunging into the splash pool at the bottom. We passed through a short tunnel and we were past Hell's Gate. The train picked up speed. From our position, high up the side of the valley we don't get any glimpses of the rapids but got a good panoramic view of the valley above the rapids. For a good view of Hell's Gate itself, you need to go to the visitor centre or take a white water raft down the river for a really close view.

A short distance further along the valley, we gazed down on an inflatable raft that had shot Hell's Gate with 'Fraser River Expeditions' written in large letters down the side. That was the same company with whom I had rafted down the river and I knew exactly how much fun they were having. They waved at the train and several passengers waved back.

We passed through Hope and by the time we reached Chilliwack, we were heading west along the banks of the river. The river had spread out and split into multiple channels between gravel bars. The valley opens out and we were soon passing through farmland and rolling countryside, as we left the mountains. The amount of urbanisation increased as we neared Vancouver with more farmhouses and clusters of modern homes.

As we approached the end of our rail journey, there were protesters, either by themselves or in twos and threes, holding up hand written signs complaining about the management of the Rocky Mountaineer train. There had obviously been a labour dispute and they were complaining about losing their jobs. The details of the dispute were a mystery to me, especially as 'The Rocky Mountaineer' is a seasonal service and other than a few permanent positions, for the more highly skilled drivers, most employees would be on short contracts. They may have had a legitimate grievance with which I agreed, but it was still disconcerting to realise that I was innocently and ignorantly supporting the management by using the train.

CHAPTER 4

Vancouver and Victoria

The train reached the terminus on Main Street in the heart of the city. I grabbed my bag from the baggage car and walked through the terminus building. I made my way to the Century Plaza hotel on Burrard Street in the West End. I had a few days in a smart hotel, but prospectors probably made their way one kilometre to the docks to the north to Victoria Harbour, a well-protected natural harbour with kilometre after kilometre of docks and wharves, to find passage up the coast.

From my hotel window, I had a great view over the city from my 22nd floor room. I got a map from reception, although admittedly it was fairly generic, not to scale and didn't show all the roads and so it was a long way from the totally accurate, informative and scaled maps that I am used in England, on sale from the Ordnance Survey. I wanted to stretch my legs after the train journey so I wandered around the immediate neighbourhood before it got too dark, checking out some of the nearest shops before retreating to my hotel room, for the evening.

The next day I set out with a more detailed map of the city that I had bought the evening before. I had been to Vancouver before so I was familiar with some of the tourist sites available in the city, but I had missed the Capilano Suspension Bridge which is one of Vancouver's most popular tourist attractions. It is located to the north of where I was staying in the West End, through Stanley Park over the Lions Gate Bridge and a short distance up into the hills, following the Capilano River.

I had thought that it was just a bridge and therefore the price seemed a bit steep on my first visit to Vancouver so I had given it a miss. It was only later, I discovered there is a lot more to see there, when I spoke to friends who had visited it. The central attraction is a footbridge 137m long suspended 70m above the Capilano River built in 1889. Originally built of hemp rope it has since been updated and now uses strong steel cable. There is only a slight movement but then that is one of the things that makes it special, not to mention the view up and down the valley and straight down to the river below.

There are a host of other things to do within the park, a visit to an unspoilt preserved area of the West Coast rain forest, cliff top walks, board walks through the trees, plus a treetop adventure on a walkway high above the ground. Other attractions included a bird of prey exhibition with demonstrations of their skills in flight, an interpretation of the lives of the First Nations inhabitants, an exhibition of early settlers and interpretation boards of some of the sights and exhibits. Plus, there were the inevitable ice cream stalls, restaurants and gift shops.

I made a trip to my favourite Canadian store, the Mountain Equipment Co-Op. There are two stores in Vancouver, plus their head office but I was heading for the store on West Broadway. I had plenty of time, so I took a circuitous route to see more of the city planning to cross Granville Bridge over False Creek on the outward journey and to come back over Cambie Street Bridge, otherwise I just wandered where the fancy took me.

I reached the store and reverted to a child in a sweet shop and had to look at everything, recognising some brands and noted a lot of brands with which I was unfamiliar. I even looked at the tents, although I was not even remotely in the market for one. Eventually, I found myself approaching the till with a few items, including a fleece having been cold in Kamloops and a generic brand imitation of a Camelbak … and as I had an armful of other items I easily persuaded myself to buy a small rucksack to carry it all in.

Prospectors would have boarded a ship and sailed up the coast to their favoured port, before carrying on overland. I didn't want a ferry for the journey and neither did I want a cruise ship of which there were plenty which plied their routes up to Alaska to view whales and glaciers. Either way, I suspected that I wouldn't see much from the ship other than the coast, some way away from the ship and had made my own plans.

My next destination was Vancouver Island which lies just to the west of Vancouver and the mainland. It is bathed in warm Pacific currents so that the maritime influence makes it much milder than many other areas of Canada. The island is 460kms long and 80kms wide at its widest point which is about the same distance in length, as London to Newcastle and as wide as London to Oxford, so it is a big island.

The next day I met up with my guide and some of the others in the group with whom I would be canoeing, for three weeks. More than a hundred years before, Captain William Moores had reached Juneau but couldn't find a ship to take him further north. So in true pioneering spirit, he had canoed from Juneau to Skagway and established landing facilities there. He is also credited with the discovery of the pass over the mountains that the prospectors would take, so I felt it was a legitimate sideways step to take a trip by canoe along the route that the prospectors would have seen, as they headed north by ship from Vancouver to Skagway.

Just to be clear, although Captain William Moores is credited with discovering the pass over the mountains, it had always been there and the local natives knew the route very well but kept it a secret. Keeping it a secret would mean that they would retain control of trade over the mountain. Although, he was probably the first non-local and European person to traverse the pass and tell other people about it.

I made my way from the centre of the city to meet up in Pitt Meadows, a settlement 40kms east of Vancouver's West End. I met my guide, Chris, a local explorer and adventurer and his wife Barbara and some of the others in the group for an equipment check. We had a spare day to get provisions and get to know each other. We had a visit to the other MEC store in Vancouver on Main Street, a long thin red painted warehouse of a building and a lot larger than the other store that I had visited earlier. For some of the others in the group, it was their last chance to add to their kit and stock up on supplies before setting off.

Back in the Ramada Hotel, in Pitt Meadows, I had some time to kill so I asked for directions to the local shops just to get a feel of a suburban shopping precinct. It was diagonally opposite, across the Lougheed Highway and Harris Road and I was given road directions as if I was driving. I interrupted the receptionist to explain that I was walking and the receptionist said that it wasn't possible to walk there. I persisted and despite her protestations, I started out anyway. When I got to the intersection, I begun to understand why she thought that it wasn't possible.

Everybody in North America drives everywhere, so there isn't provisions for pedestrians. The main highway is three lanes whilst the quitter Harris Road was two lanes but there was another lane on each road at the junction to turn right. And there were no pedestrian traffic lights and in some places, no pavement and no central pedestrian refuge.

I had to wait for a suitable moment to make my move and felt that several drivers were staring at me in disbelief whilst I dashed on foot from one side to the other, dodging traffic. I got to the shops and mooched about for a while, before making the return journey. I made a mental note that the next time I asked for directions, I would listen to the local advice given and remember that although you can see the destination, it may not be possible to get there.

The group set off in a four wheel pickup and a minibus from Pitt Meadows back towards Vancouver, crossing the Pitt River. We joined the Trans Canadian Highway and followed it across the Iron Workers Memorial Bridge into north Vancouver. From the bridge, you get a glimpse of the extent of the harbour and the extent of its wharves and in the distance, to our left, the high rise buildings of down town Vancouver.

We gradually left the urban sprawl of Vancouver behind and headed down to Horseshoe Bay and the ferry terminal. We were booked onto a ferry to take us on a two and a half hour crossing across the Straits of Georgia that separate the mainland from

Vancouver Island. I stood on the top deck to watch us depart and head out across the straits. Slowly, the coast shrank to a blur on the horizon as we got further away. It was a bright day with just a scattering of clouds but the strong breeze whipped the heat away from my face. When there was too little to make out, the features on the coast had shrunk to a smudge in the distance, I sought some shelter from the biting wind below decks.

I was tempted into the restaurant and succumbed to the siren calls of a toasted sandwich. I couldn't possibly actually be hungry, as I'd eaten a cooked breakfast in the hotel. More likely boredom, as there is so little to do on a ferry to pass the time and nothing to look at. After a couple of hours, we were approaching the port on Vancouver Island. There was an announcement made over the tannoy that we were about to dock in Nanaimo and both drivers and passengers were asked to head back to their vehicles.

The bow doors opened and a cross section of pedestrians and vehicles from container lorries, coaches and RVs, through to cars and motorbikes, poured out of the mouth of the ferry and scattered, taking their different routes. Nanaimo was a coal mining community which exported their produce to both Victoria, the capital of the island and a major port and, Vancouver, during the Klondike gold rush. They would have supplied coal to many of the steamers heading north taking prospectors up the coast.

We turned right onto the Inland Island Highway and headed north, up the east side of the island in the afternoon. The Inland Highway led into Campbell River and crossed the river after which the town is named. Shortly after leaving the town we turned off the road and parked next to the beach. This was our lunch stop and we all bailed out. A cool box was hauled from the back of the pickup and we had a picnic of bread, cheese, pate, tomatoes, cucumber and hummus plus fruit to follow together with crisps, individual chocolate and muesli bars on the beach overlooking the sea.

The road leaves the coast, cuts inland and passes through thickly forested slopes. The population of the island is 759,000, giving a density of nearly 24 people per square kilometre which is high by Canadian standards but low when set against England's density of 407 per square kilometre. This was bear country and as I was sitting in the front, I was on bear watch. We were safe in the vehicle but my job was to look out for bears, so that we could slow down and allow the whole group to get a view and take photos.

In the distance I saw an immobile bear by the side of the road and alerted Chris, who was driving and we slowed. As we got nearer, it was clear that it was a painted life size statue. Just a bit further down the road, I saw another bear and called out but this too was a statue, a fibre glass model of a bear. It was a false alarm and I learnt that the locals had a sense of humour, so I was going to be a bit more wary before calling out again.

En route, we came across some road works with several big mechanical diggers which were repairing a section of road that had been washed away. There were no traffic lights or barriers, just a woman in a reflective vest that held her hand up to stop us. Past the diggers that were moving back and forth across the road, I could see a line of traffic had stopped on the tarmac, beyond the washout. After a while, the diggers moved to the side of the road and stopped, and with a wave and a smile from the woman in the reflective jacket, she waved us through the road works.

We bumped slowly across the uneven gravel surface. I was surprised to see several other women, amongst the workers leaning on shovels as we bumped past. Women in professional roles such as engineers on construction sites is becoming more of a regular occurrence on construction sites. Whilst there is no reason that they shouldn't also have women labourers, it was novel to see quite so many and doing manual labouring jobs.

Approaching a more populated area, there were telegraph poles with wires stretching across the road. Every time the wires crossed the road, hanging from the wires over the centre of the road was a pair of trainers, the laces tied together and thrown over the wires. It was quite an achievement, as the wires were quite high and there weren't just a few, and I admit I hadn't counted them, but there were more than a dozen.

That's a lot of shoes for one person, or maybe it was a group protest. Speculating further, it could have been a bully and a lot of school children had arrived home shoeless to the anger of their parents. I doubted that, as in a small community, action would have been taken so it probably wasn't malicious. Other potential explanations include that this is a site where drugs can be bought, which seems improbable as there were so many shoes hanging from the wires but no one was hanging about ready to trade.

Another explanation that I had been given on asking, was that it was a rite of passage. When children leave school, they throw their school regulation trainers over the wires as it was the last time they would need them. This seemed an equally possible explanation but there couldn't be that many school leavers in this small community. Sadly, the true story behind the shoes on the wires would not be resolved, as we were only passing through. It would remain a mystery.

The road had crossed a watershed and we followed a river valley, down and along the shore of Nimpkish Lake. The road was going to Port Hardy but as we approached the coast, some distance short of the town, we turned right off the main road and followed Beaver Creek Road. The road surface changed from smooth regular tarmac to a surface that once had been tarmac but heavy traffic and harsh winters had severely damaged the surface. It was in desperate need of resurfacing. The road reached a railway line and turned a corner to become Telegraph Cove Road, as it followed the railway line down to the sea.

We passed a large timber yard and sawmill, where the railway line terminated in sidings with lines stretching out throughout the yard. There were railcars with flat beds and tall poles along the sides to stop the logs falling off standing in long lines in the sidings, some were loaded and others were empty There were row upon row of round timber logs stacked in long rows. There were logs floating in the water just off shore, some loose behind booms, others neatly tied together in regularly shaped rafts, some in long lines, others floating in a jumble. Piles of bark outside a number of buildings, showed where bark was removed, and judging by the piles of fresh yellow sawdust, logs were cut and planed into regular lengths, ready for the market.

The next section of road was a complete mess. The hillside had been dug away in places and trees and shrubs had been cleared and left in large piles by the side of the road. Fresh unweathered rock was exposed on the newly cut steep slopes. The surface of the road was deeply rutted and bumpy with puddles growing larger with the light rain that was falling. It was obvious that road improvements were taking place to straighten and widen the road but we would have to negotiate the road works, until they were completed. Some of the material dug out from the hill was being used to build up an embankment on the downhill side of the road.

There were no workmen on site and not a digger to be seen. This was just as well, as had we met one, we may not have been able to pass on some of the more narrow stretches that had yet to be widened for a two lane road. We made our way slowly through the puddles and bumped over the ruts to finally arrive at The Telegraph Cove Resort.

This is a fascinating place with a rich history. It started life as a sawmill and cannery. Boats would bring back the fish to be packed at the cannery or smoked and exported in boxes. The cabins and cannery were built on stilts on the shore and stretched out over the water, as there was not enough flat land on shore and the facilities needed to be near, where the boats came in to land their catch. This arrangement also eased loading and reloading of fresh fish and boxed processed fish. The cove is an excellent natural harbour. It got its name, as the place where the first Trans-Pacific telegraph cable came ashore in Canada.

Today, much of the old charm is still well preserved with a couple of dozen cabins of different sizes available for hire. The cabins are connected together by a boardwalk above the water in the harbour. Some of the larger buildings house the Killer Whale Cafe and the Old Saltery pub, although we were self-catering and so wouldn't need to rely on their facilities. We took it in turns in twos and threes to cook the evening meals. The cabins are painted bright colours and have preserved their rustic charm and although the insides are modernised, there were no telephones or TV's.

On shore facilities include a general store, offices and maintenance buildings. There is space for 140 boats in the harbour. Further back from the water there is a campsite and RV park where vehicles can connect to services. It wasn't the high tourist season so the resort was virtually empty and the pub was not open. We had two cabins adjacent to each other, towards the end of the boardwalk, although we all squeezed into the larger of the two for our meals.

I was up early the next morning, as I rarely sleep well for the first night in a new bed and strange surroundings. It was a long time before breakfast. I was not on the rota to get breakfast ready so I headed out through the campsite and RV Park to explore some of the coast, near Telegraph Cove. It was a grey dawn with grey clouds overhead, there was damp was in the air, dew on the ground and wisps of fog drifting lazily through the trees. I kept an eye out for bears.

If you meet a bear, don't make any sudden movements and it is best to back away slowly or take a wide detour, monitoring their behaviour as you go. Any talking should be calm quiet and soothing to reassure the bear that you are not a threat. Avoid eye contact, as bears may attack when they feel threatened. Bears may stand up and this is so they can hear, see and smell you better and then to try to work out for themselves, whether you are a threat or not. Bears can ran fast and climb trees so these are not escape strategies.

If there is a sudden confrontation and not enough distance to back off, a good plan is to lie face down with your hands over your neck. If the bear tries to roll you over, use your elbows and feet to try to prevent this. If the bear is successful in flipping you over, keep rolling until you are again face down.

In the wild, bears sometimes turn sideways, in order to appear bigger and avoid conflict. I have heard an alternative to utilising this behaviour, that if you move together as a group and use a blanket as a cape, to make yourself appear bigger, this may deter an attack as you appear to be bigger than the threatening bear. A useful precaution is to always be aware of your surroundings and carry bear spray which is a pepper spray as used by police and for self-defence. Another option is for at least one of the group to carry a bear gun.

This is a handgun that fires a small shell that explodes, making a loud noise and a bright flash, which is supposed to frighten the bear away. I have seen one used on another trip and Chris had demonstrated it so the whole group would be aware of its effects. I knew what was about to happen, but it still made me jump. But this morning I was by myself so I kept a good eye out for movement and returned to the cabin without any encounter.

After breakfast, we went for a short walk to the other end of the campsite and came face to face with a black bear. It was my first encounter with a dangerous bear in the open in Canada. Unknown to me, on my walk before breakfast, a bear had been seen hanging about the campsite earlier in the week. Some bears discover that there are easy pickings to be had foraging around a campsite. Rubbish bins have to be bear proofed with steel to stop bears picking through them as they are omnivores and will eat absolutely anything. Once they have found a food source, they will return and will become a menace.

In order to avoid conflict with humans, these rogue bears are captured, tagged, recorded and taken up into some remote mountainous area suitable for bears and released. They have three chances and if they are captured for a third time they may have become accustomed to humans and those easy pickings so become an additional threat. Therefore after their third capture they are shot.

This bear was in a capture trap. This is a steel cylinder, with a heavy steel grate at each end. One end opens and is connected to a strong steel spring and self-locking device. The contraption is set on a trailer and is baited. The bear climbs in and sets off the trap that slams the door shut. The next day, the bear is drugged, tagged, details recorded and then it is taken away. As I peered through the grate at the back of the cylinder I could see the glint of the bear's two eyes staring back at me and the sound of a deep growling noise. This one hadn't been tagged before so he was about to have his first journey back to the wild. Not trusting the strength of the grate I backed off and reflected whether I would have gone for a walk by myself had I known that there was a rogue bear on the loose.

We set off on a journey up the island, to collect our canoe which Chris had left in storage, with friends. Outside Port Hardy, we turned down a dirt track to pull up outside a wonderful modern but traditionally built long low log cabin overlooking the coast. We were introduced to Lynn and Daisy, the young couple in their thirties who had lent Chris a shed to store his canoe for a while.

Lynn was a tall attractive slim woman with long fair hair. Her husband was Daisy which is not what I would have expected a man to be called. It wasn't his birth name but someone had had a sense of humour and he had acquired a nickname at school that everyone who knows him uses. He stood a full head above me, no fat at all but so well built, he made Geoff Capes look thin, with size 11 feet and hands the size of dinner plates. His handshake was like having your hand crushed in a vice. He was a lumberjack by trade and could move tree trunks around like matchsticks. As a last titbit of incongruous information, in his spare time he was a tenor in the local choir.

CHAPTER 5

Voyageur canoe and Victoria

We opened the long shed set to one side of the garden and there was our canoe. This is a reproduction of a large First Nation canoe about 12m long that can hold more than 20 people. Although made of fibreglass, it is painted to represent a birch built canoe that was the material used by natives to build their canoes. These are also called war canoes and voyageur canoes. This is a French word as the first western settlers to use these were French speakers in the east of Canada. These large canoes were used to transport goods up the rivers to traders and trappers and returned with furs.

We pulled the trailer on which the canoe sat, out of the shed. We grabbed a paddle each plus a few spares and several steering paddles. The oar blades were longer and narrower than those that I am used to but I was to learn that they are much easier to use, especially on longer journeys. The steering oars are slightly larger and longer. The canoe is steered from the back and due to the shape of the canoe which turns up at the bow and aft, the last seat is higher above the water level, hence the need for a longer handled paddle. This position was traditionally taken by the chief of the tribe or a high ranking village elder.

We hooked up the trailer to the truck and headed towards a quiet cove. Many of us had paddled before but we weren't used to paddling together and in unison. The captain sits at the back and determines direction of travel. He also determines the speed by telling the paddlers how fast he wants them to paddle. The stroke is set by the lead paddler who sits at the front, usually on the right and paddles at the speed required by the captain. Everyone else tries to mimic the lead oar and his speed so that all the paddles rise and stroke at the same time.

If a paddler gets out of sync, there is a clash of paddles and sometimes bruised knuckles. If paddlers get out of sync they should stop completely whilst they try to get the rhythm back, but they only have a brief moment to get back in the rhythm. The power of the two sides differs and the stronger side will start to turn the canoe making travelling in a straight line difficult especially if one or more paddlers stops paddling for any length of time.

This differential in power can also be put to good use to turn a canoe by paddling only on one side thus making a tighter or faster turn or even paddling in opposite directions, on either side, so the canoe can be made to spin on the spot.

The canoe can be brought to a hard stop by back paddling so all paddlers must listen for commands so as to be prepared for the next order. It should be remembered that tired paddlers will not like a captain who sets a fast pace, then demands frantic back paddling only to set off again. Anticipation of the water conditions and an understanding of the crew's ability is required on the part of the captain to ensure harmony.

We donned our buoyancy aids, grabbed a paddle and loaded up the canoe with day packs and cool boxes. We pushed the trailer into the water until the canoe floated off the trailer and we clambered aboard. We were also towing a kayak, as I had asked that if one was available, I would like to do a bit of sea kayaking.

For our first time on the water together, Chris was captain, his wife Barbara was the lead oar and we chose our preferred positions. If we were being competitive, we would be paired by height and weight to get a balanced crew but we weren't heading for those competitive heights just yet, just getting a regular rhythm would suffice.

We headed out and tried out some manoeuvres, turning left and right and changing speed. Except for an occasional clash of blades, we seemed to be doing alright. There were some islands facing the cove a few kilometres offshore and we headed towards these. The first one we came to, we made a steady turn and circumnavigated it in a smooth circle. I think we are doing really well as a team, although it is probably the steering skill of the captain.

We stopped on one of the islands, approaching the beach at a slow controlled speed, having been told to stop paddling some time beforehand. Therefore, we gently run aground with the front non lead oarsman, jumping out with a mooring rope to hold the canoe against the beach. This is essential to stop the canoe drifting away. As buoyancy returns and people get off, wind and currents could push it offshore.

We knew better than to all stand up and try to get out at once which would destabilise the boat, although that would have made for a better story. The cool box was carried ashore to set up lunch and the canoe was tied firmly to a large dead tree that had been washed up onto the beach. We were grateful to take off our bulky buoyancy aids. The beach we had landed on was largely pebbles and gravel with a few larger rocks sticking through.

At the high tide mark, there was a mass of driftwood from small twigs to whole trees, plus a few cut logs that had escaped the foresters' attempts to corral them near the sawmill. All of them had had the bark stripped off and been bleached almost white by the sun. I was surprised when Chris gathered up a number of the smaller bits and lit a fire, especially as it was on the beach (typically not allowed on UK beaches or forests but it's a legal minefield but if in doubt, don't light a fire).

I am used to seeing 'no fires' signs and warnings all over the place back home, with perhaps the exception of accredited scout campsites which are one of the few places you can experience the fun of a camp fire. Other than perhaps a bonfire in your back garden to get rid of a lot of garden waste which is not the same at all. Besides, this is now widely collected by the municipal authorities to be composted and sold back to you.

In Canada, needless to say, the rules are different and provided you are not reckless, it seems that few people mind. The weather had brightened and it was a sunny day with only a few scattered small clouds and the driftwood was largely dry. Cedar is an especially good wood to burn, as the essential oils within the wood make it easy to start a fire, even in the damp.

We had great fun in gathering wood and keeping the fire going. There is something magical about watching a fire, seeing how it consumes the fuel, enjoying the heat and sometimes having the ability to cook over it, or heat water for a hot drink. And even if a fire is not used for cooking, it still forms an attraction, as the centre piece of a group around which we can chat.

After lunch, the cool box and other equipment was loaded back into the canoe, the fire put out and everyone got back into the canoe. I took the opportunity to paddle the kayak and chose to follow the canoe and take a few photos of the team in the water. We set off and from my vantage point in the kayak, looking over to the canoe I had to admit, that as the paddles rose and sank on the stroke, it looked really impressive, as if they had been paddling together for ages. We headed along the coast in the afternoon sunshine and we were enjoying ourselves.

We were joined by at least one whale somewhere nearby. We could hear the occasional blow as the animal surfaced and exhaled, throwing clouds of steamy breath into the air. This was followed by the suck in of breath, before it dived again. We saw plenty of clouds of warm steamy breath being thrown into the cool air. Unfortunately, we were so low in the water that we never actually got to see the animal itself, only the results of its breath from a distance.

In the late afternoon, we turned around and headed back towards our launching point. Paddling your own canoe or kayak by yourself is tiring, especially if you haven't done it for a while. It uses a particular set of muscles which, speaking for myself, I hadn't used for some length of time and I was ready for a break. At a convenient point, I swapped the kayak for the comfort of the canoe. I managed to get out of the kayak and into the canoe at sea, without falling in and once again, the canoe was pulling the kayak behind it.

We reached the shore where we had put in and followed the sequence of events in reverse order, first gently beaching the canoe, getting out, unloading then getting the canoe back into its cradle on the trailer and securing it ready for transport. We threw our buoyancy aids and paddles into the canoe and we changed out of wet shoes to dry our feet and put on ordinary shoes. We had an early meal in a local restaurant with Lynn and Daisy, before hooking up the canoe on the trailer with the kayak inside and headed back to Telegraph Cove for the night.

For the next few days, we headed along the coast, paddling the large canoe, in which were our supplies and baggage. We would stop in the late afternoon at what looked like a promising location and unload the canoe, making it secure and building a fire, gathering driftwood for the fire and pitching our tents. We cooked using gas and from experience, it was a lot easier to control the heat and therefore, the cooking. When camping, another issue, is cleaning and it's a lot easier to clean the pans after using gas than an open wood fire.

Despite cooking on gas, we still had a fire and after the meal we would gather round the fire, for both warmth and a chat. As for pitching tents, there was always competition for the best pitches, as flat land was sometimes hard to find. Most of us did not want to be in bear country and too far from the fire and the other tents. Consequently, some good looking pitches further away from the fire were scorned, in preference for lumpy pitches which were nearer the centre of the camp and the fire.

As we progressed along the coast, we met other paddlers coming in the opposite direction and they were all intrigued by our large canoe. Such a large canoe is an unusual sight and they just had to come across and have a brief chat. Several kayakers we met had fishing rods and would stop occasionally, to try their hand at catching fish and had been successful, proudly showing off their catch that would be supper that evening. Along the coast, we saw plenty of seals and sea lions, either lazing in the sun on rocks or at sea, who would quietly surface and watch us with curiosity, before continuing with their lives.

It was a rich fishing ground and we saw several small trawlers. One small trawler was built of aluminium, called the Harvest Moon which we watched for a while, whilst plying its trade. It would send a small one man boat to anchor its net on a large rock on the shore. Then it would lower its nets and lay them in a large arc, coming back to the anchor point. Then the nets were hauled in by the winch gear and the resulting catch, unloaded on to the back of the ship.

Here were hands waiting to sort the catch, often with a crowd of noisy gulls waiting for cast offs. It was fascinating to watch the action in close up from the canoe just metres away and the fishermen didn't seem to mind. Conversations with the fishermen were shouted across the water and a lot of waving, whilst waiting patiently as we negotiated our way out of the arc of their nets.

One afternoon, we had stopped to camp early at a particularly promising camp site and had decided to go for a walk up into the hills overlooking the water. On the centre of the trail was some poo with some berries clearly discernible, buried amongst the droppings that had not been digested. Chris came along and explained the field craft to us. This was bear poo and as it was cold, light brown and dry, it was several days old so no problem. Apparently, you only have to be concerned if it is warm, damp, black and shiny and then it is fresh so you need to exercise all the bear precautions that we had been told about earlier.

Not much further along, in the centre of the trail was a small pile of damp, black and shiny poo. No one was prepared to touch it to test the temperature but we all looked at each other and knew what it meant. I found that I was out in front of the group and no one else seemed to want to take the lead. The path was easy to follow and so from a navigation point of view it was easy to follow but I kept my eyes peeled for bears as I was on point duty.

Despite the nerves, all was going well on our afternoon walk, until I saw movement in the bushes, just ahead of us adjacent to the trail. I put my hand up to signal to those behind to stop. The leaves continued to move and not from the wind. None of the other bushes and branches were moving at all and it was the only bush whose leaves were quivering. There was definitely something there but I couldn't make out what it was and walking backwards was difficult, when people behind you want to see what's happening. Anyone can be brave when there is somebody else in front of them.

Chris came forward and asked what the problem was. I indicated the bush and the moving leaves. He looked serious for a moment and said that he would take over. He tiptoed forward right up to the bush, turned around and suddenly jumped up and down, waving his arms about and shouting, scaring the living daylights out of all of us.

He knew exactly what the movement was and it wasn't a bear. There were some chipmunks who were biting off nuts from the tree above and letting them fall to the ground to collect later. As the fruit hit the leaves it caused them to move which was the movement that I had seen. He had played along to give us a fright. He split his sides laughing at our terror as he had started jumping up and down, shouting his head off.

We did see bears down by the water's edge, but from the relative safety of our canoe out on the water. We saw a large black bear with two cubs in tow. Bears can also swim but happily we were down wind and the bear looked in our direction but their eye sight isn't that good and apparently the bear saw nothing to threaten it so it went on searching along the beach.

We stopped paddling and drifted in the light swell to observe it for a while from a short distance off shore. What amazed me was the ease with which it can roll aside quite large rocks with a single paw with apparently no effort. Later, after we were sure that the bear had gone, we stopped on the beach for a break. I tried to roll aside a similarly sized rock and could barely move it, let alone roll it aside.

Another incident occurred a couple of days later when we had finished dinner and tidied up. It was late and we were about to head off to our tents. Chipmunks are cheeky little animals, similar to squirrels and they will eat anything. They are so persistent that nothing can stop them if they want to get it. They can sniff food out from tens of metres away and will eat through the canvas of your tent and backpack to get at food, chew plastic and ruin insulation to get to food and especially, anything sweet.

We were in bear country, so we made sure that everything was washed clean of any food remnants and the wash water was carefully disposed of. All food plus toothpaste, perfumes and toiletries are stored in a sealed box, and hoisted into the trees on a rope and away from the centre of camp. Therefore there should be no food in camp and no tempting target for bears.

One night I happened to be sharing a tent with Steve who had a sweet tooth. I got back to the tent to go to bed and found it infested with chipmunks. I shouted out and waved my arms around like a madman trying to frighten them away. Steve was still by the campfire and I shouted back at him whether he had any food in his rucksack. It was a stupid question, as it was obvious that there was some food in it, as evidenced by the persistence of the chipmunks inside the tent. Very cleverly and not wishing to lie, his answer was 'Ermmm…maybe'.

Back on the water as well as seals, we saw whales that came to the surface to breath before plunging back down beneath the surface to continue their search for fish. Sometimes, they were rather distant and unlike our first encounters, sometimes they were really close. It might be exhilarating, watching them from a larger craft but it could be a bit menacing when you are in a relatively small canoe with them so close. When they were close, the light swell that they created rocked our canoe. But they left us alone, as they fed and breathed and we had a great up close and personal view.

We saw a lot of fins breaking the water's surface but it was great fun in retrospect when the animals surfaced nearby and breathed out showering us with fine spray which was a unique experience, getting us quite wet in the process. I tried not to think about the accompanying bogies.

We turned around and headed back towards Telegraph Cove. We all had the opportunity if we wished, to try our hand at lead oar or being the captain if we wanted. My personal crowning paddling moment was when we were nearing Telegraph Cove, towards the end of the last day of our trip, along the inside passage on the water along Vancouver Island. Chris called me up to the back of the boat. He gave me the steering oar and said that I was in charge.

By using a 'J stroke', so called because of the pattern that it makes in the water. I guided the canoe along the coast across various bays as we headed home. Around the last headland was the harbour mouth, a narrow gap between jagged rocks. The crew knew where we were going and after several days of paddling together, knew almost instinctively what to do from the speed and feel of the canoe. We negotiated the opening of the harbour and gently made our way around the berths, towards the slipway.

I told the oarsmen to stop paddling with just an occasional order to pull a stroke or two to maintain direction or to help a turn. And I had judged the speed and momentum just right, as we glided ever so gently towards the concrete slipway for the front oarsman to jump out with the rope to hold us against the slipway. I had successfully manoeuvred the 12m long canoe around the headland, past the rocks, through shifting currents at the mouth of the harbour and through the harbour negotiating the different quays and moored boats to arrive at the slip way without gouging a hole in the bottom of the canoe and not a single back stroke. I was elated at my success.

The next morning we hooked up the trailer with the canoe on it to the truck and headed back down the length of the island. We passed underneath the trainers on the telegraph wires again and this time I was not caught out by the statues of bears by the road side. We turned off the Inland Island Highway and found a pleasant spot on the coast near Fanny Bay to have lunch.

Later, we continued straight past Nanaimo, as we were heading towards the city of Victoria and whilst the city was not on most of the prospectors' routes to the goldfields, it was still a major port so would have been visited by some of the prospectors coming up the coast from further south. It is such an interesting place that it deserves a mention, as you can't visit Vancouver Island and not visit Victoria.

We arrived in the late afternoon and checked into our hotel, not far from the city centre. Victoria is the island's capital and with a metropolitan population of over 344,000 which is nearly half of the island's total population. It is the oldest city in the northwest being established in 1843 and incorporated as a city in 1862. During the Fraser River gold rush, starting in 1855, it was the major port and fitting out centre for miners on their way to the Fraser River gold fields.

The 1886 completion of the Canadian Pacific Railway terminus in modern Vancouver and the excellent port facilities nearby was too much of an attraction and whilst Victoria continued to prosper for a while, further development and investment took place in Vancouver. Victoria was eclipsed as a Victorian and Edwardian city but without later developments which took place in Vancouver, so in part this makes it such a pleasant and unspoilt city frozen in the Edwardian era.

There were a few days to explore the city, prior to heading back to Vancouver so I spent a little time researching what I would do next. The rest of the group had wanted to go whale watching from a larger boat and to get some photos looking down on the animals, rather than being at sea level as we had been on most recent encounter. I had done this before and although I had thoroughly enjoyed it, I wanted to experience more of the city and its culture. Besides which, even if we had had some memorable close encounters with whales just a few days earlier, it's not every day that you get some free time in a historic city.

We headed down town in a large group all together by public transport towards the docks. We got to near the bottom of Douglas Street, not far from the docks and got off the bus. We made our way westwards, down to the docks of the inner harbour. We found the boat that was to take the rest of the group whale watching for the day. They dressed up in bright orange, all in one waterproof overalls and buoyancy aids and got on the boat. Together with a few other passengers, the boat cast off and made its way out of the harbour and off into the distance to find some whales as I watched from the wharf.

As they disappeared out to sea and from view, I walked up the waterfront to the harbour airplane terminal, a short distance away. I had chartered an airplane for a journey around the local area, but the thrill for me was that this was a sea plane or a float plane with floats instead of wheels that takes off from the water, rather than a tarmac runway. It was a rather expensive option, but I wanted the experience, so I had paid up. I checked in at reception and was shown towards a private reception area, but I was not allowed to enter before I had been subjected to a search and body scan.

After a short while my pilot entered the waiting area and introduced himself as Jack. We left the warmth of the terminal building and he accompanied me outside, to where the plane was moored and it was gently bobbing up and down on the swell against the jetty. I was helped aboard, not that I needed helping but no doubt he was making sure that I didn't slip and drown before I had taken my flight.

I strapped myself into the seat next to the pilot's seat, as Jack climbed in and made some final adjustments. He made the final flight checks and ensured that we were safe and ready to go. He handed me a headset and put his own on before he started the engine. It roared into life and then he throttled back to a gentle purring noise. He checked with the harbour air traffic control and indicated to the ground crew that we were cleared to go. The tether holding us to the wharf was released by the ground crew and we inched forward as Jack added more power.

We left the jetty and had to negotiate the Inner Harbour, avoiding some of the many water taxis to reach the take-off area designated on sea charts and reserved for planes. I have often wondered on the mechanics of getting enough lift and speed to enable the floats to escape the drag of the water, but have yet to meet an engineer or physicist who could answer some of my probably inane questions. Of greater concern though, is on landing when the floats suddenly met the friction of water. Why do the struts not break with the sudden change in speeds between the body of the aircraft and the now suddenly slowing floats? Or, as the water grabs the floats, why doesn't the plane just nosedive into the water?

We passed Laurel Point Park on our left. Other than the passenger terminal, most of the harbour is marina, open shoreline or modern buildings looking across the harbour's water. Only near the exit to the sea on our left, were there industrial wharves and jetties with a few large ships loading or unloading.

Out in the open water we passed some buoys and turned again. Jack checked with control and then revved the engine and we accelerated forward. We gradually picked up speed and pulled away from the grip of the water and we were finally airborne. It was noisy and there was some vibration, but both reduced as we levelled out along the coast. We headed out to sea to find some whales.

After flying for a while, Jack pointed off into the distance but I must admit I only saw some smudges bobbing on the water. Flying closer I could clearly see several bright orange whale watching boats and from the air, I could see the black forms rising towards the surface ready to exhale, before the spectators on the boats watching them. We circled clockwise for a while so that I could have a view out of the side window of the whales, as they came to the surface to breath and then sink back into the depths.

Some of the boats and whales got really close to each other. Occasionally, I could see the spray from the whales, blow over the whale watchers. One of those boats may have had my friends on it but I hadn't taken sufficient notice of the particular boat that they had set out in, to be able to positively identify it. The whales eventually all dived and the sea became calmer with just a few boats rocking in the swell. Bow waves appeared as two of the boats were under way tracking the whales using sonar. Jack asked if I wanted to see more whales but I opted for a tour of Victoria and the island.

We headed back towards Victoria and followed the shore, first east and then north. I gazed past the pilot's shoulder, trying to make out landmarks in the city below and especially Craigdarroch Castle which was where I planned to visit later in the day but either didn't recognise it or I wasn't looking in the right direction. There were more whale watching boats just a short way off to our right, but we couldn't take a closer look as that was USA airspace and Jack hadn't filed a flight plan to cross the border so we continued to head north over various islands and away from Victoria.

It was fascinating to look down at the leisure craft and larger commercial shipping, navigating their way across the sea and around the many islands. From the air, it was easy to see the metropolitan area made up of industrial estates, blocks of flats and housing estates and the like. This thinned and there were swaths of farmland and forest bisected by highways.

As we turned over the islands, Jack pointed out several and named them, but I forget all the names and I was just enjoying the view and the trip. We headed down Saanich Inlet, towards Butchart Gardens. Jack asked whether I wanted a closer look and the answer was 'Of course I do'.

I had read about the gardens and had wanted to visit but I didn't think I would have time, as they are over 20kms away from Victoria and not so quick and easy to get to by public transport. By air, it was just a few minutes. Robert Butchart manufactured cement and moved to Victoria from Ontario, attracted by rich deposits of Portland limestone needed for quality cement. It was an ideal location for the ease of shipping from here to the growing markets of Vancouver and all the way down the coast to San Francisco. He started manufacturing here in 1904 and continued until 1916 when cement manufacturing ceased with the exhaustion of the quarry.

It was his wife who had gardening designs and transformed the obsolete quarry into a sunken garden. Other themes followed, a rose garden, a Japanese garden, a Mediterranean garden and later, there were concerts and firework displays held regularly in the grounds. From the air, the gardens looked neatly kept and colourful. The two large car parks were busy with cars and coaches, of the more than a million visitors that these award winning gardens attract annually which is open all year round.

Jack checked with the air traffic control and dropped a little height and flew a slow clockwise circle. I got a great aerial view of both the house and the gardens. I was almost disappointed, as the view was great but I was missing out on the close up view and the smells of the flowers. I could make out the different areas of the garden and racked my brains to try to determine which was which, which was only resolved later, on my return to the hotel, where I could check a plan of the garden. But at least I had seen it. I regretted that I had not made more time and effort to add it to my list of things to do whilst I was in Victoria.

We regained height and headed back to the terminal. I got a little bonus as there was some congestion and rather than heading straight back to the landing area we were told to make an arc westwards and I got to see some more of the island and some forest, west of the city before turning and making our final approach. We taxied back to the jetty, Jack turning off the engine and after the propellers had stopped he got out ready to be received by the ground crew as we gently drifted towards our mooring.

A line was thrown and we tied up against the jetty. I took off the headphones, undid my seatbelt and climbed out back onto the jetty. I thanked Jack for a great flight and was shown through the security gate and back to dry land. It had been expensive but well worth it.

I made my way through the streets of Victoria on my way to Craigdarroch Castle. I knew the story but I wanted to see the reality for myself. The castle is built in the tradition of a Victorian version of a Scottish baronial mansion and had some great stained glass windows.

It was built by Robert Dunsmuir, who was born 25th August 1825, in Scotland. He had become a wealthy coal merchant who had mined coal in Scotland, before arriving in Canada. He had struck lucky near Nanaimo, with a rich coal mine which he had staked out. He later invested in railways and built a line that was to stretch from Victoria through Nanaimo and Wellington and onto to Courtenay, on the north east of the island.

His business empire continued to expand and as he grew ever wealthier, he commissioned an architect to build Craigdarroch Castle. Robert Dunsmuir died on 12th April 1889, ten months before the castle was completed. He is reputed to have said that "money is no object, just build what I want." Granite was imported from British Columbia, tiles from San Francisco, and a staircase in oak pre-fabricated in Chicago. All of this opulence in the building was set in the grounds of 11 hectares. He had died before the buildings completion but his widow, Joan, moved in ten months later, in February 1890 and lived there until she died in 1908.

The estate was then bought and sub-divided into lots to be sold off, but the building luckily survived intact with a number of different uses, being a military hospital building and a college until 1979 when it became a museum. It has a host of artefacts from the age when it was lived in as a house and the tour around the house is fascinating and well worth a visit. Also, Robert Dunsmuir's son, James Dunsmuir, commissioned the building of a castle, to be called Hatley Castle which was completed in 1908. It was subsequently used by various branches of the military, until its current use as part of the Royal Roads University.

I left the Craigdarroch Castle and headed back to the waterfront, taking an arc through back streets to get back to the jetties. I hung around until the rest of the group, on their whale watching tour, got back to the jetty. They were later than scheduled but by the beaming smiles on their faces, I could tell without asking them that they'd had a great time. I asked whether they had seen a small float plane fly over them and they said yes, and there wasn't that many float planes in the sky so I was sure I had seen them from the air.

We moved to a cafe on the waterfront to trade stories and catch up on news. It was getting towards dusk so we decided to stay down by the wharf and have an early evening meal by the wharf. It was still early and the sun had passed behind the mountains to the west, but there was still some light. Even at this early hour in the evening, several of the most popular locations overlooking the water, were fully booked but eventually we found a restaurant on the water front that served seafood and had space for all of us. We had a wonderful meal of seafood, crabs, shellfish and white fish before heading back to our hotel.

Some of us stayed in the local bar longer than we had anticipated, so the next morning was a bit of a shock and a challenge to get up and pack, ready for our departure. The trailer with the canoe was hooked up to the pickup and we set off out of Victoria, to get back to the mainland. We headed out of Victoria in the early morning and there was a steady drizzle falling from the sky. We headed up the Patricia Bay Highway due north from Victoria for the 30kms drive to Swartz Bay and the ferry back to Vancouver.

It was a cold, wet, early morning start. We were waved into our lane, ready for boarding and parked up, waiting for the call to board the ferry that had not yet arrived in port from Vancouver. We headed for the small cafe that promised hot drinks and burgers, but it was not open this early. Eventually, the ferry arrived and traffic flowed off it past us. There was a break and we watched anxiously for the call to board the ferry and were elated, when we got the call to board and get into a warm dry environment and a hot breakfast.

As soon as the pickup with the canoe and the minibus had stopped, we were up the stairs and heading for the cafeteria to warm up, to get a hot drink and some form of hot cooked breakfast. I chose the full English cooked breakfast with coffee which was not my usual healthy breakfast option, but I needed the calories. I hardly looked through the windows which were streaked with rain as the ferry manoeuvred past several islands on its voyage, through an outlying range of islands, off the coast of Vancouver Island on the route to Vancouver.

After leaving the last of the islands off the Vancouver Island coast and just over two hours later the ferry terminal at Horseshoe Bay was visible. An announcement over the tannoy asked drivers and passengers to re-join their vehicles. The ferry docked and we drove off as instructed, along the causeway back to mainland and my next stop was Alaska.

CHAPTER 6

Juneau

I arrived in the Alaskan capital of Juneau, late morning. The weather was cold and damp with spits of rain that got heavier, then eased off again. Planning to have so little time in Juneau was one of those difficult decisions that on reflection, I may have taken a different decision, but given time constraints it seemed reasonable at the time. It was not on my list of places that I must see, neither was I aware, there was some magnificent 'not to be missed in a lifetime' attractions, that warranted a visit but like so many places, they have their pearls but sometimes you have to be in the know.

I was due to visit the Mendenhall Glacier at 3pm so I had time for a walk around the town and lunch. The Juneau metropolitan area is claimed to be the second largest in the USA, although much of it, is forest and steep mountainside and not at all urban. It is the capital of the state after the US Congress in 1900, said the state capital must move from Sitka, the original capital under Russian rule, to Juneau. Juneau was a larger city and more economically developed than Sitka, at that time. Juneau is also unique, in that, it is the only state capital without a road link to the rest of the USA or indeed, with the rest of the state, of which it is a capital.

It was founded as a mining settlement in the 1880's after gold was discovered in nearby unimaginatively named, Gold Creek. Neither is Juneau a large population centre as the largest urban areas in Alaska are Anchorage and Fairbanks, before Juneau with its population of just 32,000. It is also an odd choice, given that Alaska is a large state but the capital sits at the southern end of a panhandle in the very south eastern corner of the state as opposed to a location nearer the centre of the state or a coastal location nearer the mainland area.

My first target was to get to the wharf and find a cafe selling local produce. My prime aim was to find some king crab. Most of my initial knowledge of this fantastic sweet tasting crab meat was generally set by the TV series Dangerous Catch. This series of programmes featured fishermen braving the Arctic weather, the swell, the cold, the dark, and the hard work to trawl the seas for king crab.

There are several species of king crab that are common in Alaskan waters. The body shell can be the size of a man's foot and the leg span can exceed 1.5m. Broadly, they are giant crabs whose legs are really tasty. I must admit that I am neutral on the morals of the fishing industry, the quota system, sustainability, or a fair distribution of quotas and jobs. But, I am a supporter of Hugh Fearnley Whittingstall's campaign in Europe, against discards but right now I just wanted some crab meat.

Down in the harbour, just off Franklin Street, is the public library and behind this, is Tracy's King Crab Shack, right on the water front. There were some seats outside with umbrellas to try and keep the rain off and a small shack with a serving hatch. The smells from the kitchen was all the advertising they needed. There was quite a selection that took a while to absorb. I was joined by three other people, a mother and daughter and her friend, who all wanted to taste king crab. They were Americans from California, who were on a cruise and their cruise ship had stopped off that morning, to allow passengers time for a quick visit to Juneau.

I chose some fresh king crab, a homemade (and prize winning) bowl of king crab bisque and garlic bread. We sat down in the rain and chatted whilst our food was freshly prepared and cooked. And when it came, it was well worth waiting for. The bisque was rich, smooth and creamy with generous lumps of crab meat and it was hot, just what you want on a cold wet day. And the crab meat really was sweet and succulent, just like the books say and at long last, I was tasting fresh locally caught king crab.

I said goodbye to my fellow travellers and headed off to explore some of the town. My next stop was the Red Dog Saloon. It is reputably the oldest tourist attraction in the town, having been established here for the early miners. It has the true ring of a western saloon with bat swing doors painted red, wooden walls and tall bar chairs lining the bar. On the walls are all sorts of paraphernalia, stuffed bear heads, moose horns, stuffed king crabs, glass floats, life belts and everywhere, paper bank notes of all sorts of denominations and currencies, from all over the world.

It also has on display, Wyatt Earp's revolver. He was visiting Juneau on his way to Nome, a gold mining town, half way up the west coast of Alaska on Norton Sound. This gold rush started with the discovery in 1898 of gold in the sandy beaches of Nome and of all the gold rushes throughout the area, this one is the best known of all the Alaskan gold rushes. It also attracted many people from Dawson City, who didn't have valuable claims and still believed in the gold prospectors' dream of becoming rich. It was relatively easy for them to float down river and along the coast or chance the sea journey, straight across the bay from St Michael to Nome.

This location on the coast, made it much easier to reach than the Klondike goldfields near Dawson, in the depths of the Yukon forest and the gold was easy to get at and extensive. The discovery of older gold bearing former beaches, higher up the shore line prolonged its life as a gold producer for more than a decade. The story of Wyatt Earp's gun is that he landed in Juneau on June 27th 1900 and handed his gun in, at the local marshal's office, as was required by the city's rules. He left on the SS Senator at 5am, two days later, which was before the office opened so he left without being able to reclaim his gun.

I walked down the road southwards, along the water front to the Mt Roberts Tramway. This started operations in 1996 and its two cable cars take visitors from the cruise ship terminal, over 550m up Mount Roberts, where the top terminus ends at the top of a tower that gives marvellous views over Juneau, the port and the Gastineau channel. There is also a gift shop, an interpretation of local native life and a restaurant. There are various trails through the forest and up to the summit of Mt Roberts, but I didn't have time to go trekking.

South of here, the steep mountainside, presses back towards the sea, so the flat stretch of shore narrows and there is little development so I turned around and headed back towards the centre of town. I am surprised at the number of jewellery shops, for a small town but given the number of cruise liners visiting the town, the footfall must be sufficient for them to stay open and be profitable. I have an impression that cruise liner passengers must be rich and have nothing better to spend their money on than more jewellery. I headed up Main Street, up a steep slope to the State Capital building. I wasn't sure quite what to expect but I did expect to see a building a hundred years old that an architect had had permission to provide some form of impressive facade in order to make a statement.

In the event, I found a six storey building, the bottom two stories were stone clad and the top four had a brick finish. Other than four marble columns, stretching two stories in height at the entrance, it looked rather plain and a lot less impressive than the picture I had conjured up in my mind's eye. It was a functional, rather than a landmark building making a statement. I made my way in an arc back to Egan Drive and followed the waterfront back to Marine Way.

Right on time, my coach arrived and I climbed on board for the short trip of a few kilometres to the Mendenhall Glacier Visitor Centre. We drove along the main highway, parallel to the coast and just past the airport, we turned right up the Mendenhall Loop Road, climbing upwards and we reached the Mendenhall Glacier Visitor Centre.

The glacier starts high up in the mountains, in the Juneau icefields and flows for 19kms to terminate in the Mendenhall Lake from which flows the Mendenhall River. The Lake started forming in 1931 and since then, the glacier has retreated nearly 3kms and, as a consequence, the lake has slowly increased in size.

The Visitor Centre shows maps and models of the glacier, information boards on the local environment and a video presentation. As for visitor facilities, it has a cafe and a gift shop. There is a view across the lake and up towards the snout of the glacier. For those wanting a closer look, there are walks through the forest and along the lake shore, and, up nearby Nugget Creek which enters the lake just below the snout.

Since the glacier's origin is in an ice field, there is a lot of ice in the glacier and not too much rock so other than a few darker lines of moraine or dust on the glacier's surface, there is a fair amount of white and blue ice to be seen. The lake is peppered with lumps of ice, icebergs that have fallen off the leading face of the glacier in a process called calving and float in the lake, gradually moved about by wind and currents across the lake.

The Juneau Ice Field Research Program monitors the glacier and its retreat but the retreat is not steady. Increased moisture levels have led to greater snow fall on the ice field, high up in the mountains. It is still cold up on the mountains and the increased snow fall may add to the glacier and stabilise it or even push it forward. However, as the temperatures continue to rise, the rate of replenishment may be exceeded by the rate of melting and the glacier will continue to retreat.

There are platforms and elevated boardwalks for viewing wildlife. The salmon running in the late summer that attract bears hoping for an easy meal and there are a number of viewing points but I saw no bears.

We got back on the coach and headed back towards the airport and turned back onto the Glacier Highway. We followed the coast for about 40kms crossing Eagle River, towards Yankee Cove. We turned off the highway and headed down a short slip road, to the shore of the Lynn Canal, not a canal despite the name, but a wide and deep flooded former glacial valley or fjord that leads up to Skagway at the far end of the channel, about 110kms away. Moored to the single pier jutting out into the water was the boat that was to take me to Skagway.

It was a gleaming white, 20m long fast twin hulled catamaran custom built, locally owned and operated by Fjord Express. The last passengers got on and we set off up the channel. It was warm and comfortable inside with comfy seats, large windows all around and an outside viewing platform. Complementary drinks were available and there were loads of reference books on Alaskan wildlife, birds, fish, whales, flowers and the like, for customers to peruse.

Not far out from harbour we came across a buoy bobbing up and down and sideways, on its mooring in the swell consisting of a buoyancy device on top of which, was a pole with a warning light on top for shipping. Nothing unusual about that, but the captain pointed it out to us and as we approached, the engine noise and vibration decreased as we slowed down.

As we crept towards it, we could see that several seals had pulled themselves out of the water and were using the flat surface of the buoyancy device to rest. We got quite close and everyone had their cameras out. The seals raised their heads and stared at us but none of them moved, they just watched us and we watched them. When everyone had taken enough photos, the captain set off again on the original route.

Later, we passed a gravel bank on one end of a small island, in the channel and as we passed, we could see a colony of seals, some in the water but with most of them on the land and we could clearly see several bull seals with their heads held high and distinct, as they dwarfed the females, who were smaller and lying down resting in groups.

It was a smooth ride and we seemed to be making good time. Off our starboard bow, there were three boats just drifting in the light swell. They were whale watching boats and they had found a pod of whales and had ring side seats for the action. We veered off our course and the engines were cut and we slowed down to join the other boats and drift in the swell as we got near. There were several whales, their fins showing above the water surface, were clear to see, as they swam along the surface, showing off their tails when they dived.

The tail fins were all of different sizes, indicating a family group with youngsters. Every now and then, one would come to the surface to breathe, emitting a distinctive noise of a whoosh and a great cloud of spray, as they exhaled before breathing in and diving into the depths again. They were fascinating to watch from the comfort and safety of the catamaran. Gradually, the activity dropped off, as they went diving into the fish rich depths of the channel. With no more action to watch, the captain throttled forward and powered the boat forward and returned once again towards our original course.

The captain made an announcement over the tannoy whenever he noticed some interesting wildlife. There were not only sea lions and whales but there were several announcements regarding the birds that flew around the coast. There were eagles, hawks and other birds and there were lots of individuals to see. A few of my fellow passengers had the foresight to bring binoculars and so could view them for longer and kindly lent me a pair but you still had to get the direction and elevation right on a moving target. Usually by the time that I had got a pair of binoculars in my hands they were moving away, so I seemed to miss most of the sights.

One of the crew must have noticed my lack of skill at ever becoming a twitcher and kindly opened one of the books on birds and showed me what I had missed. It was kind and I was appreciative, but it wasn't the same as seeing the real thing close up for yourself.

We passed close to Eldred Rock lighthouse. This stands on a craggy rock, forming a small island with steep cliffs on three sides, but rising no higher than ten metres above sea level. The island sits right in the middle of the channel and was a dangerous navigation hazard. The lighthouse was one of several completed along the Lynn Canal, this being the last to be completed in 1906. The base is a two storey octagonal shaped structure, housing living quarters and store rooms with the lighthouse tower rising through the centre of the sloping roof for another two storeys with the light room on top. It was the only one that was built of concrete and is well preserved.

As we passed close to the shore, we slowed down and saw more seals and sea lions resting on the rocks. Sometimes they were surprisingly hard to see as they were camouflaged against the rocks, sometimes lying by themselves, or twos and threes, or grouped together in quite a large number along the same piece of rock. I can't say beach as these were few and far between, as the rock often plunged straight into the sea.

The captain nosed the ship as close as he could so that we could get good close up shots of the seals and sea lions, and on one occasion, backing us up to the rocks so that the rear viewing platform was closest to the action and everyone could get to see the animals. The animals might raise a head or two but largely seemed unconcerned about our curiosity. This was more of a wildlife cruise than a functional ferry. Judging by the number of people who had brought their own binoculars, they must have known that this was less of a ferry and more of a sightseeing tour of Alaskan wildlife.

It was getting towards dusk, as we approached a stretch of coastline with electric lights spilling out of buildings against the darkness of the evening to stop at a port. This was Haines on the western side of the channel. A drop off point for a few passengers before heading on to Skagway. The channel splits into two arms and we headed up the left hand arm to drop off some passengers at Haines.

We spent little time in Haines, just enough to drop off a few passengers and then we were off up the right hand channel. The walls of the valley closed in quickly and seemed to get higher and the width of the channel became much less, although still big enough for cruise ships to reach Skagway and turn around.

It was well after 8pm and our scheduled arrival time in Skagway, but we had taken time out to see wildlife sights and none of the other passengers seemed to mind. There was still some natural light, but it was fading fast. We passed several cruise liners moored against their terminals with lights blazing out lighting up the route to the small berth that we were heading towards.

I thanked the captain and crew for the memorable journey and headed into town to find my hotel.

Luckily, it was not a big place. By heading up the main street and turning left, I soon found my lodgings for the night, Sergeant Preston's Lodge on 6th Avenue. I hurried, as it was raining and didn't want to hang about. Annual rainfall is about 70cms, over two feet, with about a third of that falling in September and October, so if you want a dry visit, choose another time of year.

CHAPTER 7

Skagway

The next day I took an opportunity to investigate the local surroundings. Skagway is only one of two towns, where the whole town is a designated national site (the other is Harper's Ferry). It has a short history in time terms, but a long and sometimes violent history in human terms. It has a winter population of about 850 but this more than doubles over the summer, by casual labour and seasonal business owners that head into the town for the summer season. Skagway is a version of the local Tlingit language name for the area that was too difficult for new English speaking prospectors to pronounce correctly.

The town was first developed by Captain William 'Billy' Moore, a former sea captain and he was the first white settler. He was a member of the 1887 boundary expedition who had also explored the pass over the mountains that was later to be called the White Pass. This pass and the nearby Chilkoot Pass, had been kept a secret by the local population, to preserve their monopoly on trade but as with any great discovery, it could not be kept quiet for very long.

The boundary between Canada and Alaska had not been defined and even after the Alaskan purchase in 1867, the border was still unclear. Canada had requested a survey in 1871 when the neighbouring territory, formerly joined Canada as the state of British Columbia. The proposal was rejected by the USA, as being too expensive and whilst there was little economic activity in the area, the boundary issue did not get a high priority. The matter drifted for a few years as still unresolved.

Captain William Moore recognised that gold had been found in other areas, similar to those beyond the pass and had a hunch that gold would be discovered around here as well. He staked a 160 acres (64 hectares) homestead claim and built a cabin, a sawmill and a wharf to receive ships, ready to make money out of the prospectors, as they passed through. He preferred to make his fortune this way rather than facing the hazards of the wild interior and search for gold himself. He had experience of other gold rushes and had made money out of the Fraser and Stikine gold rushes plus a host of others. He had marvelled at the legends of the gold of the Incas and being a sea captain, he had sailed to Peru.

He had grand designs for a new town and developed plans for a town on a grid pattern, calling it Mooresville and had dreams of a railway as well. The border dispute continued unresolved but there was no catalyst to resolve it until the news of the discovery of gold on the Klondike River in August 1896, finally reached the outside world on 15th July 1897. In just two weeks' time, the steamship Queen docked at Moore's wharf on 29th July 1897, bringing the first prospectors to Skagway, on their journey to ultimately Dawson and the Klondike River.

In no time at all, there were whole waves of prospectors who landed and took over whatever space was available without regard to Moore's original plans or land, planting their tents on the flat land behind the wharf, setting up businesses and trading amongst themselves. There was no police or other authority to enforce Moore's claim to his land and his original plan as the population swelled from a tiny village to eventually, over 30,000, just a few years later. The area became a lawless place and the NWMP had described the town as hell. Land swapped hands irrespective of its original rightful owner and there were many cases of individuals jumping a claim and Moore was side lined.

Some of these potential prospectors were put off by the prospects of a difficult journey ahead when measured against some of the profits to be made from the overly eager or desperate miners, to be made in Skagway. They decided to make their money from those passing through the town, either by legal means or fraud.

Just a year later, in June 1897, the population of Skagway was 8,000 but as there was no census or other reliable count, with constant arrivals to be set against those leaving for the goldfields, estimates range up to 20,000 in the early years. People were making money out of the prospectors who were moving through the town on their way to the goldfields at perhaps the rate of 1,000 a week.

They were dissatisfied with some of the practices of entrepreneurs, exploiting them for goods and services and set up a council to protect their interests. The council was not very successful, as it might have had great aims but it had little power or authority. There was no continuity, as its members constantly changed, as they took to the trail to get to the gold fields. There was a power vacuum forming and it was to be filled be one particular opportunistic fraudster, who saw big bucks to be made.

In walked 'Soapy' Smith or to give him his birth name Jefferson Randolph Smith born 2nd November 1860. He was charismatic and plausible and sold himself in great displays. He halted lynchings, helped widows with alms and sometimes enforced the law breaking up fixed games of dice and cards but probably just to eliminate the competition.

He earned his name 'Soapy' from a scam that he had practiced years before. He would set up a stand to sell bars of soap and around several of the bars of soap, he would wrap dollar bills, ranging from a single dollar to a hundred dollar bill. Then, he would wrap them in plain paper and sell them for a dollar … of course holding back the bars that he knew had the big value dollar bills. When he judged the time was ripe, he sold one of the valuable bars of soap to a confederate, at which point they would publicly and loudly announce a 'win' in order to encourage further sales.

As sales flagged, he would announce that a hundred dollar bill was still unclaimed and he would auction the remaining bars, but as is often the case with scams, his accomplishes would win the vital bar of soap but the story tells how Soapy Smith got his name.

By this method, he had built several gangster empires, his first was in Denver Colorado. Regulation became too tough and he fetched up in Creede, Colorado. There was a silver bonanza under way and he could see that money could be made but conditions became too tough, as reforms were proposed, so Soapy returned to Denver. He survived for a while but he was too well known and eventually even corrupt officials were unable to protect him. As conditions for him to use his exploitative skills waned, he moved his base of operations and turned up in Dyea, adjacent to Skagway. He used card or pea and shell tricks on the White Pass trail but was forced out and fled to the east coast before returning to Skagway in January 1898.

In Skagway, he had a network of conspirators to fleece prospectors of their money. In another operation, his telegraph office offered to send telegrams to anywhere in the world for $5. But the innocent and duped clients didn't know that there was no telegraph cables to connect Skagway to the outside world.

He had a string of businesses such as saloons, casinos and tobacco shops. He controlled an army of spies and villains. In Skagway he controlled the press, the marshal's office, a bunch of thugs under the title of the Skagway Military Company and a random group of fraudsters, con men, dice men and card sharps, who were on the prowl to fleece those passing through Skagway.

But he didn't have it all his own way. A returning miner named John Douglas Stewart, with a sack of gold was persuaded to join a crooked card game run by three of Soapy's men. When he had to pay his losses, the card sharps grabbed the bag and ran off. Stewart complained to everyone he could about his loss and several citizens approached Soapy to persuade him to pay the gold back, which he refused to do, saying that Stewart had lost the gold 'fairly'. A citizen's meeting was announced to be held down on the wharf on 8th July 1898 and Soapy tried to muscle in on the meeting and was confronted by four guards whose job was to identify and stop Soapy's gang members from joining and disrupting it.

Among the four guards was Frank Reid, Skagway's city engineer and Jesse Murphy. There was a confrontation between Soapy and Frank Reid and suddenly firing started. Several shots were fired, the first two almost simultaneously. Both men received bullet wounds with reports of the time differing, but between five and nine. Jesse Murphy picked up Soapy's Winchester and shot him through the heart. Soapy was killed and his reign was over, Frank Reid died of his wounds, twelve days later, but Jesse Murphy had the accolade of killing Soapy Smith although later, historians support Frank Reid.

Walking up from the docks, the first sight that you see are several railway tracks, locomotives and a snow clearing locomotive, Rotary Snowplough No. 1 perpendicular to the road, painted a shiny black with twelve blades at the front with the windows, doors and the surrounds of the blades picked out in red. The blades are connected to a central shaft that rotates and throws snow to the sides of the tracks to clear them of snow, to enable trains to pass. It was built in 1898 by the Cooke Locomotive and Machinery Co in Paterson, New Jersey. This and the other locomotives on show all belong to the White Pass and Yukon Railway, the WP&YR.

The WP&YR was a 176kms long narrow gauge railway from Skagway, over the White Pass through tunnels, over bridges and trestles, with steep gradients and tight cliff edge turns to get through the mountains. Finally, it skirts lake shores and on to Whitehorse via Carcross. It closed in 1982, as metal prices had fallen so low that there was not enough freight to keep the railway open. It re-opened in 1988, as a tourist attraction but now only runs 108kms from Skagway to Carcross. In its first year, it carried 37,000 passengers and this had swelled in 2010 to 365,000.

The history of the railway starts with the arrival in Skagway of two men at the same time and who met by chance in the St James Hotel. One was Sir Thomas Tancrede representing the English investment bank of Close Brothers in London. William Brooks Close had paid £10,000, against the advice of his solicitors, to the government for the right to build a railway from Skagway to the Yukon.

The other man was Michael Heney who was an experienced railroad engineering contractor who had worked for the Canadian Pacific Railroad. He was the engineer that had pushed the CPR rail network west across the prairies and through the Rockies.

Tancrede had thought that building a railway through the rugged terrain was not possible, but Heney persuaded him otherwise. By a chance meeting, of money, talent and vision, the White Pass and Yukon Railroad Co, the WP&YR was founded in April 1898.

In May it had brought the right of way along the toll road built by George Brackett and construction began. Technically, construction was handled by three subsidiaries set up in order to satisfy the different legal requirements of the different jurisdictions through which the route lay, starting in American Alaska, crossing the as yet, still undefined border, into Canada's British Colombia and finally into the Yukon.

The route climbs from sea level to the summit of the pass at 873m over 32kms and there are a number of tight turns of up to 16 degrees so only a narrow gauge railway would be able to manage the turns so a three foot or nearly a metre gauge was selected. Work was challenging with thousands of men working on the project to lay track bed, blasting through rock using a total of 450 tons of explosives and the construction of two tunnels. In places the rock face was so steep, workers were lowered on ropes to hack away at the rock to build the track bed.

Work continued through the winter months, although the cold conditions made for slow progress. Between the two tunnels on the ascent towards the summit, is Dead Horse Gulch. Engineers had to build a steel cantilever bridge across the gorge 65m above the river. Timber had to be cut and manhandled across rough terrain to build the trestles. About 35,000 men in total worked on the construction of the railway although daily work force varied between 700 to 2,000 with 35 losing their lives.

There was little trouble in the work camps as alcohol was not allowed, but otherwise the work force was treated well. Pay was three dollars a day and the workforce was a mixture of those who were saving up to head on towards the gold fields or those who were saving up to pay for their passage home, either way, the work was welcomed. Soapy Smith's gang caused trouble in the camps by trying to fleece the workers of their cash but this ceased when he was shot dead and his gang was run out of town.

It is known that Sir Thomas Tancrede and Michael Heney met with Soapy and it must have been obvious that he was a bad character that could cause disruption in their workforce. However, it is not certain whether the pair had any influence over the vigilantes and the final demise of Soapy.

In July 1898, just two months after construction started, WP&YR ran their first train. It was a passenger train, along the first 6kms of track that had been completed. News of a gold find on Lake Atlin, just a hundred kilometres away, instead of the 800kms to the Klondike caused many of the workers to leave, sometimes taking the WP&YR picks and shovels with them, who headed off to Atlin Lake. More labourers were hired and work continued. They continued to extend the new track and reached the summit of White Pass in February 1899 and in July, it had reached the shores of Lake Bennett.

Another construction team had started in the summer of 1899 in Whitehorse, heading towards Skagway making better progress as the ground conditions were not so difficult compared to the route up the pass which was largely solid rock. But getting heavy rails and equipment to the second team was a challenge. Materials were taken by train to the end of the line and then transported down the lake by boat, to be unloaded at Carcross.

The two teams met at Carcross in July 1900. In just 26 months the railway stretched 176kms from Skagway to Whitehorse. By the time is was completed, the original gold rush had peaked with most of the area having been staked out. The diehard gold rush prospectors without a claim, were heading for Nome but the mines on the Klondike still operated. Many small claims were amalgamated into larger corporate enterprises which the WP&YR serviced.

In later years, the railway was also an important link in the supply chain, assisting the US Army to build the Alaskan Highway and associated airbases during the Second World War. Locomotives changed from steam to diesel with the delivery of their first diesel engine in 1954 and continued until the collapse in mineral prices and therefore, ore freight demand caused it to cease operations in 1982.

Just up the road from the rail depot, on the corner of Broadway and Second, is the Skagway Visitors Centre which assists visitors with accommodation, trekking routes and tourist information, plus exhibitions and videos of times gone by. It is also where I discovered that I would need a permit to trek across the Chilkoot Trail into Canada. All the permits had been sold and none were available. The money raised from the permits goes towards the cost of maintaining the trail.

I discovered that it is a very popular trail and permits sell out months in advance. I could of course, take pot luck but if apprehended without a permit I would be subject to a substantial fine. Alternatively, permits were not required at the end of the season but I had neither the time to wait nor the appetite to risk a fine, so I would have to make my onward journey by road or rail.

Almost next door on Second is the WP&YR offices where there are further exhibits and information boards about the WP&YR plus importantly to me, where you can book tickets for the rail journey through the pass to Carcross. I made sure that I could continue my journey onwards by rail rather than trekking and made a booking.

I discovered that the railway used to come down from the pass and go straight down Broadway, the main street. It was only in 1942, when the US army took over the town, that the tracks were moved eastwards to the outskirts of town to leave the main street free of trains. This was necessary, due to the increase in train traffic with up to twenty trains a day heading north up the pass to move supplies for the army as it built the Alaska Highway.

The town has the feel of an old gold prospecting town. The buildings are single or double storey often with large false fronts in the style familiar with film goers watching westerns. They are all made from wood with over lapping planks for walls. Further up the main road, away from the main tourist centre there are corrugated walls of buildings but no high rise buildings and no modern concrete and glass structures.

I wandered up and down Broadway and along the side streets that led off it. There were a few vehicles but not many, but plenty of people, as there were two large cruise ships in port whose passengers were also investigating the town. Just as in Juneau, I noted a lot of jewellery stores plus a significant number of gift shops, of one type and another specialising in native art works, souvenirs, paintings, artisan work, woollen goods and more bars and restaurants that a small town would be able to support by itself.

On the opposite side of Broadway from the Skagway Visitors Centre is the original Jeff Smith's Parlor, the building owned by Soapy which also served as his office. It was originally located on 6th but moved here in 1964 and has been converted to a shop. On the diagonally opposite corner from the Skagway Visitors Centre is the Red Onion Saloon. This was built in 1897 and was the classiest bordello in Skagway. There were ten small rooms upstairs which were as decorated as the rooms downstairs, but each was different as they were decorated by the girls themselves.

Clients would select their girl in a unique manner. Each of the then girls upstairs had a doll that represented them behind the bar. The client would choose his girl and the barman would lay the doll on its back, to indicate that that particular lady was busy entertaining. When the client left, the lady dropped her earnings down a copper tube, from her room that went directly to the cash register. Then the barman would set the doll upright again so other potential customers would know that she was available.

There is an intriguing array of bed pans displayed along one wall and there is a Brothel Museum displaying a number of historical artefacts, documents and photos of the Red Onion, Skagway and of times long gone. A lady in period costume will take you on a personal tour and relate some of the stories associated with the Red Onion's past. Nowadays, it's a bar and restaurant with a range of local beers, plus nachos, sandwiches, soups, salads and pizza. I chose the Gold Rush Chilli and sampled several locally brewed beers, but noted that the range of services on offer upstairs in the past were not on offer today.

It was not always on this site. Originally, it was on the corner of 6th and State Street but when the railway was built, the centre of town literally shifted southwards to be nearer to the railway terminal which became the best location to be. Consequently, this building, along with several others were physically moved from its old site to its current location. One last observation about the Red Onion, is that the opening hours change, depending whether there is a ship moored in the harbour or not.

On ship days, it opens at 10am and stays open all day, till late in the evening (at least 10pm but arbitrary depending on the amount of custom). Conversely on non-ship days, it opens at 4pm or noon at weekends. It's not hard to tell when it's a ship day, as any cruise liner moored in the harbour towers several storeys above the rooflines of the buildings in the town and can be seen from all over town.

Just a few doors up the road is another wooden building, decorated with more than 8,800 pieces of driftwood nailed in patterns across the front facade with the words picked out in more driftwood of Camp Skagway No 1 with the date 1899 and the letters 'AB' on its second storey and repeated at the very top of the facade.

The story of this building starts in February 1899 on the steamer 'City of Seattle' on its voyage towards Skagway. Captain William Connell was dining in the ship's dining room with several of the passengers. There was much drinking and the captain suggested that there ought to be a great brotherhood of the north. The idea caught on and the eleven founding members of the brotherhood went on to sign up to the Arctic Brotherhood. Articles and a constitution were drawn up which expressed the object of the fraternity which was to encourage and promote social and intellectual intercourse and benevolence, amongst its membership and to advance the interests of its members.

The initiation fee was a dollar to join and the emblem was two crossed flags, the Union Jack and the Stars and Stripes, a miner's gold pan, crossed pick and shovel and the letters AB. Its motto was 'No boundary line here'. Membership grew and Camp No. 2 was established at Bennett Lake and Camp No. 3 at Atlin Lake as their members increased and spread out across the area.

They received criticism initially but it was realised by those critics that they really did look after their sick members, bury their dead and improve social conditions in the camps for their members. Soon there were more than 30 camps or lodges throughout the northern areas and more than 10,000 members who were active into the 1920's and all from a suggestion made over a dinner on board a ship.

Further up Broadway, I came to the Bonanza Bar and Grill, I entered but it was noisy and crowded, with many fat customers from the cruise liners, whose ambition seemed to be to eat and drink as much as possible, before returning to their ships in the harbour for even more food. With their more than ample frames, rolls of fat that flowed over the tops of waist bands and the edges of chairs. They lent on the tables and ate with their mouths open. It was crowded and the restaurant didn't have an inspiring sea food menu so I just chose a beer and as soon as I was finished I left. But opposite this restaurant is the Sweet Tooth Cafe, open for an early breakfast and lunch. On another day, I made my way there and had a great cooked breakfast with friendly service, it was cheap and had no pretentions of grandeur.

I had several days in Skagway before catching my train over the pass so I wandered around the town. The architecture was fascinating and I noted all sorts of different designs and additions to make an otherwise functional square box into something with character. The old centre of town has a wealth of old wooden buildings with bright colours. The Wells Fargo bank on 7th has a modern outside but there is a plaque outside detailing some of the history of the Bank of Alaska which was eventually incorporated into Wells Fargo, known today. Inside, there is a well preserved traditional bank counter with grills to protect the tellers and other paraphernalia although adjacent to this there are more modern facilities for current customers.

Wells Fargo is now one of the top four banks in the United States but also has its roots in another gold rush. Henry Wells and William Fargo were no strangers to business and were well known names in business as they each had an express mail business which they merged in 1850 in Buffalo, New York together with another business owned by John Butterfield to co-found another well-known name in business, American Express.

John Butterfield didn't want to expand into California so in 1852, Henry Wells and William Fargo founded Wells, Fargo & Co. offering banking services and express mail, including buying and selling of gold. It opened its first bank in the booming gold rush port of San Francisco. As the port grew and prospectors known as the Forty-niners spread out across the newly formed state, they built new towns and Wells Fargo expanded with them.

It had a reputation for honesty and promptness. It transacted business swiftly and used the fastest methods possible to complete transactions. In 1858, it co-founded the Overland Mail Co also known as the Butterfield Line which later ran the famous Pony Express. For those who know the banking industry, there is a Butterfield Bank founded in Bermuda in 1858 with operations in Guernsey and a private banking arm in London, but the name is a coincidence and unrelated to the Butterfield that started American Express.

After the Wells Fargo bank building, there started to be gaps between the buildings, residential houses with front lawns and no more commercial premises. I passed a few trailers parked up and at 15th, the town ended, Broadway became a rough track, the steep valley side was just a few metres to my right with the WP&YR tracks on the edge of the flat land before the steep wooded valley sides towered above me. The route out of town was the Klondike Highway that was a continuation of the next street across on State Street.

I walked over to State Street and up the road. At the top of the road on the outskirts of the town were the WP&YR sidings which was the functional end of the operations as opposed to the trains, down by the docks to greet cruise passengers which were the smartly painted nicely restored trains to show off the WP&YR to visitors. Here there was a collection of engine sheds and associated buildings, several locomotives largely diesel in corporate colours of green with a wide band of yellow along the middle but also one or two steam locomotives but not as presentable as those on show downtown.

There were strings of carriages, plus several Casey cars, a functional small diesel train, no larger than a car for an engineer and a few crew, plus hand tools whose job it was to check the track before the first service was sent through in the morning. And surprisingly, there was no fence and no graffiti so perhaps there was no need for a fence.

Continuing up the side of the sidings is Alaska Street and following this, the road crosses the railway and reaches the cemetery set amongst the shadows of the forest trees on gently undulating land right next to the tracks. Here is where Frank Reid and Soapy Smith are buried plus many others with dates of death dating from the gold rush era onwards. Some of the graves are plain including Soapy's, a surprise considering his notoriety and the gangs that he ran. Some grave markers are made of wood and others are quite ornate stone with one boasting an obelisk 3m high. Frank Reid's I would say is a little more ornate than Soapy's but not the largest by any means.

Heading back to the Klondike Road, I walked over the bridge, across wide shallow ribbons of river that flowed past gravel banks towards the sea and noted that the number of buildings had thinned. By the time I reached the junction with the road to Dyea and the start of the Chilkoot Trail, there were no more buildings and the forest had taken over and despite the bustle down by the waterfront, just 3kms away, it was quiet and deserted here.

Other than the tarmac of the road, it was wilderness. I turned round and headed back towards the port and civilisation. I took a deviation through a residential area heading westwards and finally was blocked by the last road and detached houses with well-kept gardens that backed onto the Skagway airstrip. I continued down State Street and back to Sergeant Preston's Lodge.

The next day, I joined a walking tour of Skagway with a guide and a few other visitors. We started at the WP&YR offices. Right next door, is a wonderful cream painted building with the doors and windows picked out in black with lovely ornamental curlicues at the top with a name and date at the top, Railroad Building and 1900. It is now occupied by the National Parks Service and has displays and exhibits inside. We headed up Broadway. The guide was entertaining with local knowledge and interesting anecdotes. Buildings were picked out and some of them I had already identified and knew the story behind them.

Others were new stories such as the Golden North Hotel on the corner with 3rd, a three story building with a dome and at ground floor level home to several stores. One of these was the Russian American Co, an upmarket jewellers who specialise in contemporary and historical Russian art, crafts, gifts, matryoshka dolls and amber as well as jewellery whose bright displays had caught my eye earlier. And as with many other buildings I was to discover that this one was not originally built on this site but was built in 1898 and moved here in 1908. The third storey was added before opening as a hotel. The dome was added as a landmark to help illiterate visitors find the right address.

The Mascot Building is painted pink with the doors and window surrounds picked out in red standing on the corner between Main and 3rd. It was a saloon and one of more than eighty in Skagway at the height of the gold rush. It closed in 1916, with the introduction of Prohibition. It is owned by the National Parks Service and is open to the public and appears to be a bar but is in fact a reconstruction once you get inside together with piped music, recordings of people talking in the background and mannequins of customers and staff.

On the corner of 4th is the Pack Train Building which is yellow and the window frames picked out in green with a hardware store on the ground floor with a square bay window on the first and second floors on the corner of the building. It was originally part of Camp Skagway but was abandoned when the military moved to Haines across the Lynn Canal in 1904. The building was moved here in 1908 and had several uses over the years, one of which, was as a saloon called The Trail and hence the inscription in large letters painted down the side 'U AU TO NO THE TRAIL' which dates from this period. It wasn't missing any letters but it was the owner's spelling version of 'You ought to know The Trail'.

Just around the corner, visitors can see the difference between the grandiose quality of the craftsmanship and design of the painted facade of this building and the functional plain weathered horizontal planks of wood that make up the side and back of the building which is so common in all of the older buildings.

Looking up at the hillside, on a bare cliff of rock, there is a picture of a pocket watch and the word Kirmse's. This is an old advertisement for Kirmse's jewellery and curio store on Main Street which dates from the gold rush. It is still there a little further up Main Street, on the corner between Main Street and Spring Street.

Opposite The Trail is the St James Hotel, where Sir Thomas Tancrede and Michael Heney had that chance meeting to establish the WP&YR which other than its history has little to distinguish itself from the many other old wooden buildings. Two doors down is The Barracks, one of only ten of the more than 80 barrack blocks that the army built in the town when they occupied it from 1942 to 1946 and built the Alaskan Highway. It is best described as a long shed and I don't suspect for a moment that it was more than functional for those stationed here during the war.

On 5th is Captain William's Moore's Cabin built in 1887 when he settled here and staked his homestead claim. It is literally a log cabin, nothing to see inside and about the size of an average sized living room. His son, Bernard Moore, to give him his birth name but also called Ben, built the rather more sophisticated, although largely single storey clapboard house next door, in 1897. It had a single upstairs room where Moore could sit and watch the ships in the harbour.

This seems improbable today as the docks are some distance away but the seashore was closer in his day. Following heavy glaciations and the huge amounts of snow and ice of the glaciers, the land had been pushed downwards by their weight. After the melting of the glaciers and the release of the pressure, a process of isostatic readjustment is allowing the land to slowly rebound again at a rate of perhaps 2.5cms a year. The land he claimed had been overrun by prospectors but he made money from the dock, the warehouse and sawmill that he owned. He stayed until 1906 before moving to Victoria where he died in 1909 at the age of 87.

We passed the McCabe College, worthy of a mention as unlike all the other historical buildings that I had seen, this one was built of neatly trimmed granite blocks and opened in 1899. It was a Methodist School named after Bishop McCabe but it was beset by financial problems and lasted only a year before closing. It is now occupied by the Skagway Museum.

Several other houses followed on our tour including the Nye House and some had interesting stories but their history was after the period of the gold rush that interested me. Some I had seen the day before and although I didn't know the story, the sight of some of the buildings was not new and I think my interest was waning.

But I did listen more attentively when we came to the First Presbyterian Church, built in 1901 and the only surviving gold rush era church, a white painted clapperboard building with a small spire. It had started as a Methodist church but when they moved out in 1917, the Presbyterians moved in after a fire at their original church just the year before. But from the beginning of the gold rush, there was only one church in Skagway, the Union Church, but other denominations followed eventually, but for several years despite the growth in population, it was mammon and filthy lecher rather god that was on men's minds.

Having seen several of the historic buildings in Skagway, Soapy's saloon, his grave and other places where he might have been, no walk around Skagway would be complete without visiting the place where he met his death. On a corner of 1st and State Street there is a marker to commemorate a spot nearby where Soapy was shot and killed. There is not much to distinguish this corner from any other, there is some grass and trees on one corner, a couple of parking lots and a small building behind some trees. I wasn't sure what to expect but I felt somewhat cheated after seeing a lot of history and then be left between two parking lots nearby, where he had fallen with nothing to see.

CHAPTER 8

WP&YR over the White Pass

It was a cold damp morning with rain falling as I walked down to 2nd where the WP&YR offices are located and just behind it is the station or depot as it is called locally. This early in the morning nothing was open and no one was about. There is no station to talk of or any evidence of it being a station other than the fact that the offices also serve as a waiting area. Behind the building there is some concrete hard standing at ground level adjacent to the railway tracks. There was no train there so I waited in the offices out of the rain. Gradually other travellers arrived and we all waited in eager anticipation.

The train reversed into the depot. There was a diesel locomotive in corporate green and yellow and six restored traditional carriages with square windows and small rectangular windows in the central raised central section of the roof running the length of the carriage. At each end, there were steps up to an open platform and a central door into the carriage itself. The conductor who was dressed in period costume put a moveable step on the ground opposite the bottom step to make it easier to get on board.

We got on and could sit wherever we liked. Inside, it was much as it would have been in its heyday. There were few passengers so there was plenty of space and we could all have a window seat if we wanted. Just inside the door at one end was a small stove with a stack of wood beside it. It had been lit and was throwing out a lot of heat but it had yet to make much of an impression on the temperature at the far end of the carriage.

The conductor came round and checked our tickets. He picked up the step and stowed it under one of the seats. A whistle was blown and we gently pulled out of the depot. We made the first turn and passed the back streets of the town as we headed north. We passed the last houses on the outskirts and got a good view of the railway sidings at the north end of town. We crossed a level crossing and amongst the trees we could see some of the headstones of graves in the Skagway cemetery. We were following the Skagway River which was flowing gently off to our left and we caught glimpses of it through the trees.

The track had already started climbing and reaching the East Fork Skagway River, the track turns up the side valley and crosses the river and cuts across the valley slope through trees to re-join the main valley higher up above the river. There are great views across and down the valley but the low cloud base obscured the peaks. On a vertical smooth face of rock on the far side of the valley, just below the US Customs post, on the Klondike Highway there are the words 'On to Alaska with Buchanan' in large capital letters picked out in white paint.

The sign can't be seen from the road but this is Buchanan Rock. The story behind the sign starts with George Buchanan who was a coal merchant in Detroit and had made a fortune. He wanted to teach children the benefits of earning money and being thrifty. He was a self-made man and said that he got his education by 'going and seeing things'. As a teenager himself, he had saved some money and borrowed some and made a trip to Europe and this may have been the inspiration for him to start his Alaskan tours.

His idea was to take a group of boys and girls and give them a holiday to experience the wonderful wilderness that they would remember but they had to be resourceful and to partly pay for it. The children would have to earn money and save it, so that they could afford a third of the cost of the trip. Their parents contributed a third and Buchanan would contribute a third. The group had about 50 children, initially boys only but there was such outcry from their sisters that they were also allowed to join.

The group would set out from Detroit to travel by train across more than three quarters of the width of the United States to Vancouver. There was a three day steamship trip up to Skagway, a trip on the WP&YR and finally a boat trip to Atlin on the shores of Atlin Lake. Here, they would stay for several weeks and walk in the mountains, visit glaciers and experience the wilderness. The first trip was in 1923 and they continued every year for the next fifteen years. One group of boys painted the sign to commemorate Buchanan and later groups maintained it and repainted parts as necessary.

At the edge of the track at Black Cross Rock there is a memorial to two workers who lost their lives working on the railway. On 3rd August 1898, there was an accidental black powder explosion that buried the two under 100 tons of granite. The grave and its black cross mark is their final resting place. Just after this, we passed through Heney Station with nothing much to see but I recognised the name as the station was named after Michael Heney himself. The Skagway River makes a 90 degree turn eastwards and the track also makes a turn and follows the valley.

It passes through Glacier Station which consists of a wooden former rail wagon without the bogies with a door and a window that can be rented as a trekking base. In earlier times steam trains would have stopped here to fill up with water from a tank that is filled from the river that flows off from the glacier above. Steam engines would use a lot of fuel whether it was wood or later coal and needed a lot of water for steam to climb up the valley side. They had the nickname of hogs reflecting their thirst for fuel and water. Consequently the engineer that drove and controlled the engine was called a hogshead.

The track continues across a bridge that spans the river and turns back on itself as it heads on up the valley slope on the opposite side. Looking back across the valley, we get a good view of the track below us as it climbs up the other side of the valley.

We crossed a trestle high above Glacier Gorge and disappeared into Tunnel Mountain, the first of two tunnels en route. The weather had already turned and there were wisps of low cloud which occasionally masked the view across the lower valley. The remains of the old steel cantilever bridge could just be seen through the thickening low cloud which was built in 1901 and used until 1969 when the route of the track was altered with a new bridge and tunnel constructed a little further up the valley. We crossed Dead Horse Gulch which inspired Jack London to coin the phrase Dead Horse Trail.

John Griffith 'Jack' London was born 12th January 1876 in San Francisco and had worked long hours in a cannery. He then became a pirate oyster fisherman until his boat was shipwrecked. On 12th July 1897 aged 21 years old he sailed north and joined the gold rush. His first books including 'The Call of the Wild' and 'White Fang' were based on his experiences in the Yukon and he went on to publish several other books and years later one of his plots was used as the basis for a Hollywood movie.

The track levelled off and there were a few cuttings. There are bare rocks and the soil is too thin to support trees. The few we saw seemed to be stunted. The terrain is rocky with pools of water in some of the low hollows between the rocks. We reached White Pass Summit at 873m above sea level. The border dispute was finally settled as largely the highest point of the watershed between the two countries but during construction the builders faced another problem. The workers reached the summit but were confronted by a single NWMP constable who repeatedly told them that they could not enter Canada.

News travelled from the workers facing the policeman to the supervisor and onward up the chain of command to William 'Stikine Bill' Robinson, a friend of Heney's, who was the general manager of the WP&YR. He gained his sobriquet as foreman on a project to build a railway along the Stikine River which was doomed to failure but he left with his reputation intact and the name 'Stikine' Bill. He bought a gift of whisky and cigars and went to see the policeman. When the policeman awoke, two days later, he discovered that construction had already crossed the border and was overlooking the shores of Summit Lake a mile beyond his post.

The terrain was rough, rocky and open with the mountain tops on the horizon. At least the cloud base had risen a little, although there were still wisps of cloud around the higher slopes.

There were a few trees but largely there was a bleak rocky outlook from the windows of the train. The grade was flat or an imperceptible gradient unlike the steep ascent that we had made to get up to the pass.

We passed Meadows, a rocky place and nothing like the name might suggest. This is technically the highest elevation of the track at nearly 900m. White Pass Summit is the highest point of the pass but the old trail slopes away over rough ground and twists and turns whilst the railway sticks to the higher ground for a better route for a train through the terrain, high up on the valley side. We rolled down into a place named Fraser and stopped for a while.

This was where the Canadian customs post was situated and where the railway and roads met. Our passports and documents were inspected and I had no problem but there was a delay for some nationalities who needed to buy visas. This is the point where walkers on the Chilkoot Trail could have taken a side step away from the Chilkoot Trail across the mountain and get a lift back to Skagway or on to Whitehorse and there were a few who were waiting for the train.

Some passengers had either only wanted to see the pass, had not wanted to enter Canada or didn't have the time for a longer journey due to their cruise ship's departure and there was a coach waiting for them to take them back to Skagway. Those of us that had opted for the full rail journey had the opportunity to stretch our legs and view the local surroundings although there was little to see and the cold damp weather was a discouragement to attempt a wider investigation other than the area immediately around the train stop.

After a while, the formalities were complete and we continued our journey towards Whitehorse. The rugged scenery continued with rising ground to our left and flatter terrain to our right passing Bernard Lake where I noticed that the trees had reappeared after the rather bleak and barren terrain devoid of trees between the summit and Fraser. A short distance after Shallow Lake and just after Maud Lake, the Klondike Highway crosses the track and heads east towards the Yukon Suspension Bridge and along the shores of Lake Tutshi through the small village of Conrad, towards Carcross. The railway turns west along the valley with mountains to the left and rugged flatter terrain to the right, towards Bennett.

We pulled into Bennett on the shores of Bennett Lake. We were due to stop here for over an hour for a hot cooked lunch. The station had a central two storey building, with wings of a single storey, all in wood painted a light crimson with windows and eaves picked out in white. Inside, the place settings were laid on long trestle tables and we were treated to a buffet style three course lunch with complimentary soft drinks or alcohol available from the bar. After lunch there was an opportunity to look around the old town or what was left of it.

Bennett was where both the Chilkoot Pass and the White Pass trails met. Here a great tented camp sprung up as prospectors waited for the ice to clear and for the trip to the Klondike could be continued by boat. A town sprung up to service their needs and Fred Trump opened the Arctic Restaurant and Hotel. He was the grandfather of the famous late 20th century billionaire and 21st century presidential hopeful Donald Trump.

He wasn't the only famous person to make money in the gold rush. Martha Louise Munger was born 24th February 1866, into a wealthy family in Chicago but the gold bug attracted her and her husband, Will Black. They were pulled towards the Klondike goldfields but her husband, Will, who had planned to make the journey with her, ultimately decided to head for the warmer climes of Hawaii.

Martha continued with the original plan. She struggled over the Chilkoot Trail whilst pregnant, to arrive in Dawson and in January 1899 gave birth to their third son, Lyman. After a short trip back to the east coast, she returned where she had staked several claims, operated an ore crushing plant and bought a sawmill to provide an income for her and her family.

Meanwhile, around the shores of Lake Bennett, trees were cut down for both fuel and for construction. Boats and rafts were built to take the prospectors and their years' worth of supplies down the river. Some of the prospectors that had come down the Chilkoot Trail had chosen to pitch their tents and build their crafts adjacent to Lake Lindeman a short distance upstream of Bennett but to get their crafts to Lake Bennett required portering them the short distance from Lake Lindeman to Lake Bennett to avoid some rapids.

By May 1898, when the ice had cleared, there were 7,124 craft of various designs and quality of construction ready to set out. In 1897 there were already 96 NWMP constables in the area but the authorities had sensed that the sudden increase in the population making its way to the Klondike, would require some form of control. By 1898, there were 288 policemen stationed there to keep the peace. After the initial launching of many vessels and subsequent drowning of several travellers in the White Horse Rapids and Miles Canyon, the NWMP applied new rules and inspected the craft for their robustness before their launching.

After lunch, I had some time and there is a short walk around what was the centre of the town. Besides views of the mountains and the lakeshore, there was a wonderfully preserved wooden church, St Andrew's Presbyterian Church, built in the midst of the gold rush era with exquisite craftsmanship displayed in the wood working. It was built in 1899 by the Rev James Sinclair. Although nominally Presbyterian, it was also a popular meeting place for other denominations and also served as a community centre and a place to get out of the cold and wind for a while for those who were living in a tent.

There is also an intricate sprinkler system of plastic pipes suspended on poles above head height surrounding the structure through the trees that surround the building to protect it from wild fires which are common in the area from lightning strikes. We got back on the train and waited for the whistle to sound to signal departure.

Leaving Bennett we followed the lake shore on a level grade all the way for the 43kms to Carcross. On our right was the mountain slopes cascading down to the shoreline and on our left we had views across the lake to the mountain slopes beyond. The track bed is often at the water's edge with the lake's edge lapping at the track bed's ballast. There are times where there are promontories sticking out from the mountain side into the lake.

There are cuttings and a few sharp curves. We passed Pennington Station with a couple of buildings, well preserved, but we didn't stop to investigate. It is an unlikely location for a station as there is no settlement, no flat land for farming and no gold. But every now and again the original steam locomotives on this route would need to stock up on water for steam and wood for fuel and this was such a stop.

Shortly after Pennington, we crossed the state border line between British Columbia and the Yukon, but there is no sign and no ceremony. We continued down the last 26kms of railway between Pennington and Carcross which hugs the shores of Lake Bennett and we can see the approach into Carcross where the modern line terminates. Here the Bennett Lake meets the Nares Lake over a river crossing called the Nares River connecting the two. From the train you can see a foot bridge and beyond it is the railway bridge, a solid steel arched structure that spans the watery void of the Nares River that flows out of Lake Bennett.

We slowed to a halt at the Carcross Station on the far side of the steel bridge and the end of our heritage railway journey. We disembarked with some of the passengers disembarking only to walk across the tarmac to board a waiting coach to take them back to their cruise ships in Skagway. Meanwhile, I had time to check out Carcross on foot before my coach to Whitehorse was due to leave. The town was originally called Caribou Crossing but the name was shortened to Carcross.

The station itself was a two storey building with single storey extensions on both sides, painted a dark red with the windows and door frames picked out in black. Inside was a ticket office and gift shop with pictures of the railway on the walls. Next door there is beautifully restored 0-3-0 steam engine on display with its name 'The Duchess' painted on the boiler.

Opposite the station was a single storey general store with Matthew Watson General Store painted above the door and a two storey section to the right. From the front the building appeared to be originally three stores judging from the roof lines and the three doors but it had been knocked together into a single shop. It had a false wooden front and around one side, the wall and roof was made of corrugated sheet metal. It sold gifts, local artisan products and bric-a-brac and offered ice cream and coffee.

Other than that shop that was about it for the centre of town and walking further afield, I didn't find anything further of note. I found the path to the footbridge across the Nares River and walked across to get a look at the railway bridge downstream just a few metres away. I also had time to look around the WP&YR sidings at Carcross where there were several locomotives and carriages of different eras parked in the sidings.

On the road that connects the town to the Klondike Highway, is the little clapperboard church of St Saviour, established in 1901 by Bishop Bompas. He had lived at Fortymile, below Dawson, before the gold rush but seeing so many people making their way to Dawson, he set out as a missionary and headed south to evangelise despite being past retirement age. This particular building was built in 1904 and floated across the river, to its current location in 1917.

There were also several hulks of paddle steamers that had been beached here and left like stranded whales on a beach. They were interesting to view and on one part of a steamer that was partially restored, you could still see the scorch marks of the fire that had destroyed most of the original boat but had not destroyed the bows. There were some interpretation boards, one with a picture of the SS Tutshi, a magnificent ship but all that was left were the bows and behind an incomplete modern interpretative structure, of just the main beams but it was difficult to picture any of the history of these monoliths when there was so little preserved. There was a new wooden building just beyond which was yet another gift shop.

I continued along the river bank, keeping an eye on the bus stop, in case the coach arrived early. I reached the Klondike Highway and paused on the road bridge across the river and where the river widens and becomes a lake to take in the view. In the distance, I could see that there was a coach coming down the main road so I turned round and headed back to the bus stop.

There were a small handful of other passengers waiting and I hurried over to the bus stop to board it for my onward journey to Whitehorse. I climbed aboard and bought my ticket. The coach set off and the driver introduced herself as Francis and that she would point out features of interest on the journey.

In no time at all, we came across our first sight. Francis pointed out the hillside off to our right. There on the rocky cliff edge were some white angora goats. Somehow to me they looked rather immobile and posed and didn't move as we drove along the road and had the air of painted concrete or fibre glass which after my previous experience of concrete bears on Vancouver Island I thought I had some expertise in this area.

I am sure Francis was following instructions and I would be interested in reality but I had no appetite after a long day to be hoodwinked and deceived so I ceased to listen. We passed Cowley Lake, a distinct semi-circular lake and popular tourist attraction and turned onto the Alaska Highway that would take us into Whitehorse, the state capital of the Yukon. The outlying areas are located at an elevation above 690m on the bluff above the town but the main centre is located next to the river at 640m where I was dropped off at my hotel.

CHAPTER 9

Whitehorse

The population of Whitehorse in 2013 was nearly 28,000 whilst the population of the whole of the Yukon in 2011 was only 34,000 making Whitehorse by far the largest population centre in the state. It was incorporated as a city in 1950 and also became the state capital in the same year when the capital was moved from Dawson. It took its name from the Whitehorse Rapids whose waves looked like the white manes of horses. These were flooded as was the Miles Canyon that had drowned so many prospectors when a dam and hydroelectric plant were built in 1958 creating the resultant Schwatka Lake.

The lake was named after Schwatka and his expedition down the length of the Yukon River through Canadian territory which alarmed the Canadian government especially as the borders had not been defined between the Yukon and Alaska. They called on Dr George Mercer Dawson (1st August 1849 to 2nd March 1901). He had studied geology and palaeontology in London and returned to Canada to be a professor of chemistry at Morrin College in Quebec. He later surveyed areas of the country including joining the International Boundary Survey 1872–76. In 1883–4 he surveyed the major peaks, mountain passes and rivers on an expedition in the Canadian Rockies. In 1887, the government sent him to survey the interior of the Yukon and he produced some of the first maps of the area.

There were several things that I wanted to do whilst I was in Whitehorse. I had missed some of the views across White Pass and had not seen the Chilkoot Trail partly due to the weather and partly as the permits had all been sold. So I chartered an aircraft to take me for a fly past so I wanted to check out the airport. This seems extravagant but aviation fuel is cheap and as the distances are so large, every community has an airstrip. Taking an air taxi or special charter in this area is an everyday event and I booked a two seat Cessna with wheels for the next day.

The easiest way to get to the airport was by bus so I headed into town on the same route that I had taken to day before. Between the road and the river there are some tracks originally laid by WP&YR and on it runs The Whitehorse Waterfront Trolley from the north end of Whitehorse where I was staying to Rotary Peace Park. It is painted bright yellow with window frames picked out in white. The electricity to run it comes from a generator pulled on a trailer. It was originally built in 1925, but restored and has operated during the summer season since 2000 and takes only a few minutes from one end to the far end and the conductor dresses in period uniform and rings a bell by hand to alert pedestrians near the line.

From the city centre, I caught the bus to the Erik Nielsen Whitehorse International Airport, renamed in 2008 after a popular local politician. It only took a few minutes and dropped me right outside departures. I walked round the outside of the perimeter fence and found Loadstar Lane and Whitehorse Air, the company that would be taking me up tomorrow. I now had a bus timetable and knew how long it would take to get to the offices tomorrow.

I walked back to the Alaskan Highway and along it to the Yukon Beringia Interpretation Centre in a new, modern building. Beringia was an ancient ice free expanse of land that stretched from Siberia to the Yukon during the Pleistocene era, the geological epoch starting about 2.5 million years ago and ending just some 12,000 years ago. The Beringia name was first coined by Eric Hulten, a Swedish botanist in 1937. Great glaciers and ice sheets had formed and covered much of the northern hemisphere areas but not this particular area.

With large amounts of water trapped as ice on land, the sea level dropped and what is now the Berings Sea between Alaska and Siberia was dry open steppe. It is thought that this area wasn't covered in ice as although it is a long way north, it was in a rain shadow so there was not enough rainfall for the winter snow and ice to build up over the years and so escaped glaciation.

Trees couldn't grow but grass could and it was a large expanse of open grassland. It was home to mammoths, mastodons, giant short faced bears, deer and bison. With the herbivores came hunters such as the scimitar cat and humans. This land bridge between present day Asia and North America was a crucial link in the story of humans. The land bridge allowed humans to move out of Asia across Beringia and down through North America.

With the melting of the ice, the lower parts of Beringia were flooded but there are plenty of fossils and bones that attract scientist to excavate and undertake research. The centre has examples and displays, information boards and a collection of more recent human artefacts. It is compact but there is enough to give a good insight into some of the history of the area.

Just south of the city centre, next to the river lies the SS Klondike, a traditional sternwheeler. It sits in a park next to the river and today it is a museum. It was completed in 1937, using some parts cannibalised for an earlier SS Klondike that had run aground the year before. The SS Klondikers were owned and operated by the British Yukon Navigation Co, a subsidiary of the WP&YR. They transported freight between Whitehorse and Dawson until 1950 when a reasonable passable alternative road connection was completed. This meant that it along with several other sternwheelers were decommissioned. Its tonnage was 1,226 tons, length 64m, beam 12.5m and can navigate sand bars in just 1.5m of water. It was able to carry 270 tons of freight.

It was converted from a freighter to a cruise ship but this wasn't a commercial success and it was beached at the Whitehorse shipyards in 1955. It was donated to Parks Canada and slowly restored until restoration was complete and it was moved to its current location in 1966. Visitors can see most of the ship, both inside and outside, on a guided tour. This includes the boilers, areas where the wood was stored for the boilers and the freight carrying areas together with boxes, sacks and barrels to give a real idea of what life might have been like on a working steamboat.

The upper decks are where individual cabins could be booked for the journey but at a price. There are plenty of artefacts on board that really make it easy to understand how life on the ship may have been like, when it was in operation with clothes and chests in the cabins. There is a first class dining area with wicker chairs and ornamental fake palms and a second class dining area in painted plain white, a lot more cramped with ordinary chairs. Some cabins had baths, and the kitchens look like you could cook in them today. The view from the wheelhouse on the top deck must have been panoramic when the boat was on the river.

An interesting aside is that Whitehorse is the highest point in the world up a river that ships can navigate to, starting from sea level and rising to an elevation of 640m. Although as there are no current sailings to Whitehorse, the current regularly used highest point that is navigable continuously from the sea is between the Hipoltstein and Bachhausen locks in Bavaria on the Rhine–Main–Danube canal at 406m.

Walking back towards the hotel, I passed various parked cars and I couldn't help noticing wires sticking out from the radiators of all the local vehicles with Yukon number plates. The winters are so harsh that it was explained to me that this is to stop the engine freezing. When the driver gets home in winter, they plug their vehicles into the mains to stop the radiators freezing and some versions also keep the seat warm for the driver when he comes to start the vehicle in the morning.

Not to miss out on at least viewing the Chilkoot Trail from the air I chartered a light aircraft to take me to have a look at the pass from the air. I arrived at the airport and walked along Lodestar Lane to Whitehorse Air's offices. They were at the end of a range of industrial buildings that had been painted blue some time ago but were now faded to almost grey. There were no cars outside which wasn't a good sign as I had learnt that everyone drives everywhere.

I knocked on the door and tried the handle. It was locked. There was another door to my right and that too was locked. I was a little early but by mid-morning, I had expected there would be someone about. I checked that I had the right place and the right day. There were some more industrial units further along but these were also deserted. I ambled about to fill in the time and to keep warm as unlike yesterday, it was cold, grey and overcast and smelt like rain.

A large pickup came round the corner and turned off the road to draw to a halt outside the offices and two men got out. The owner, Chris, introduced himself and introduced his passenger as Teak who was the pilot who was to take me up. He unlocked the door and we went in and I was ushered into the office and shown to a settee that had seen better days. Meanwhile, Teak was out the back making coffee.

It was lucky that I wasn't in a hurry, as it was now half an hour after the time that I had booked and they didn't look like they were in a hurry but I had little else to do that day so I just waited for things to happen. On the walls were maps and charts, advertising photos and posters of aircraft, tours to glaciers and photos of friends and family in planes and around planes.

Teak had been on another job with a float plane located down at Whitehorse Water Aerodrome on Schwatka Lake. He had flown north to a lake where a holiday maker had spent two weeks at a camp next to a lake taking photos and fishing. But it had taken quite a while to load all his camping gear, plus a canoe, on to the plane and then unload it at the other end and hence the delay.

There were a few general questions and a few specific such as did I still want to go up? Yes of course I replied. What did I want to do? Fly along the WP&YR tracks to White Pass and back along the Chilkoot Trail. Had I seen the weather reports? No … and I sensed an almost audible downhearted 'Oh'.

It was explained that there was a front coming in and there were strong winds and rain forecast and a low cloud base which meant that we might not see very much. That was no surprise as

117

I had been in Skagway a few days before and except for the memory, that there was one afternoon that was sunny, it was largely overcast and had rained or drizzled most of the time. Perhaps I had been a little naive to expect to be able to see very much from the air when there is so much rain expected at this time of year but I still wanted to go.

I followed Teak through the back of the office and a maintenance area to a padlocked gate in the perimeter fence of the airfield. Going through the gate we were on some hard standing where there were several small aircraft parked. I watched as Teak got the aircraft ready, untying the wings held firm by rope to the chocks on the wheels and removing the engine and cockpit windscreen covers. He checked the fuel and wheeled over a barrel. Using a hand pump, he pumped some more fuel into the fuel tank. He unlocked the chocks from eye hooks cemented into the hard standing and pushed the plane around to face towards the taxi way to the main runway.

I climbed into the passenger seat and strapped myself in. Teak primed the engine with a couple of rotations of the propeller by hand then he climbed in. It was a bit cramped and would be uncomfortable if you were any larger than average size. He turned and leaned over the seat and picked up two headsets and plugged them both in so that we could talk to each other and I could listen in to the exchanges with air traffic control. He started the engine and it roared into life. He made a final check of the various dials in front of him and then rolled forward a short distance and stopped. He requested permission to leave the parking area and taxi to take off from air traffic control.

We rolled to the end of the runway and waited. Just landed was a Thomas Cook airbus under the Condor brand from Frankfurt that had to turn and came back up the runway to get to the terminal. It rolled ever onwards straight towards us and towered above us menacingly before making a turn off the runway to reach the terminal. We were cleared for take-off, the engine revved, we rolled forward down the runway and we lifted off leaving the ground disappearing below.

We passed the perimeter of the airport and over the forest beyond. We climbed and off to our left was Schwatka Lake, below were some gravel diggings surrounded by the forest. Further away from the airport, there were well spaced residential developments with large plots with the buildings placed amongst the trees. Teak asked a question and I answered but obviously he didn't hear my answer and asked again. He gesticulated to the microphone built into the headset and told me over the headset to push the microphone closer to my mouth. I thought it was already pretty close but that last centimetre made all the difference and I suddenly realised that I could speak and be heard.

Teak was in his late thirties, a well-built chap in jeans and a check shirt. He had flown since a teenager as his father had also been a pilot and had given him lessons. He had had his own business but business lately was thin on the ground so he now worked part time as a pilot for other companies to make ends meet.

The Alaska Highway was below and the Yukon River off to our left. The junction with the Alaska Highway was clearly visible, the Alaska Highway headed eastwards and we continued to head south roughly following the Klondike Highway. The former track bed of the WP&YR railway cut a line through the forest around lakes and hills although the metal rails and wooden sleepers had long since been pulled up. There were lakes surrounded by trees and a tributary of the Yukon River meandered through the forest to eventually join Bennett Lake.

We reached Carcross but already there were wisps of clouds even at our low level that obscured the vista. We circled around Carcross and some of the local valleys but the views weren't great. We headed up Bennett Lake but on the northern side of the lake. I asked if we could fly along the line of the WP&YR track on the other side of the lake. Teak said we would go and have a look. It seemed an odd answer, as I expected a simple yes as I was the client paying the bill but he was the pilot in charge.

It became obvious that he also knew the local mountains and the air currents. As we approached the other shore line, the plane began to be buffeted by strong cross winds with some of the bumps causing me to hit my head on both the window and the roof. I could see Teak struggling and manfully fighting with the controls to keep the aircraft level. After I had taken a few rather poor photos, because of the buffeting, he asked whether I had had enough and would like to go back to the calmer air on the other side of the lake. I answered yes without hesitation and we duly returned to the other side of the lake where the air currents were a lot quieter.

We flew over Bennett and there was a train in the station with the passengers having a lunch inside the station. Even from here looking up towards the White Pass in the distance I could see thick black clouds down to ground level. Teak said that he was not even going to try to fly through that and it would be pointless as I would see nothing. Instead we circled Bennett and took a detour to circle the Yukon Suspension bridge tourist attraction on the Klondike Highway but the turbulence had increased and we needed to get back towards Whitehorse.

We reached Carcross and the clouds had blown away so after a quick referral to air traffic control in Whitehorse we lost height and descended to a few hundred feet above the town. We had a great view of the town, the railway sidings and the surrounding buildings. It really was a small town, largely on the Whitehorse side of the Nares River but with a few houses on the far side. In the forests surrounding Carcross along the valleys were a few outlying houses and cabins nestling in the forest but even with this hinterland the population must be tiny.

Teak checked in with air traffic control before regaining height and reappearing on their radar. We retraced our journey along the path of the Klondike Highway and into the approaches to Whitehorse International Airport and landed to taxi past the terminal and back to our parking stand with the other private light aircraft.

Teak parked up and we got out. He took me through the perimeter fence and back through the office and I thanked him for a great flight. It was a great experience to be in a small aircraft but a bit disappointing that I hadn't seen the pass from the air. Next time I book a charter, I will also check the weather. My flight around Victoria had been unaffected by winds but in Whitehorse it was mountain country and although it was calm at ground level that is no indication of conditions higher up in the air.

That evening, I was in the bar and got talking to some of the other guests, who were going on a guided trek and I was determined to have one last try at getting to see the Chilkoot Trail and I got some numbers of local guides. It took a bit of patience and following dead leads but eventually after phoning around, emails and rearranging plans, I had found a guide and his company had an unused permit, so I would be following the Chilkoot Trail up the Golden Stairs in a few days' time.

Back in down town Whitehorse, I made my way to McBride Museum of Yukon History on Front Street. It is a fascinating place which from the outside looks like a small log cabin but the exhibits area stretches back a long way from the entrance. It is a cornucopia and all sorts of exhibits, some fossils and geological specimens, First Nation artefacts, photographs of the gold rush and a host of valuable items that prospectors had brought with them or those who had made a fortune had imported. There was a lot to see and as the museum closes at 4pm there were some parts that I had not fully investigated.

I had noted over the days of rummaging through my bag that somehow, I had lost my canoeing shoes, basically waterproof sandals, plus, despite my purchase of a fleece in the MEC in Vancouver, I could do with another fleece as the temperatures were a little lower than I had expected and the summer was unusually cool and wet; as I would be camping for a while and further north, I might need to wear more than just one fleece. There was no MEC on Main Street in Whitehorse and there was an outdoor shop but the brands didn't grab me and they didn't have wet shoes.

On my earlier meanderings, across town I had noted a Salvation Army store on 4th and it was the size of several shops so must have a lot of clothes, just right for the local environment. I entered and searched through the store. There was indeed, lots of winter clothing for men, women and children, padded boots, gloves, hats and the like and a modest selection of T shirts and shorts for summer time. As well as clothes there was an array of books, household goods and all sorts of other donated items looking for a new home.

I was also surprised that there were quite a few customers in the store looking through the selection of clothes. I was in luck and found a fleece that fitted which wasn't a tasteless colour and a pair of water proof sandals. I had just what I needed at a fraction of the cost of new items. I handed over a ten dollar bill against the ridiculously low price requested and as the cashier was counting out the change I was glancing around the store at the customers who probably could only afford to shop here. The size of the store suggested that a large shop floor was required for the amount of custom that they expected. So to salve my guilty conscience, I told the cashier to keep the change as a donation and headed back to the hotel.

I had some time before my trek, so I walked along the waterfront avoiding the trolley past the original location of the WP&YR Whitehorse station and terminal sidings. It is a pleasant wooden building and across the front, was an advert for the Yukon Quest, the international thousand mile long dog sled race. This is a long challenge to run a dog team from Whitehorse through Dawson and beyond to Fairbanks in Alaska. Here was where you put you name down to enter the forthcoming season's quest.

When you travel across snow on skis, it is called skiing and if you use a snowboard, it is called boarding but if you use dogs it's not called dogging as it should be since that expression has already been used. It is called running dogs or dog sledding which I have done before. I would jump at the chance to do this quest but I don't have my own dogs and I don't have a sponsor but I am open to offers. I briefly considered putting my name down but today I was concentrating on trekking up river to see a notorious section of the river for those prospectors coming down from Bennett.

En route I crossed over to Riverdale and through some forest to reach the longest wooden fish ladder in the world. A dam and hydroelectric plant was built across the river in 1958. In order to allow fish migration up and down the river and allow access to spawning grounds, a fish ladder was installed. It weaves its way from the river, up the side of the valley and eventually connects with Schwatka Lake behind the dam. There is a small but interesting interpretation centre and you can watch fish making their way through the ladder.

I crossed the Millennium Bridge and around the power plant to reach the trail up the left hand bank. There are a lot of buildings here as the HEP potential is supplemented with additional power generating plants to cope with low water levels or exceptional demand. The plants have recently been converted from oil to gas and there were three new giant gas storage cylinders on site.

The trail passes the area reserved for float planes to land and take off before climbing up the side of the valley overlooking the lake. It then curves around the lake hugging a steep slope with picturesque views across the lake and the comings and goings of planes and water craft. Boat tours of the lake and Miles Canyon are advertised but the MS Schwatka stopped running some years ago.

The lake suddenly ends and there is the deep flooded gorge of Miles Canyon and beyond now under the lake waters are the Squaw and the Whitehorse Rapids that proved such a stumbling block for early pioneers. The trail goes through trees high above the gorge but there is a spur to a lookout above a spot where the gorge suddenly widens into a roughly circular hole in the ground before the waters plunge back into a narrow gorge.

A suspension bridge allows access to the far side and views from above the water along the gorge. The trail wanders through the forest alongside a wider stretch of valley and the site of the now flooded Squaw Rapids to arrive at the site of Canyon City. This was a popular name used several times along the route and can be confusing.

Having crossed the Chilkoot Trail, the Klondikers would build rafts at Lindeman or Bennett lakes and paddle along Bennett Lake, Lake Tagish and Marsh Lake to arrive here. Canyon City was a miner's camp that was situated just above Miles Canyon.

This was the last take out point before the rapids. The NWMP insisted that only experienced pilots could take boats done the rapids due to a number of drownings. In the spring and summer of 1898, 7,080 boats went down the river. The pilots could be costly and there was still a risk of losing you boat with all its provisions so most people opted to bypass the rapids. The city grew as people took a break unloading their boats and carrying their supplies past the rapids.

Norman Macauley was one of these prospectors who had nearly drowned when his boat capsized and one of his partners was drowned. He saw a business opportunity and built an 8kms long tramway from Canyon City to the bottom of the Whitehorse Rapids which came to be known as the Macauley. The rails were round logs laid end to end. The wagons had grooved wheels to help them hold the rails and were pulled by horses. There is not much to see today at Canyon City but there is a short section of track and two wagons to view.

Not long afterwards, John Hepburn built a 10kms long tramway on the other side of the canyon using squared timber rails known as the Hepburn. This was later sold to Norman Macauley shortly after construction. Both tramways were made redundant when the WP&YR reached Whitehorse in June 1900 and Canyon City was abandoned.

CHAPTER 10

The Golden Stairs

I was met at the hotel by Matt, my driver who was going to drive to Skagway for the start of the Chilkoot Trail, across the mountains which is one of the most beautiful journeys in Canada. With him was Benny who was to be my guide, a French Canadian who spoke both French and English. We wasted no time and loaded my rucksack into the van and we set off for Carcross to view the Carcross Desert.

The Watson River drains into Bennett Lake at Carcross and brought a lot of sand and silt and deposited it where it drained into the lake. When lake levels were higher, a lot of the sand was deposited higher up the now exposed slopes. It is fine and drains well so only deep rooted trees can survive here. The wind picks up the loose sand and blows it up the slope away from the lake and creates dunes thus creating the illusion of a sandy desert.

After Carcross we stopped at a view point on Lake Tagish overlooking Bove Island. The correct pronunciation was lost on us whether it should rhyme with dove or Bovey until the information board told us that it was named by Schwatka after an Italian naval officer and explorer, Lieutenant Giacomo Bove, hence it should be a two syllabled word. He had also renamed the lake as Bove Lake, but the First Nation name survived Schwatka's renaming. As we drove through this pass through the mountains, there was snow on the sides and tops of the surrounding hills.

We crossed the Canadian–US border and descended into Skagway. I opted not to spend any more time here since I had already visited but we needed to sign in at the ranger post, check the latest reports and collect our permits. Then it was a drive for the last 16kms to Dyea. There is a viewpoint along the road that looks out over the whole of Skagway and it is easy to pick out the major sights. The harbour with two huge cruise ships in port, the roads laid out in a grid pattern, the railway and directly below the airport.

The tarmac soon finishes and the rest of the route to Dyea is a dirt track. This town was once a thriving place but there is little to see there today. Skagway became the larger settlement and people started to relocate when the railway was built. The harbour at Dyea is silting up and since Skagway harbour is so much deeper and accessible, there was little to keep people in Dyea.

We were dropped off at the trail head and said farewell to Matt and started out onto the Chilkoot Trail. The Chilkoot Trail is a National Historical Site and is jointly administered by Parks Canada and the US National Parks Service. The whole trail is littered with artefacts left by the prospectors and is said to be the longest museum in the world. The trail had originally been used by the local First Nations peoples as an ancient trade route. During the gold rush promoters argued that the White Pass was lower and less steep and therefore better but in reality it suffered heavier snow falls in winter and become muddy in summer so was frequently impassable.

We set off up the Taiya River and initially the gradient was easy. Just as a reminder of the dangers, we hadn't been walking for half an hour from the start of the trail when we came across a pile of fresh, black shiny bear poo. Proof if you ever wanted it that we were in their territory. How fresh I wasn't sure but definitely this afternoon's so we talked a little louder and continuously as we didn't want to surprise a bear on the trail.

The trail had started flat but soon started raising as it twisted through the forest with the river never far away from us to our left. The path is well maintained and just to emphasise the point, we came across a pile of tools, some gravel in large one ton bags for the path and a wheelbarrow suspended from a high wire, tied to some of the trees to assist moving the gravel around. Although there was no one here when we went past.

A bridge crossed a wide stream and the path traversed a low lying area of forest which had flooded with recent heavy rains. There was an elevated walkway, a metre above the ground level made from rough sawn and squared off tree trunks, two trunks wide, across this low lying area to keep your feet dry. There was a series of old beaver dams that kept the area above this permanently under water and the walkway continued across a series of these stretches of water for what seemed like several hundred metres.

We arrived at Finnegan's Point, just 8kms up the trail from Dyea. Pat Finnegan, together with his two sons, established a ferry service here in 1897 and later built a bridge and a corduroy road up to the Point and charged a toll for people to use it. Finnegan's Point today is an official stop on the route. There is a canvas tent with wooden walls that can be used to shelter from the rain and to prepare meals in the dry but you are asked not to sleep in it. There are also some bear safes, strong metal cabinets that can resist a bear attack to store all your food and your wash bag. Bears are attracted to all sorts of smells and will happily eat toothpaste, perfumes and creams hence these need to be locked away as well.

We weren't stopping here but going on to the next camp, Canyon City, 12kms further on. The area is temperate rain forest with both deciduous and evergreen trees. The constant damp encourages lichens and moss to cover great swathes of the forest floor and grow in the trees. There were some stone steps to get down the side of the valley to the Canyon City campground, situated on the banks of the Taiya River where a small creek joined the main river.

There was a constant drizzle as we arrived. The camp site here has a permanent wooden cabin with a few bare beds for sleeping bags on a first come first served basis with a potbellied stove. There is a canvas tent with wooden walls for cooking which was identical to the one we saw at Finnegan's Point plus some bear safes. Set away from the camp and well back from the river were the inevitable two outdoor privies, small huts reached up a few steps with a door and inside a hole in the floor and a deep pit underneath.

We pitched our tents a little way into the forest behind the cabin and used the picnic tables to prepare the evening meal which we ate standing up as the benches were so wet. There are views allegedly of the Irene Glacier on the far side of the river but the cloud cover was too low to see anything.

We sheltered in the cabin and chatted to our fellow trekkers. First to arrive and take their spaces in the cabin had been Layla and Neil, a Canadian couple who were going to share our air taxi from Bennett Lake at the end of the trek. David and Annette were trekking the trail for their first time despite having lived in Whitehorse for a number of years, together with their teenage granddaughter Kiara. Last to arrive was an extended family, Peter and his wife, Marjorie with the youngest three of their six children and his brother Byron and his wife Cali, who all came from Alaska. It was great to chat but we were all tired and there was no electricity. We had all warmed up and got a little drier around the fire but it was time to go to sleep and for those of us who hadn't bagged sleeping positions in the cabin, time to climb into our sleeping bags, in our tents.

Benny and I were up early and left before anyone else had got up for breakfast. Just a short walk up the trail we crossed a modern wood frame and steel cable suspension bridge to visit the site of Canyon City itself. The telegraph that was built in 1898 to connect Skagway with Bennett and Log Cabin came through here. There was a hospital, telegraph office, a post office, bars and hotels plus a host of tents. The population was said to range up to 8,000 people at its peak. It was also a terminus for an aerial ropeway and for those that could afford it, you could have your goods transported over the Chilkoot Pass.

The massive boiler to operate the ropeway is still there as are a great numbers of other artefacts lying in the undergrowth. There was a metal range or double oven, pots and pans and miscellaneous bits of metal and cable. Some of the piles in the undergrowth are the collapsed remains of cabins, although a couple date from after the gold rush.

On the main path there are several creeks to cross, luckily all with wooden bridges and a few steep but short climbs, with steps put in for the steeper sections. All around, there were thick blankets of moss covering the ground and rocks where the trees thin and allow light through. These were especially noticeable at Rock Garden where there are fewer trees struggling to grow throughout an area covered with small boulders.

We walked through Pleasant Camp, so named as this is an area of level wooded plateau which made a difference after struggling up several steep climbs and patches of mud on the lower trail. It had a similar set up as Canyon City with a wood cabin with potbellied stove, a wood walled canvas tent, privies and bear safes but we weren't stopping here. We crossed another suspension bridge to head further up the trail.

The flora started to change with fewer ferns and less moss. There were fewer trees, they were smaller and the canopy is less dense allowing in more light.

We passed a ranger station, a modern well-built cabin with solar power and radio antennae and reached Sheep Camp. This was a First Nation hunting camp, used to hunt primarily the dall sheep and mountain goats that roam the tops of the mountains in this area. There are a few artefacts to be seen in the undergrowth and the remains of a cabin but without its roof. There are only a couple of wood walled canvas tents but at least these have potbellied stoves although like all the camps, you have to supply your own wood. Demand for flat pitches out strips supply on the rugged site, so there are a number of small wooden platforms on which you can put your tent.

Early arrivals have a choice of the best pitches but later arrivals have a poorer selection but everybody are provided for due to the permit system. We began to see familiar faces that we had seen at other camps such as the family from Alaska and a young group of three men and two women from Germany and Layla and Neil.

We had a talk from the ranger that evening, primarily, to advise on bear activity and weather conditions, but also to give a short talk on history and flora, and to be on hand to answer any questions. The area has six out of the top ten best savoury mushrooms and with the expert on hand, it was easy to identify and sample some of the more commonly found examples although when confronted with a specimen without expert advice on hand I reverted to form, if in doubt, don't touch.

The next day was to be our longest walk day. The ranger had explained that the climb can be quite gruelling and to ensure that you have enough daylight left. To minimise the avalanche hazard, he recommended starting early. The guide book indicates that it is only 13kms to the next camp, Happy Camp, but there is the steep pass itself to cross, at altitude and a long clamber up a jagged boulder slope. From Sheep Camp to the summit it is a change in altitude of over 850m. The weather is unpredictable and often bad, so allow more time. We had always planned to leave early so that came as no surprise.

We set the alarm for 5am (we were still working to Yukon time and there is an hour difference so local time was 4am) for a big cooked breakfast to set ourselves up for the day. We packed way our tents, filled our water bottles and we were on the trail before 7am). I was surprised that we saw no one else until we were leaving so there would be no one behind us for some time.

We had only just left camp and the trees had already started to thin noticeably. There was a damp in the air, overcast and a low cloud base but at least it wasn't raining for a change. The trees became gnarled, twisted and stunted earning this area the name of the Enchanted Forest. They struggle to survive here as there are strong summer winds and such heavy snowfalls in winter to bury them under several metres of snow.

All around us, we could see white water gushing down steep streams leading down from the mountains towering above us obscured by the clouds. Somewhere amongst the trees is the old Treeline Sign, now surrounded by trees but an indication that the weather used to be cooler and the tree line was lower but soon we were above the present day tree line.

The valley floor became steeper but the sides were wider and had gentle slopes only partially covered by patchy grass interspersed with lots of bare rock. Along the path is evidence of lots off artefacts discarded by miners as non-essential and not worth the extra effort to get them any further along their journey. Snow lies in patches even on the lower slopes of the valley sides and it is noticeably cooler. Above our heads we can see the wind pushing clouds up the valley towards the summit.

Perched high on the cliff on our left hand side is what looks like a jumble of wood. This is all that remains of one of the many towers that made up the aerial ropeway from Canyon City across the summit and down to Crater Lake. We weren't carrying 50kgs of supplies at a time to move a miner's one ton of supplies that he was required to take but it must have been disheartening to see other miner's goods being transported effortlessly and quickly over their heads whenever they looked up. Without the undergrowth it is easy to spot artefacts along the route, pots and pans, empty tins, steel cable and an occasional pulley, discarded or lost in the snow.

There are several known avalanche danger areas as you near The Scales and The Golden Stairs. One such avalanche occurred on 3rd April 1898 which claimed 70 lives and the victims are buried nearby. Some victims were not found until the last of the snows melted in the spring. This is known as the Palm Sunday avalanche area. A little further and we arrived at The Scales, where the Canadian Mounties weighed the goods of each person entering the Yukon to ensure they had their mandatory one ton of provisions before being allowed to continue.

A 'ton of supplies' was considered to be more than half (min 520kgs) of food per person and the rest was other essential items such as tents, cookware and tools to help you survive and be self-sufficient for a year. If you didn't have it, you would be turned back. It was not popular with some of the miners but the Mounties insistence on this probably saved a lot of cheechakos (a Tlingit word for greenhorns).

We paused at The Scales to soak up the atmosphere and inspect some of the artefacts. The wind had picked up and was blowing more clouds up the valley. Looking back down the valley, we could see a fair way but as yet there was no one else on the trail. The trail ahead leads across a large patch of snow and to the base of a steep boulder strewn incline at about 60 degrees. This was the start of The Golden Stairs. This is where the iconic photos of the long lines of men and women bent over from their toil, were taken in 1898. It's a tough climb, scrambling over and around large boulders.

In winter, the boulders were covered in a thick layer of snow. A pair of brothers cut steps in the snow and for a fee miners could use the steps. The brothers hired labour to look after the steps such as re-cutting them as necessary as they were worn. The slope is wide at the bottom but narrows and passes through a cleft in the rocks above. If you stepped out of line for any reason then the person behind would move up and you might never get back into the line for the rest of the day. Hence if there was a hold up further along the line, everyone just waited in a queue.

There was an alternative route up the Pettersen trail to the right of the Golden Stairs. It was less steep but a greater distance and like the Palm Sunday avalanche area below, both the Petersen and the Stone Crib area above it were subject to avalanche so it was dangerous as well. It also did not benefit from any cut steps and with drifting snow the path could become easily obscured and you could lose you way. Hence people preferred the more costly but safer Golden Stairs route.

The visibility had dropped so I did not have a view of the start of the Pettersen trail. I could only see the base of the Golden Stairs, so I was robbed of a view of the height above me that I would have to scramble across. The point of the trek was the personal challenge to recreate a prospector's journey which I was embracing but it still would have been nice to have a view as well.

There were route marker poles sticking out at regular intervals, but in the poor visibility you could only see the next post and the post beyond it was out of sight until you nearly reached the one that you could see. The markers are there but how you get from one to the next is up to the individual to clamber across which ever rugged angular boulders you think gives you an easier route. More often than not, I would choose what I thought to be an easy route only to be confronted with apparently nowhere to go.

An apparently easy route might not be so easy once you tried to scramble along it. Add to that was the surprise when the boulder you were about to put your weight on would wobble as you transfer your weight. Better therefore if you avoid clambering up directly below another climber so choose another route or wait until the person above makes a traverse.

There are a few false summits where you think you are about to get to the top as you can see no more boulders above. Then you reach it to find it is only a flatter section across the slope and it continues above you. All the time we struggled on in the low cloud, the rock was damp, cold and slippery to the touch. The exertions of pushing and pulling your own weight up plus your rucksack with all the weight of camping equipment and food for the rest for the journey was beginning to make my muscles burn. The extra effort meant breathing was heavier which was harder in the thinner air at altitude. I had regretted not packing any gloves but the thought never occurred to me that I might need them. And importantly gloves plus a few other items that might have been useful were not on the suggested kit list.

We preserved and pushed on towards the top wherever it might be above us. Some of the clefts in the rocks were filled with snow so you had to avoid any fissures that had been covered over with a thin covering of snow. Some of the edges of fissures and where the wind had carved out gaps between the snow or ice mass and the solid rock were unstable and also had to be avoided. In a strange way, it was safer in winter when you could rely on a thick, deep and regular coating of snow. Putting your foot down between some the rocks might result in twisted ankles to broken legs.

We finally reached the cairn which is the border between USA and Canada although there is no border control here but this was where the NWMP claimed the border was at the time. A bit further on is an information board, announcing that this was the true summit. Between February and May 1898, the local NWMP post checked 13,000 stampeders. That is over a thousand people a day. A bit further on still, is the modern ranger post and nearby, a rest cabin. We left our rucksacks outside and went in to get out of the mist and wind for a break.

The weather looked a lot better down at Crater Lake with breaks in the clouds and even sunshine so it might also be warmer and drier. I was eager to push on but Benny thought it better to have a bit more rest and to relax, some more food and a hot drink before setting out again. Of course he was right but then you don't hire a guide and then ignore his advice.

I read as we waited that for those that could afford to do it, on the 2,575kms from Seattle to Dawson, only 53kms had to done on foot and that was along the Chilkoot Trail. But even here some distance could be saved by using Crater, Long and Deep Lakes plus Lake Lindeman before reaching Lake Bennett and the river to Dawson. If you had a boat and were prepared to load and unload it several times you could cut the distance that might have to spend on your feet.

We set out again and as per advice travelled as quickly as we could through this area without lingering as there is still an avalanche potential above Crater Lake even in summer. On 5th December 1898, there was an avalanche here and five people were killed and I had no intention of adding to the statistics. The descent on the far side is gentler and less painful on the knees and muscles.

We carefully crossed several snowfields, ensuring that we dug our heels in and avoided obviously icy sections as best we could. The weather was better but it only seemed to be better on the other side of the valley which was bathed in sunlight where there were gaps in the clouds. On our side of the valley there were still a thick, grey mass of clouds racing over our heads.

We crossed several small streams although the greater challenge was crossing areas where the stream became braided and crossed very flat rocky and muddy areas in a myriad of rivulets to ensure that you didn't get water over the tops of your boots. There were several more small lakes off to our left. The patches of snow thinned and the number and size of grassy patches increased as we made a gentle descent.

By early afternoon, the sun had broken through and we came across our first trees after crossing the summit. We climbed a small ridge to find a grassy patch and settled down for lunch. We could see back along the path and still there was no one behind us. Looking down the trail we could make out Long Lake and therefore somewhere this side of it was Happy Camp, so we knew it wasn't much further. We had conquered the worst of this section and camp was within sight and it was only early afternoon so we boiled some water for a hot drink.

We reached Happy Camp and chose a pitch and set up our tents. It was the same system as at Sheep Camp with wooden platforms scattered around the thin forest of stunted trees near the cabins. I went down to the river for a swim and after testing the water settled for a wash. Not surprisingly the water was mind numbingly cold and I washed as quickly as possible, but there is a certain satisfaction in being clean and refreshed as you put your clothes back on. We left our tent fly off to dry separately and angled our boots towards the sun to help them dry off.

Throughout the rest of the afternoon the other groups that we had seen at Sheep Camp came down the trail and chose their pitches. One Swiss group walked on through the camp and on to the next campsite as they were eager to get to Bennett Lake and their scheduled air taxi. Another couple with a dog also just lingered long enough to rest and have a hot drink before they too carried on down the track. Layla and Neil plus the group of five Germans had all arrived in camp as had David, Annette and Kiara.

By the late afternoon we had accounted for everyone but notably by their absence was the extended family from Alaska. We knew that they had set off as several people had passed them en route but they had yet to arrive in camp. So Benny and I took the first aid kits and some dry sets of clothes and went back along the trail to see whether they needed any help followed shortly after by Layla and Neil who were following behind us.

Some way back along the trail and a long way off in the distance, we could see a couple of people walking but with no one behind them. We hurried on fearing the worse as if they were coming along the trail to fetch help. As we got closer we saw that it was Peter and his elder son. When we met and greeted each other to our relief, no, nothing had happened but they were just walking at different speeds so had each gone at their own speed and therefore they had slowly drifted out along the trail. The pair of them had gone ahead to set up the tent so it would be ready for the others when they arrived.

After another fifteen minutes walking, we met Marjorie with her daughter. Gradually as we went back up the trail we met the whole family with Byron being back marker. I thought the point about being in a group was to be available to look after each other and to give assistance and moral support if required. No matter this time as no harm was done but we had become concerned.

We offered to carry their packs or at least some of the weight but they were all determined to complete the trek without assistance which was very commendable. Back in camp, we had hot drinks in the cabin which although there was no fire as there was no wood, the heat given off by the cookers and body heat warmed the small cabin and we exchanged stories.

The morning followed the usual pattern in that Benny and I were up early, we had eaten breakfast and had packed away our tents before we saw anyone else. At least there was someone to say goodbye to, as we set off down the trail and alongside Long Lake. The trail has gentle gradients for the most part except for a steep descent before Deep Lake and a footbridge, over the river emptying into the lake, so that we would be walking along the other side of Deep Lake.

It is not named Deep Lake because it was known to be deep but due to its deep blue colour thought to be a result of deep water. On the far side of the bridge was a notice warning of bear activity. There had been sightings of both a grizzly and a black bear feeding in the locality and dated less than a week old so they might be long gone but if food was plentiful, they may still be around so we kept our eyes peeled. The date was actually immaterial as all kinds of bears are known to be frequent visitors to this area.

There were plenty of healthy trees and the forest was growing well along the shore. At the far end of the lake was the remains of a boat that had been abandoned here. The owners must have struggled to get it up and over the pass and then carried it between lakes to this point, only to find that the river flows into a gorge and then over a waterfall, followed by numerous cascades down the gorge. It would be miles downriver before they could refloat the boat on the river. In winter the river freezes and is covered in snow, so it is passable by sled.

They must have arrived after the spring melt otherwise they could have used it as a sled. They must have been gutted. None of the wood of the boat survives but the metal around the gunwale and strips from the gunwales around the hull to hold the planks together still exist and give a skeleton outline of the boat that was left here.

We topped for lunch at the end of the lake about level with the waterfall. The group of five Germans passed us as we sat sipping tea. They were going past Lindeman, our next stop to camp at Bare Loon so didn't want to stop to join us for a hot drink. The trail down the river stays high and back from the gorge so we have good views down Moose Valley.

The gradient is gentle and the sun was shining and we know that there are no more difficult sections to deal with so we are happy and relaxed and so can enjoy the views. My personal opinion is that every day we are getting a little fitter and our packs are getting a little lighter as we eat our way through the supplies so ruck sacks cease to be an issue. And now that the sun is shining, we can really enjoy the vistas.

Down by the lake the ground flattens out and in fact there is a choice of two camp sites adjacent to Lake Lindeman when you reach the end of the trail down the valley from Deep Lake and Deep Lake Gorge. Turn left and you reach a sheltered campsite and two cabins overlooking a bay on the lake. Turn right and follow a path to the lake shore with views down the lake and a larger single cabin which is more exposed to the wind with less shelter from any trees but tends to be quieter as many people favour the other option. We went for the lake shore with a view option, hoping that it would be both quiet and not windswept. As it happened there was only Benny and I, David, Annette and Kiara at this site so it was intimate and quiet.

This option is also closer to the ranger camp and information tent with a host of books, photos and information boards about Lake Lindeman. At its height, there was an estimated 15,000 people staying here. All the photos show a mass of tents that housed hotels, cafes, post offices, hospitals, churches and everything that a town might need. But two things stand out in that there are few, if any, trees or permanent buildings. The trees had been cut down for fuel or to build boats.

No one expected to stay long as they are all moving through and didn't expect to stay. Even for the hoteliers and store keepers etc. who hoped to make some money from the migrants knew that they could only make money until the potential prospectors ceased to pass through. When the numbers of potential prospectors dropped or ceased, they would also go so there was no point in building a permanent building for the future.

Some people built their boats here, confident that they could manage the rapids between Lake Lindeman and Bennett Lake whilst others opted to move on to Bennett before constructing their boat and thus avoid at least one set of potentially dangerous rapids.

We walked back up the trail to visit the other camp site to chat to our fellow trekkers but what was noticeable on the way over, was wherever we looked as we walked, there were artefacts strewn across the ground. After more than a hundred years most of the organic artefacts had long disappeared. Nowadays, all that is left are the inorganic remains and a few robust items such as the soles of boots, but the rest of the items were inorganic, discarded pots and pans, rusty round tins, rusty square tins with handles, rusty square tins with openings in one corner and plenty of other unidentifiable metal objects. Anything else, having long since weathered and decayed away to nothing.

Up a small path on the valley side, overlooking the flat ground around the lake shore was a small cemetery. Most of the small number of graves had wooden gravestones which had weathered other time, so any painted or written record on the headboard had disappeared. One grave had a stone headstone that recorded that it was the grave of William S Kent from Aberdeen, Washington who died on 16th May 1898. What was significant about this particular grave, was the Masonic sign on the gravestone that had caught my eye, a compass and set square with the letter G in the middle.

This was the final day's hike to our final destination. We rejoined the trail that went parallel to Lake Lindeman but we were often out of sight of the lake. It was a gentle gradient all day, through forests and occasionally over bare rock, on which trees could not grow but the trail was high enough up the side of the valley to give some great vistas through gaps in the trees, of the surrounding mountains and glimpses of lakes.

Our first stop was at Bare Loon Lake campsite where the group of five Germans had been planning to stay. The campsite was empty and over looks Bare Loon Lake, so we settled down for our morning break in the open sided mess shelter. It was here that Layla and Neil caught us up and joined us for a hot drink. We set off again together towards Lake Bennett. The trail crosses first some rocky terrain through trees and then the ground becomes loose sand with little undergrowth and in contrast to the rocky sections of the trail, it is not so easy to walk upon.

We came across a fur trapper's cabin and the door was unlocked. It was a simple one room affair with a window at both the front and the back. Inside was a bench down one side, a couple of tables and a wood burning stove. It was simple but it would be very welcome if it was raining. We continued down the trail, through forest with soft sand under foot. We took a detour to go down to the lake's edge, where there was a landing stage overlooking a small bay with a sandy beach. It was a pleasant little spot for fishing, swimming and even for landing a float plane.

Along the side of the trail was an embankment that used to carry the WP&YR, until they realigned the track to shorten the journey. Now it is just a flat topped embankment that the forest is slowly reclaiming. There was a grave yard nestled in the forest with a small handful of graves of people who had died on the trail and a memorial to five workers who died and were buried here, whilst building the WP&YR.

Most had wooden markers but one was a stone headstone with the same Masonic mark that we had seen the day before. This was Laughlen McLean from Richmond, Quebec who had died aged 62 on 14th May 1898, just two days before his fellow Masonic member, William S Kent, buried in Lindeman City on 16th May 1898. Since they were in the same fraternity, in the same part of the world, it is inconceivable that they never met but we will never know for certain.

On a rocky outcrop devoid of trees was a great view overlooking Lake Bennet and providing a great view up and down the valley. Whilst we stood there admiring the view, a float plane circled and came in to land on the lake. We were well ahead of our scheduled pick up time so we guessed that it was not coming to pick us up.

As we descended towards the lake shore we came through the settlement of Lake Bennett and the wooden church that was built during the gold rush and dedicated as St Andrews that I had seen earlier. It is designated as a Presbyterian, but in reality all denominations used it and used it for a lot of other social activities and not just worshiping. It is a testament to the Reverend James Sinclair, who built it, in that he was able to persuade passing hopeful miners who were also skilled craftsmen, to build it. They were all eager to arrive in Bennett and build a watercraft to float down the river to reach the goldfields. However, they would be left with time on their hands if they arrived early and had already built their boat, stuck waiting for the spring thaw.

I had already seen the church a few days earlier with its intricate sprinkler system against spreading forest fires but it still had a fascination and this time, I had more time to look around although there was little left from the gold rush other than a lot of rusted metal spread throughout the area. I also had a look at the campsite and the mess shelter where we had lunch looking out along the lake.

We walked on and rested on the platform of the railway station and waited for our float plane which would land and tie up opposite the station. There were some cleaning and maintenance staff and they let us use their toilets but they were not open, as there were no passenger trains due through that day. However, there was maintenance being undertaken on the tracks and we saw two Casey wagons and an engineering train pass through.

The next person to come down from the church towards the station was Kiara, by herself, walking strongly with a big smile on her face. It had been her wish to walk the Chilkoot Trail and she had done it. It was a great personal achievement for her and she was thrilled to bits and over the moon. David and Annette turned up a bit later and whilst they had also enjoyed the trek, it was nothing to the elation that Kiara was still radiating an hour later. They stayed for a short while before heading off to Log Cabin which is on the main road, where they had left the car.

A float plane appeared coming up the lake and it flew over us to turn above our lookout point above the lake and landed on the water and taxied to where we were waiting. We loaded our gear and with Benny sitting on the baggage at the back, Layla and Neil in the passenger seats and me next to the pilot, we took off.

We flew down the lake with great views of the WP&YR tracks following the edge of the lake just below us. Instead of reaching Carcross at the end of the lake, we turned left up a creek and followed the Watson River, through a gap between the mountains for a more direct route to Whitehorse and were once again following the route of the former railway. We could see the main airport but we veered eastwards and straightened up for a landing on Lake Schwatka, the reservoir created by the Whitehorse Dam.

It was an exhilarating landing and I doubt I will ever tire of the excitement of flying low level in small planes. We were picked up by taxi and taken to our respective hotels for a good bath before a final farewell meal that evening, since for some of us, this was the journey's end but it was just the start of the next section of my journey, recreating a prospector's journey to the goldfields.

CHAPTER 11

Canoe to Carmacks

The group that I was going to paddle with for the first section of the Yukon, met up in the hotel in downtown Whitehorse the night before. It was an introduction to our guides and to each other, an opportunity to ask questions and to ensure that we had the right kit.

There was the usual introductions around the table where you gave your name, importantly your paddling experience and level of skill, something about yourself, why you booked this particular trip and what you expected to get out of the trip in general.

Our guide was Benny, the same guide that had taken me along the Chilkoot Trail just a few days before. With him were two assistant guides, Jonas and Simon, both German but all young. Next was Gisela and her husband Michael, also from Germany. The two thirty-something sisters were Julie and Jen from Kelowna, British Columbia, just south of the Yukon. They had bid for the trip at a charity auction and this was their first time on a canoe trip.

To my left were Monica, a surgical assistant from Berne and Sandro, from Lucerne, both from Switzerland but travelling separately. Bob was a veteran biologist from Minnesota and used to field trips, including canoeing and last to introduce himself was Norman from Hamburg. This was an unusual German name but not uncommon but this was potentially confusing as there were he and I with the same name.

Norman was the last of the group around the table to speak and that was the group. The German speakers were the most numerous followed by English and French. Needless to say, all the Europeans spoke good English and as Benny didn't speak German, the meeting was held in English, with any technical terms not understood, translated into German by Simon and Jonas. From our introductions of ourselves, it was only Bob and I who were going all the way to Dawson, the others were only making the first section of the trip from Whitehorse to Carmacks which would take just a week.

A kit list was reiterated to check that we all had sleeping bags, sleeping mats, wet shoes and at least one change of dry clothing. We were measured up for our paddles, signed liability disclosures, collected our tents and wet bags plus a plastic ziplock bag containing some brown paper bags and a toilet roll (more on this later).

Several of us were on longer trips than just the canoeing down the Yukon so we left surplus clothes and equipment at the hotel left luggage room and waited after breakfast the next day for the van and trailer carrying the canoes. We loaded our kit bags onto the trailer. Our first stop was a supermarket just five minutes away to ensure everyone could get those last minute items such as chocolates, snacks, drinks and fishing licences.

We took the road south from Whitehorse for the short distance to our put in point at the Takhini River road bridge, just upstream from its confluence with the Yukon at kilometre 66 or 66kms. The guide book that I was using measured the distances in kilometres from Marsh Lake, just a short distance upstream from Whitehorse and Canyon City, so my trip started at 66kms and would finish in Dawson at 752kms, or nearly 500 miles downriver.

There was a flurry of activity as canoes were unloaded from the trailer and kit sorted out. Communal gear such as food containers, propane tanks, kitchen gear etc., all needed to be spread equally across the various canoes and all tied in. We were given a demonstration of the type of knots and the method that would be required to tie the gear into the canoes.

There was a particular way to tie all the equipment into the canoe. This was to ensure that in the event of a capsizing, no equipment was lost. The first bag had a bowline knot tied to it. Then all the items had the rope threaded through handles or straps and the rope was tied in a bowline on to the last item at the back of the boat. The rope was always looped over the thwarts, the cross bars of wood that give the canoe its shape and rigidity. The idea is that the gear can float free from the sunken canoe but the very final knot is a horse thief knot around the thwart in the aft of the canoe so that the load doesn't disappear down river never to be seen again. However, the load can be quickly released by the helmsman if needed in an emergency.

It is important to get the weight evenly distributed around each canoe to maintain balance. Our packing and our knots were inspected and mostly pasted muster. Then we set off into the river. Most people had come in pairs so canoe partners was relatively easy. Gisela and Michael had not camped or canoed before so they each went with Jonas and Simon. Bob teamed up with Norman and I paired up with Benny.

We had an on shore demonstration of strokes that would be useful and a chance for a practice on dry land. There were a few rules and safety issues, such as the capsizing drill, how to float face up in the water, with your feet facing downstream ahead of you and what to grab. Then we did a number of warming up exercises to warm up and stretch the muscles which we would do every morning and we were ready to go. Benny and I got on the water first and the others followed, Jonas with Gisela and Simon with Michael, being the last two canoes in the water. We moved from the Takhini into the Yukon and started our journey downstream.

Progress was patchy, as some of us took a little time to familiarise ourselves with forgotten skills or put into practice newly demonstrated techniques. Julie and Jen were having a bit of difficulty, since neither of them had had any previous paddling experience. I would give them ten out of ten for trying something new, but first time out on moving water running at about 8kmph is a challenge.

The current moves the boat about and any wind will also have an effect. Paddling and trying to control a canoe for a novice is nothing like driving a car. A car will respond immediately to any change in direction by turning a wheel or indeed pressure on the accelerator. A canoe, takes time to respond so a novice tends to over correct. Patience is a virtue. As the boat has momentum, a correction seems to have no effect so another over correction follows. Coupled with wind and current buffeting the boat, it is hard to determine whether any change has occurred and how significant the effect of that action following a stroke by the paddler. That is, until the canoe swerves way past the intended course and further corrective action is initiated.

Jen was at the helm and Julie at the bow and between them, they were making a lot of effort but the canoe seemed to have a mind of its own making large arcs and going round in circles. Just another issue was stroke strength as they had very different strength to their strokes so a strong paddle pull from one would counteract the correct action of the other.

We had paddled for over an hour when we landed at a gently sloping beach, to tie the canoes up to bushes on shore and have lunch. There was a canoe already moored there belonging to a Swiss couple who had made camp there the night before. They were Stefan and Bolita, who were taking their time to reach Dawson. We didn't know at the time, but we would be meeting them several times as we travelled down the river.

We packed away lunch and set out again on the river. It wasn't long before the current slackened and we were about to leave the currents of the river and enter Lake Laberge. The weather was worsening so we pulled into shore at Policeman's Point, under a steep bank of alluvial material that was kept fresh and steep as the river constantly eroded its base. The intention was to ensure that everyone had their rain gear to hand or an opportunity to put it on now before the weather got any worse.

I casually looked down at the sand and gravel, and there, twinkling at me in the afternoon sun, was a flake of gold. I scooped it up and put it into a small container with a snap on lid bought for exactly that job, just hours before. I found a couple more flakes and specks of gold but had no time to do any further diligent searching before we had to move on, but this was the reason why I was paddling to the gold rush city of Dawson ... to pan for gold and I was already looking forward to more opportunities, to follow in the footsteps of those early prospectors and enjoy the thrill of finding gold.

Soon, we were at the top end of Lake Laberge. Here the fast moving river water hits the flat waters of the lake and the sudden loss of energy causes the river to drop its load and there has always been a problem here with gravel bars making navigation difficult. Piling was put in from 1899 onwards, to help navigation and encourage the river to flush build ups away. It was a good idea but it never really worked. Some of the pilings can still be seen. Another navigation hazard were the tops of roots of trees, snagged on submerged bars which are also to be avoided.

The lake has a bad reputation for cold water, strong winds and bad weather. True enough, it was living up to its reputation. The wind was licking up some white capped waves and it was starting to rain. We struggled against the wind and rain and made our way to the Upper Lake Laberge First nation village at 87km on the eastern shore, for a break and to see if the weather was getting worse or would blow over.

The village was abandoned some time ago, but there are some wooden buildings remaining, kept in various stages of repair by the First Nations peoples but time is increasingly taking its toll and several are on the verge of collapse. There was also a NWMP post here from 1899 to 1904 but that has long since been used for other purposes and only the foundations remain. The wind was on shore which kept the mosquitoes away but in the more sheltered, darker moist air of the village area, amongst the trees, there were great clouds of ravenous mosquitoes and no one wanted to spend any time in the village.

There is a trail here that starts near the village and follows an old First Nation path north eastwards to cross the Teslin River and onto Livingstone Creek over 60kms away that had been established with the discovery of gold in quantity there in 1894. Gold had first been discovered by George Holt in the area in the 1870's and had inspired further explorations ever since. Gold extraction is hard work for little rewards, but gold miners are persistent optimists, certain that they will strike it lucky soon, so will continue whilst there is something to be had.

It was only in the 1890's that Mason's Landing was built a little further down the Teslin River which was established as a supply post for the Livingstone Creek gold camp. This was an all water route and allowed sternwheelers to go down the Yukon and up the Teslin to bring in supplies and avoided the overland trail.

We waited on shore deciding what best to do as the wind was still strong and paddling would be hard but we had a long way to go and there was still a lot of sun light time left. After a while of indecision, the wind was dying down and the waves were becoming calmer, so we waited a bit longer before launching back into the lake. Even so, one of the canoes had been left too near the water's edge and the waves had broken over the gunwale so it had to be unpacked and the surplus water poured out. It was a pain to unpack and repack so we would not be making that mistake again.

There was a rearrangement of some of the crews. Most pairs were happy to swap front and back positions to give each other a chance at being helmsman. Typically, the person at the front can decide on the rate of stroke but doesn't have to think very much so can let the mind wander, or of course look for wildlife. His essential function is to provide power to travel forward through the water. He may be asked to give a different stroke by the helmsman when manoeuvring, such as a draw or pry stroke to move the bows sideways right or left in tight manoeuvring, or occasionally a sweep stroke but other than using his initiative in tight manoeuvres, his job is to paddle forwards.

The hard work is down by the helmsman at the back who decides where the canoe is going, has to keep it on a straight path towards that objective and to be alert to the situation around him to anticipate and react prior to a situation becoming an emergency. Basically, his function is to control the boat, and it's a full time job. Paddlers, paddle at different rates with currents and winds needing constant measuring and adjustment to maintain a steady course. Crew don't react well to a captain who orders a constant stream of course adjustments and hard paddling which is tiring when a few minor adjustments from the helm is often all that is required.

Julie and Jen would struggle across the lake, as it was open water at the mercy of the wind with no current to assist forward momentum and with heavily laden canoes, sitting deep in the water it could tire people out quickly. Therefore, Jen and I swapped places, Jen sat in the bows of Benny's canoe, and I helmed the other canoe with Julie at the bow.

We made good time down the lake and found a campsite for the evening. There was a procedure for landing. The head guide would land and go ashore to check for bears and to confirm that the site was free (of both bears and people). Canoes on the beach would be a good indication that a site was taken, but walkers may have taken the best pitches and gathered the nearest and driest wood, so a check is always worthwhile. Benny would land first and get out of the canoe to climb the bank and I could hear him clapping his hands and calling out to ensure that he didn't surprise any bears.

It was not a campsite in the sense that there were facilities available but these were all bush camps where there were flat pitches for tents, an area for a camp fire and an area for the kitchen. Water comes from the lake or river and toilet facilities were where you decided to go in the forest.

This is what the ziplock plastic bags, containing the toilet roll and brown paper bags were for and is part of the requirement to look after the environment. For a pee, you just wander a short distance to a bush and did your business. For something requiring a bit more privacy, a whole new dimension opens up. Near the fire at every camp would be a blue water proof bag. Inside is an entrenching tool and attached to the leather covering of the spade part is a whistle and a bear spray. You would take this, together with your ziplock plastic bag, the toilet roll and brown bag and go and find a suitable place for your business.

Suitable, means a place where you can dig a hole at least the depth of the spade blade and at least thirty metres from any water course. Otherwise, distance from camp and thickness of bush is optional but there tends to be a play off between privacy and remoteness. Remote may give the comforting illusion of more privacy but you increase the chances of encountering a bear either on the trip out or the return journey and any assistance required is equally further away. The spade only ever touches the forest soil, nothing else. You fill in the hole after you have finished and it is a curtesy to put a few stones or a stick in the ground, over the spot as a marker so that the next person doesn't choose the same place.

Any used toilet paper goes into the brown paper bag and is carried back to the campsite and burnt on the fire after having checked that the fire is not being used to cook food. A decree of modesty is effected. If you go to the blue bag and find no entrenching tool come whistle come bear spray, this acts the same as the little red-green indicator on public toilet doors, to say that the forest is occupied and you wait until said items are returned.

Other than hygiene, there is another reason why toilet paper is burnt and not left to eventually decompose, many years after its co burial objects. Squirrels and chipmunks are enormously inquisitive and think that since you went to the effort to dig a hole, you must be burying a cache of food. They will dig up your carefully dug hole and scatter the paper to blow all across the camp site and surrounding forest in their quest for your buried nuts. Another reason for the requirement to burn the paper.

True die hard woodsmen swear by sphagnum moss instead of toilet paper but you do have to be sure that there are no sharp twigs or thorns to avoid unsuspecting incidences. One last aside I will share is that campsites are often on the open shore line and benefit from a wind to keep bugs away. Mosquitoes like the calm, darker, moist air of the forest found a short distance away from the campsite, so if you are considering dropping your trousers for more than a few seconds, remember the insect repellent may be useful for some areas of the body that are not usually open to the elements.

We all survived our first night under canvas. It was light all night, although the sun did disappear from view, behind one of the surrounding mountains for part of the night. We ate breakfast, burnt all the organic remains on the fire, leaving it to die down before dowsing it with water and setting off for another day of paddling.

We passed Richthofen Island, originally named Richthofen Rocks, by Schwatka after Freiherr Von Richthofen, a member of the geographical society, thinking that it was a peninsular. Dawson came through in 1887 and although he disagreed with Schwatka's brazen renaming of Canadian locations, he kept the name, although he corrected the name from Rocks to Island. We stopped for a break in the late morning at a cove. When you are in the wild, you have to be creative to get the most out of it. Monica had erected a couple of vertical branches attached to the sides of her canoe, together with a cross piece to act as a clothes line, to ensure that her socks could dry.

Some people went for a walk to admire the view at length. I appreciated the view but after yesterday's unexpected success at finding some gold, I tried a bit of gold panning. It wasn't a serious attempt, as it was a poor spot to choose, mostly stones and no history of anyone finding gold nearby but then you never know … but I didn't find anything.

We paddled on past Hanson Mountain and gazed at the steep cliffs on this section of the lake. We stopped for the evening, just beyond Goddard Point to make camp on a stony promontory. I chose a great position high on the beach overlooking the lake only to find that the pitch wasn't quite big enough to take the tent so I had to move along the beach and pitch near Jen and Julie. All the other tents had found pitches further inland but I was happy with my beach front view and any gentle wind to deter the mosquitoes.

Most places have a history associated with their names and Goddard's Point was no exception. The owner of the Pacific Iron and Steel Works in Seattle, was an engineer called A J Goddard. When news of the gold rush broke in 1897, he bought two small prefabricated sternwheeler hulls in San Francisco and fitted then out himself, before shipping them to Skagway, where they were carried over the pass and re-assembled on the shores of Lake Bennett. He named one of the ships, the AJ Goddard, after himself.

Captain Goddard began the 1898 season by transporting miners and supplies from Lake Bennett to the head of the Whitehorse Rapids. The AJ Goddard became the third vessel to pass through Miles Canyon and descend the Whitehorse Rapids. It was also the first steamer from Whitehorse to arrive in Dawson City on 21st June 1898. His wife, Clara Goddard also worked as a pilot and business partner and is perhaps the only woman to have regularly piloted steam boats in Yukon.

The AJ Goddard was sold to the Canadian Development Company in the autumn of 1899 and continued to work the waters downstream from Whitehorse. On 12th October 1901, the steamer foundered on Lake Laberge during a storm and hence the point is named after the ship that sank nearby.

The exact location of the wreck remained a mystery, until she was discovered in 2008. Divers, the next year, found that the boat was largely intact, except for the wheelhouse and smoke stack. This is the only known example of one of the steamers that were freighted across the pass and reassembled on the Yukon.

I had a swim come wash in the lake, as did several other campers. It was cold but I would prefer to be clean and a little cold than dirty, smelly and ultimately, either way, not that warm. I also washed my shirt, or rather rinsed it through and following Monica's example that morning, I created a hangar for it to hang on, from driftwood, to be blown by the breeze to dry whilst our supper of red curry chicken and veg was being cooked. Several of the fishermen, including Michael, Monica, Norman and Sandro went fishing but had no luck.

After supper, several people went to climb the cliff behind the camp site. I had started out with good intentions but the ascent was too difficult in flip flops, so I had to return but we were all treated to a great 'sunset' (the sun didn't set, it just got low in the sky for the night) as the sky light up with various shades of reds, oranges and yellows contrasted against the dark clouds.

After a cooked breakfast, we packed camp and set off again. This time, Julie was the helmsman and was taking a little time to get used to the movement of the canoe and the different paddling strokes required to direct it in the desired direction. Needless to say, we went around in circles with Benny shouting helpful hints and me doing my best to maintain a course but effective steering from the front with a novice paddler at the back is not possible.

The rest of the group were waiting for us, further along the lake and after some more paddling to catch up, we rafted up. This is where all the canoes come along side each other and we hooked our feet or paddles over the gunwales of the neighbouring canoe, to hold all the canoes together as a single raft.

The previous evening, Jonas had spent some time creating a sail from some strong pine wood for masts and using ropes to hold a piece of tarpaulin to those uprights to create a sail. For once the wind was behind us and after setting out on the water we erected the mast. It was very effective and blew us along the lake effortlessly.

It was not to last, as the wind was fickle and changed direction. We were not able to tack in canoes, so reluctantly, we packed the sail away and started paddling again. Next stop was Lower Laberge village at 133km, a First Nation village but now also abandoned. It hosted a telegraph office built from the wheel house of the SS Caroo which had struck the bank at the end of the lake and sunk.

A transcontinental telegraph cable had already been laid by Western Union Telegraph Co across American states connecting the eastern seaboard with San Francisco by 1861. An early attempt by Atlantic Telegraph Co, led by Cyrus West Field in 1858, to lay a cable across the Atlantic had failed when the cable broke after just three weeks.

Meanwhile, entrepreneur Perry Collins, had visited Russia and noted the progress that they were making in extending telegraph lines eastwards from Moscow over Siberia. He later shared his idea with Western Union Telegraph Co with the idea of the Collins Overland Telegraph, an overland telegraph line that would run north from San Francisco, over the Canadian border to run through British Columbia, down the Yukon, under the Bering Sea and across Siberia to link America via Moscow to Europe.

The US government granted rights in 1864 and work started and continued for three years. However, the third and finally successful attempt to lay a line using modern technology and the SS Great Eastern across the Atlantic, was completed in July 1866. The need for a telegraph line to connect America to Europe via the Yukon and the Bering Sea had been snatched away from the Collins Overland Telegraph project and work ceased.

More than $3m had been spent and the project was far from complete. However, there was a useable telegraph line that reached Barkerville, named after Billy Barker, who had discovered gold near the town the previous year and the site of a gold rush in 1861. Several other towns in British Colombia were also established with the coming of the telegraph such as Hazelton, Burn's Lake and Telegraph Creek whilst the existing lines were extended to reach Dawson in 1901.

However there are still plenty of old telegraph offices along the river and for long sections the old poles line the shore of the Yukon River. In the telegraph office, we found some wildlife in the form of a porcupine in the eaves of the building. I must admit, that I didn't know that porcupines could climb and it must have been a struggle to get up there. The animal seemed content to just stay put. There was also a NWMP post here from 1897 and three of the boatmen that had drowned when the AJ Goddard sunk were buried here. At the end of the lake there is an upwelling of water from the depths of the lake and it is a popular place for birds and a great number and variety can be seen.

After Lower Lake Laberge, we were back on the river. This section is called the Thirty Mile River and after the still waters of the lake, this is a fast moving stretch with speeds between 6–10kms with some eddies at the sides which were to be avoided. Julie was helmsman and reluctant to get too close to the bank, so we were often in the centre of the river, rather than in the faster current on the outside of the bends so we needed to do more paddling than necessary, as we negotiated US Bend and Domville Creek.

This creek was named after the steamer James Domville was wrecked here in 1899 causing a navigation hazard for many years. The superstructure has been washed away but some of the hull can still be seen at low water. Other ships that perished here include the Florence S, a steel hulled vessel that flipped over and killed three people on their way to the goldfields, as were other boats in later years.

We practiced turning to face up river and ferry glide across the current maintaining the same position relative to the bank but moving away from and towards the bank. We also tried breaking in and out of the current, useful for landing. They are useful skills to know but some people just couldn't get it right, didn't listen to instructions, or just didn't believe that you could drift across the fast flowing river and maintain your relative position without too much effort.

It was late afternoon when we stopped on Johnston Island on a bend for lunch. Monica, Norman, Michael and Sandro tried their hands at fishing, whilst some of us watched them or were entertained by a wood pecker who had made its nest in a stump of a tree just yards from the picnic area. There was the constant coming and going of the parents, as they brought food for the noisy chicks inside the nest.

There were clouds over head and we were following a storm that was moving downstream, literally just ahead of us. We were dry but we could see the rain and hail just ahead of us ruffling the surface of the water. We caught up with the slow moving storm and got wet. We pulled into the Seventeen Mile Wood Camp and tied our canoes next to a boat that was already there. The ground was covered with hail stones from the storm that had thankfully now passed.

The wood camp was one of many that lined the shores of the river. The sternwheelers used a lot of wood to propel themselves up and down the river and many people made a living cutting logs into cords to sell to passing sternwheelers. A cord is a well stacked pile of cut timber four feet long, four feet high and eight feet long, which occupies 128 cubic feet but due to air gaps between the rounds or split timbers, there is only about 85 cu ft. of actual wood.

Just after Cape Horn, we landed at an established camp ground. This had outhouses, plenty of flat land for pitches, a supply of chopped wood for fuel and tall spaced out trees for shade. We unloaded the canoes and pulled the boats out of the river and up the bank and turned them over for the night.

The boat that we had seen at Seventeen Mile Wood Camp, was also there and the occupants had set up camp. They were volunteers hosting an optional check point for the Yukon River Quest, a race from Whitehorse to Dawson for various categories of boats such as single or double kayaks, canoes and larger voyageur canoes. The fastest paddlers complete the race in about 45 hours, with two compulsory lay overs.

Although the volunteers had a job to do and wore high visibility logoed shirts, it was more of a family picnic with several tents set up and a large fire. There was three generations of the same family, a grandfather, his two sons and a grandson. They took the competitor numbers of every boat and checked that the paddlers were okay and handed out water, hot drinks and crunchy bars as required although the first few very competitive paddlers were too intent on getting a good time to want to stop unless absolutely necessary.

We set our tents up further back from the river, but set up the kitchen tent on the bank overlooking the river. The fishermen had had a good day and there was plenty of grayling for all of us. It was about 10pm when the first paddlers came past. We waved and gave them a cheer as they sped past. There was a steady trickle of passing questors throughout the night, from the fifty nine boats that had entered that year's race. Some take it very seriously and train together for months, whilst for some crews, it is a challenge and an opportunity to participate, knowing that they are not a match for professional long distance canoeists. It made our three week journey look like a Sunday afternoon picnic, but then we were making our way leisurely down the river, stopping several times a day and to cook and sleep overnight.

During the night we had gained some more people in camp who had entered the Yukon Quest but had had to pull out. One was a solo kayaker, who had left a turn around an island too late and the current had taken hold of his boat and he had capsized. He was lucky, as there was another paddler nearby, who helped to rescue him but he had lost some equipment, a lot of time and so had to pull out.

The other two 'would be' contestants were a pair of female canoeists, one of whom had been taken ill during the night and was huddled in one of the tents in a foetal position under several sleeping bags with suspected heat stroke and exhaustion. Her companion was really concerned for her and bravely said that there was always next year's race, but she was busy organising a pick up for her immobile friend, under the sleeping bags.

We wished them all well before setting off. We rafted up and floated downstream for part of the morning. We stopped just above the confluence of the Teslin and the Yukon to have a look at the remains of the buildings at Hootalingua Village.

By 1896, before the Klondike gold discoveries, there were about two hundred miners in the area and a NWMP post manned by two constables was established the next year. In 1898 there were three steamers over wintering here. It was a useful transport hub as there was traffic going up and down the Yukon and along the Teslin River to the goldfields that had been established there in 1880's. Low water levels in early spring and late autumn only allowed smaller craft to negotiate the swift flowing Thirty Mile River up to Lake Laberge and only shallow draft vessels could manage the low waters of the Teslin. Lake Laberge was the last section of river to be ice free, so steamers would wait above and below it, ready for the final thaw. Hence, it became an important trans-shipment point as well as a NWMP post and telegraph office.

Now less than a third of the major buildings are still standing but they still give an indication of what life might have been like in those days. There is a lot more history to the place but I was mostly focused on the end of the century gold rush but it was all still fascinating. We had a little time, so some people fished and I looked for likely gravel bars that might contain gold, to practice some panning in the clear waters coming out of Lake Laberge, but I was not too optimistic. The river was too fast and there were no gold bearing rocks or other discoveries between here and Lake Laberge.

Several fish were caught, mostly grayling but someone caught a good sized pike. With the abundance of driftwood available, a small fire was built as the fish was prepared and we cooked it on the beach. It wasn't big enough to feed us and pike aren't so plentiful to make it worth seeing whether we could catch any more to make a meal. But it was big enough for everyone to have a taste. It is a coarse fish but it is prized in Eastern Europe and whilst it might not be my first preference, it was fresh and tasty. Meanwhile my gold panning exploits had given me nothing but cold feet and an aching back.

We moved a little bit down the river to see the ways at the ship yard at Hootalingua Island at 182kms. These were built around 1903 and changed ownership several times during their lives. They were used to haul the larger steamers out of the water for repairs or for over wintering so that they were on station as soon as the river up to Whitehorse was navigable in the spring.

It is not strictly part of the Klondike Gold Rush era but the remains of the Evelyn, later renamed the Norcros, when it was sold, was built in 1908 but it has rested here since it was laid up and never refloated less than a decade later. The names on the bow are discernible, the Evelyn very faded with the better preserved Norcros in smaller white lettering over the top. The structure is fascinating but as the years pass by, it gets a little bit more fragile and will soon be just a jumble of sawn timber.

The structure is unsafe to enter but the various parts of the ship are clearly visible with the wheel house sitting high above the decks and the wooden parts of the stern wheel mechanism intact although sagging badly. The valuable parts of machinery have since been salvaged and used as the guts of the SS Keno currently on show at Dawson.

After viewing the historical remains at Hootalinqua, we set off down river again. The Teslin joins the Yukon here and the waters are very different. The water coming from the lake, down Thirty Mile River is clear, whilst the water in the Teslin carries a lot of muddy silt. At the confluence, the two streams there is a distinct water line between the two but as they move downstream they mix to become just a muddy grey brown.

The river is also wider with more water in it and the banks are further away so there is less sense of speed. We saved ourselves some effort from paddling and rafted up. Every now and again, the four oarsmen on the points of the rectangle that the rafted up canoes made might need to paddle to turn the raft into the current or away from the bank and other obstacles in the water. One thing that is memorable, is the silt laden water washing against the hull of the canoe. The silt rubs against the polyethylene of the bottom of the canoe and makes a low background noise like sizzling bacon.

All down the left hand bank had been a massive forest fire and there were just the bare trunks pointing skyward. The fire had happened some years before so there is green undergrowth that contrasts with the thin blackened trunks. The current is over 10kmph and with just a few corrections to keep us away from the banks we drifted for over an hour and still the uninterrupted charred remains of a fire were visible.

Whilst we were drifting, we were startled by a sound like a builder's lorry tipping out gravel for several seconds, and we all looked up to see what the noise was. Just down river, part of the bank had collapsed leaving a fresh scar on the bank and a cloud of dust drifting out across the river.

Along the river bank were sand and gravel banks, raising tens of metres above the water line, with their foot in the water where the river would continually undercut them. This causes new material to be exposed, including occasional ancient tree trunks and mammoth bones. In places, it exposes permafrost which whilst icy, it can support more weight and at a steeper angle than loose sand and gravel. As it melts, water seeps down the face of the cliff and creates a damp patch so these areas are easy to identify. As it melts further, it becomes unstable and eventually there is an avalanche. The sound that we had heard was one of these avalanches and I would witness more during the trip. Needless to say these are not good places to pause so we hurried on by.

As we were drifting, we also had a chance to relax and watch some wildlife. There were plenty of bald eagles and other birds just watching us pass. Only if they were low down near the water's edge and we were drifting past, near the bank, did they bother to fly away. Some people jumped into the river from the canoes with their clothes on. A multiple function of cooling off, washing themselves and rinsing their clothes. Luckily, it was a warm sunny afternoon so they might dry again before we got to camp.

At Klondike Bend, 196kms are the remains of the SS Klondike (No 1) built in 1929 sitting in the river. In 1936, with an inexperienced pilot at the wheel, she failed to successfully negotiate Fish Eddy, a bend a short way upstream and crashed into the bank, putting her out of control. She hit the banks several times more before grounding where she lies today. Much of the cargo was washed overboard and lucky scavengers picked up pieces all the way down the river as far as Fort Selkirk. The crew tapped into the telegraph and a rescue boat, the Whitehorse was sent to pick up passengers and crew to continue their journey to Dawson.

At the first opportunity of low water, the valuable parts of the wreck were salvaged such as the engine, boiler and parts of the super structure. These were used as parts for the ship's replacement, SS Klondike No 2. The remains are visible at the surface and on a previous trip I have moored to the structure and walked around on deck and peered through holes to the lower deck areas. On this trip, the water levels were higher and the deck was visible through more than a foot of water but it was too dangerous to stop, so we gave it a wide berth and paddled on by.

Around Vanmeter Bend, there were some hoodoos. These are thin, tall spires of rock that rise from the surrounding rock.

They are typically formed from softer rocks, topped by a harder less easily eroded cap rock that protects the column from the elements. The difference between a hoodoo and a pinnacle or spire is that hoodoos have a variable thickness like a totem pole whilst a spire has a smoother uniform thickness that tapers from the ground upward. Both can be multi-coloured depending on the different minerals within the rock, but these particular ones were just plain sand stone colour.

After looking at the hoodoos, we missed our proposed lunch stop on the right bank so had to cross the river to reach a small island just above Keno Bend, with wide shallow shelving beaches. Jen was helmsman again and I was in the bow. The way to cross the main channel is to do a ferry glide. The helmsman angles the boat up stream at a slight angle to perpendicular in the direction that you want to travel and the crew paddle at the same speed as the river flow to maintain your position relative to the bank and gently move across the current to you desired landing point.

That was the theory, but Jen didn't have the experience and despite me trying to tell her she shouted that she knew what she was doing and pointed the canoe straight at the new proposed lunch stop site on the other bank and shouted at me to paddle harder. She shouted at me several times to paddle harder, especially as we could see that others were on course but we were being swept downstream. Some strong paddlers worked hard together as a team and whilst not a perfect ferry glide, they did make their way across the current to land, not too far downstream from the lunch stop site.

Meanwhile, we were beam on to the current and carried a long way downstream and eventually made the bank, but out of sight of the rest of the group. In some slack water we were able to paddle a short distance upstream, but eventually I had to get out and drag the canoe by rope through the shallows. The atmosphere was a bit tense between us as we blamed each other, my fault for not paddling hard enough, whilst she hadn't learnt how to ferry glide or listen to and act on instructions.

We had a bit of time to relax, after we had put the lunch things away, so some fished and others went for a wash come swim. I was only knee deep in the water, when I spotted something glinting in the water so I dashed back to get a pan. I persevered panning the finer gravels but came to the conclusion that those glints that I had seen were just mica reflecting the sun and not gold.

We rafted up and drifted down the river, all except Simon and Michael who were too far ahead and couldn't slow down to let us catch up and we couldn't pick up speed whilst rafted together to catch then up so they just drifted 50m ahead of us. We reached an island opposite Fyfe Creek at 223kms where we would rest for the afternoon as we planned to have an evening cum night time paddle to try and catch some wildlife.

This was easier said than done, as the access to the camp on the island was facing the outside of the bend and should have been a gentle bank but a quick check of the guide book advised that the best landing spot was on the other side of the island, as the bank was steep. We were committed and too late to change direction. This was going to be a difficult landing so we spread out and we all swung around to face up river but near the bank, ready to ferry glide to the camp site.

Luckily I was helmsman so no repeat of the lunchtime disastrous attempt to ferry glide. Benny was in front and Julie and I were second. There was a two metre high vertical bank plunging into deep water and I thought this this was crazy to try and land here. Suddenly Benny shouted and started to paddle frantically. The access to the campsite was over grown and he had missed the small cleft in the bank, where it was only a metre high but still a long way, when you are sitting on the water. Luckily, I was near the bank and was able to turn us into the bank and Julie grabbed an overhanging branch and I plunged my paddle into the river, hitting the submerged foot of the bank to stop us drifting further so that we could get a better mooring position.

Benny had reached the bank and was struggling to pull his canoe up to where I was opposite the small cleft in the bank by pulling his canoe standing waist deep in water. The others behind us had had more time to react and they had all pulled into the bank and were using over hanging branches or jamming a paddle into the riverbed, to slow their descent. It had been a frantic moment, but we all made it without anyone capsizing or missing the mark completely.

We set up the kitchen and built a fire but didn't put up tents, as this was going to be just a restful afternoon before our evening paddle. The forest on the island was quite thick with fallen trees and uneven ground under foot. Beyond the small campsite, there were no paths, only virtually impenetrable forest but I was going to investigate anyway.

Movement was slow, but I was determined to get to see the far side of the island, stooping under fallen trees, going around scratchy and thorn leadened bushes and avoiding marshy ground, ready to do some panning. Tantalisingly close, but out of reach across the water, just downstream is Cassiar Bar, named after the Cassiar goldfields in BC, where gold was found in 1886 by well-known prospectors, Thomas Boswell, Howard Franklin and Michael Hess (who all have places named after them). There were no gravels to pan on this side of the island, just mud and reeds, so I had carried my pan through the forest for nothing.

Back in camp, Bob had found a spot overlooking the river and got out his penny whistle. I had heard someone playing before but wasn't sure who it was or even whether I was hearing things. He was just practicing and it was pleasant to listen to, but I didn't disturb him so I left a respectful distance as I walked past his spot as he played.

Our early evening meal was ribs in a succulent rich sauce and sweet potatoes before packing everything away. We would have set out earlier, but Benny lost his sunglasses and it was a while before we had all combed the camp ground and the surrounding forest to retrieve them. It was Gisela who had sharp eyes and eventually found them. The sun had gone low on the horizon and it was dusk, but being this far north in the summer it never got dark.

CHAPTER 12

Bear Encounter

We rafted up and set off down the river. We wanted to see some large wildlife such as moose, elk or bear. There were a few birds singing but nothing was flying in the evening air. We were told to be quiet, so as not to scare the animals away. It must have been the first time that the group was awake and no one was saying anything to one another. It just seemed a little spooky for such a large and usually, noisy group, to be so quiet.

We kept ourselves on course in the river but paddling if required very gently and quietly. Instructions were given by hand and eye so as not to disturb the peace. There were a few taps on the shoulder, to make people realise that someone was trying to tell them something. There were plenty of gesticulations from some to indicate potential wildlife sightings. They turned out to be false calls since as we approached, the suspected bear or moose turned out to be a rock or tree stump bobbing up and down in the rivers current. False calls came less often, as people got used to the gloom and the ever present tree stumps imitating animals.

We passed the confluence of where the Big Salmon River joins the Yukon. It had been raining further upstream and as we passed the mouth, the water levels were noticeably much higher in Big Salmon, as it joined the Yukon. Gold had been discovered upstream here in 1881, by George Langtry and Patrick McGlinchy, who were the first white men that these native villagers had seen. When Frederick Schwatka came through in 1883, he was told that the First Nations name meant Big Salmon but despite this he renamed it d'Abbadie after a French explorer. He had a habit of arbitrarily renaming places but some stuck and some reverted to their previous names and this river reverted to its English translation of its previous name.

Here is the Big Salmon Trading Post and Village as announced by a sign with neat lettering on a cabin, situated on some flat land below where the Big Salmon River joins the Yukon River. This is an abandoned former trading post with a couple of cabins with roofs. There was a NWMP post here from late in 1897 and a telegraph office. Inside one cabin, were several shelves crammed with every type of empty spirit bottle that you could imagine. Other cabins had collapsed and were just jumbles of planks. There was a modern half built cabin, made from plywood with an open door but no one was about.

Further down the river, are a number of islands, bends and sloughs. This required some careful navigation as it all looks similar when you are on the water and looking for landmarks in the gloom is not easy. Benny had to stand up several times in the canoe to get his bearings. We managed to get around the islands avoiding eddies and over hanging trees and not find ourselves beached in a slough.

It was here that we saw a beaver. We had heard several warning slaps of tails on the surface of the water as we had come down the river. However, here on a small creek where for those who were looking the right way, we saw a beaver with its head out of the water, as it swam for a moment before it too beat the water in warning and disappeared.

Just after 4th July Bend on the shoreline, on a flatter section of bank were the remains of a dredge, a rusty boiler and a rusty half buried tractor with the words 'Caterpillar' in raised letters on the top of the radiator. There was a sign on the shore giving details of the history of this particular site. In 1940, Laurent Cyr and Boyd Gordon built a small dredge in Whitehorse, then floated it down river for a summer of gold mining.

Using true Yukon ingenuity, they had improvised the dredge from a stripped-down Caterpillar tractor, a car motor, buckets bought from Vancouver and other various home-made or cannibalised parts and mounted them on a basic hull. The bucket line dug up gravel that was then screened by a rotating trommel and then sluiced, leaving gold-bearing concentrate. Although the two partners mined 72 ounces of 'flour' or fine gold from the river bars which was worth at the then current price of $32 an ounce, they made $2,300 but the dredge had cost $10,000 (at today's prices their gold would be worth nearly $100,000, not bad for three weeks work).

At the end of the season, they pulled the dredge onto land and planned to return the following season. However, they did not return and the dredge has remained here rusting away ever since. The river has undercut the bank and soon it will disappear in the waters of the Yukon to remain just a story in history.

We negotiated Hendricksen Slough and the islands just below and passed another sunken dredge owned by McKurdy which operated for just one season and was a contemporary of Cyr and Gordon although with the high water level, none of this dredge was visible.

We reached Erickson's Woodcamp around 4am in the morning and moored the canoes. Then we lugged all the tents, kitchen equipment, boxes and baggage up the steep slope and set up camp for a short sleep before a late breakfast.

We'd had a good night paddle, but most of the group were tired and a late breakfast was scheduled for 10.30am and we didn't get on the water until just after midday. The river was fairly straight and unchallenging, so we rafted up and drifted with several people dozing in the canoes as we drifted.

It was already 5pm by the time we passed Five Mile Bend and the Little Salmon River to land at the cemetery, for the Little Salmon river village, which was still occupied so we were not allowed to land any further down river. The settlement existed well before the gold rush and Taylor & Drury had opened a trading post here in 1902. Frederick Schwatka had renamed the river as Daly River after Chief Justice Daly of New York but Dawson renamed it Little Salmon when he had the opportunity to do so.

The tradition was typically to cremate the corpses but to leave treasured possessions in spirit houses so that the spirits could access the goods inside. There were a number of funeral houses built above graves, some with personal artefacts inside. Most of the graves were surrounded by balustrades and open to the sky. Many of the first Nations had been converted to Catholicism in the late 19th and early 20th centuries and so had more European style graves, but there were still some graves that looked recent, but in the local traditional manner.

After visiting the cemetery, we could see the left bank further downstream with smoke starting to rise above the tree line. As we approached, the smoke was getting thicker and we realised that a forest fire was starting. It was still small and set back from the river so we beached the canoes and investigated. We first checked the immediate area for safety and that the fire was not about to cut us off from the boats. A few tens of metres inland from the river was a warm campfire with several beer cans discarded in the ashes which were also still hot to the touch.

A few tens of metres beyond this was the actual forest fire, which was burning and seemed to be gaining hold on the dry forest. Trees and bushes nearby were already steaming from the radiated heat as it dried them out further. There was the acrid smell of smoke everywhere and it seemed to linger amongst the trees. The fire was spreading through the undergrowth and leaf litter and showed no signs of running out of fuel to burn.

Every now and again the heat would reach up into the tree canopy and suddenly the essential oils in the trees branches and pine needles would burst into flames and radiate more heat as the whole tree seemed to erupt into a Roman candle and add more heat to the burning mass. This was quite frightening, as it didn't necessarily happen in front of you as you faced the fire, but could happen above your heads. Cinders and sparks would climb into the air and then fall back again. The inrush of air, caused by the heat rising from the main fire, acted like bellows on these larger sparks that fell on the dry forest floor and would set off new additional fires.

It was a larger fire than we could manage, even with a willingness to act and though there were quite a few of us, we lacked equipment and expertise. We called the local emergency services and although no one replied, we left a message together with the location. The fire was beginning to spread more rapidly so we evacuated the area.

Once safely on the water, we tried another number to contact the emergency services and left another message and thought that our efforts were to no avail. However as we paddled away, after nearly an hour after first seeing the smoke, an emergency helicopter flew over us and it circled the forest fire to assess the danger and we felt that our efforts had eventually got through to the right people.

We stopped at Beaver Creek, where there was a good camp ground set high above the river and adjacent to a creek where there were several beaver dams, although the builders did not seem to be in residence. I pitched my tent away some distance from the main camp, on the end of the bluff between Beaver Creek and the Yukon with fine views up the river. Some of us went exploring up the creek but didn't get very far before we were confronted by a sea of burnt forest with ash on the ground and some plants most noticeably fireweed only now growing through the thick layer of ash.

Michael and Norman had gone fishing where Beaver Creek emptied into the Yukon and both had caught some large pike and were delighted with their catches. Meanwhile, a slack line had been set up in camp and whilst some had gone for walks or to go fishing, the rest of the group had tried their balancing skills. And now that we were back in camp it was our turn. I am sure that it is a natural ability or something that can be learned but most of the fun is just watching people just giving it a go and falling off.

We were ahead of schedule so there was time to walk up the mountain behind Beaver Creek. Not everyone wanted to go, so we left some people in camp and started out. We passed the beaver lodge and in no time, we reached the burnt out area and trekked through the thick ash that covered the ground kicking up small clouds of ash as we passed. It was a desolate sight, for as far as we could see.

The fire had been intense and killed off the trees over a huge swathe of forest and only a few plants had so far reclaimed the area. There was no trail but the lack of undergrowth and tree foliage gave us the chance to pick our route and bush whack our way up to the top of the hill. The ash and its nutrients would contribute to the regeneration of this area and it would soon be reclaimed by the forest.

It was quite a way and steep in places, but we eventually got above the last of the burnt trees to be able to view the Yukon valley in its full splendour. The fire had come this high but there was little to burn just here, so there was little ash, just a few scorched patches and a lot of bare rock. We had a great view of a tributary valley as it meandered its way down to join the main river with different terraces clearly visible. We were on the wrong side of the hill to see north but we had a great view southwards back the way we had come. And importantly, back towards Little Salmon Village and a spot nearby that had been on fire, but now there was no smoke rising from the forest fire that we had discovered yesterday.

We passed Eagle's Nest Bluff, the English translation of the native name although in true form Frederick Schwatka had no hesitation in naming it Parkman Peak after the well-known Professor Francis Parkman, an American historian but his name change did not survive. The outcrop is distinctive, as it consists of a light grey rock and rises 170m above the river and surrounding forest. According to the map, the Campbell Highway was not far away from the bank and it goes behind this bluff but from the river, we never saw or heard the main road.

Next feature down the river was the Columbian Slough, named after a disastrous shipping accident. The SS Columbian was steaming from Whitehorse to Carmacks in September 1906, with a load of three tons of blasting powder, to be off loaded at the Tantalus Mine. One of the ship's crew borrowed a repeating rifle and tripped, with the gun going off straight into the black powder. There was a massive explosion, throwing several crew members over board. The resultant fire was intense but the captain was able to beach the vessel on the bank and secure it. Luckily, there were no passengers but six of the crew died, either at the time or from burns suffered.

We were still ahead of schedule, so we decided to have two easy days of paddling rather than arrive a day early in Carmacks. Therefore, we hadn't gone far when we reached some islands and gravel bars just a bit further on. We pulled our canoes out of the river onto a gravel bar in the river. It was flat and stony, a few spindly young trees with a scattering of weeds and thin willow saplings. Despite only having a few trees on the gravel bar, there was plenty of driftwood that had been washed down the river and bleached almost white by the sun to gather for firewood. Here and there, the gravel was covered with a thin lens of sand overlying the gravel and these were the best places to pitch a tent.

There was a gently shelving inlet and some of us took the opportunity to have a good wash and we stripped off and waded into the water. It was cold but I washed my hair and I rinsed it by sitting on the stony bottom and leaning back. Standing in cold water and having a splash is one thing, sitting down and getting your shoulders and whole body under water is quite another. Once back on land and drying myself with a towel, it didn't seem so bad and I felt very refreshed.

That evening, there were a few scattered dark clouds and blue sky beyond. The sun was setting and there were some spectacular reds, oranges and yellow clouds reflecting the setting sun nicely juxtaposed against the darkness of the clouds with light blue sky to the west ranging to dark blue sky in the east. It was only spoilt for a moment, by the whine of an outboard motor as a boat sped pass going up river.

We would be having an early dinner and we were sitting round the fire when someone spotted a bear on the far bank. We crowded round the bank, above the beach but stayed within the shadows of the few bushes so as not to alert the bear. It was unusual to see bears down by the river, at this time of year as they usually work their way up the mountains and only move back down the slopes to find winter hibernating dens.

We watched it for a while as it wandered up and down the far shoreline. Amongst the group, we only had two pairs of binoculars but these were passed round continuously to view the bear on the far bank. We had some good views of it, as it came down right into the open to the water's edge. It eventually moved off back into the forest lining the shoreline.

Even when we could no longer see it, as it had wandered back into the forest, we continued to watch. Bears can run fast and climb trees but they are also good swimmers, so even across the wide river we were not necessarily safe from a close encounter with a bear. We ate our dinner but many of us cast anxious glances across the river to where the bear had been seen.

More wood was gathered and we sat around the fire chatting until it got late and it was time to go to bed. The guides are usually the last to put up their tents and as the best pitches near the fire would have been taken, they are usually furthest from the fire. This time I noted that the guides put up their tents on the well packed earth right next to the fire instead of finding a good pitch further away. I settled down and lay awake in my sleeping bag. I was near the river's edge and the furthest tent from the fire. I could hear the water running past the bank and catching in the tree roots and branches that dangled in the river.

The sighting of the bear played on my nerves and all night, I was trying to decipher whether what I was hearing was a danger or not. I wondered about the noises and whether what I was hearing was a bear. Had it swam across the river and was climbing out of the water, dripping water onto the beach or the forest floor ready to come and attack me? I could also hear the noises of animals, working their way through the night of the forest. Was it a fox, a wolf, a lynx, rodent or a lemming or something that I could at least frighten away? And what did a bear prowling through the forest sound like?

Worst still, in the middle of the night, I had to get out of the tent for a pee. Not a problem usually, but was I about to be pounced upon, to be squashed or slashed to death, by an angry bear. I didn't go far before returning to my tent. Another camper was awake and shouted out at my approach, but I reassured her that it was just me and that there were no animals about … I might have sounded convincing but I wasn't so sure myself. I got back into the sleeping bag, but I continued to listen to the noises of the night, grasping my open Swiss Army knife.

I heard an animal slowly approaching my tent as it rustled through the leaf litter on the forest floor. It came closer and sniffed my tent a few times, but it continued down the trail and judging by the light short steps, it probably wasn't a bear but that was little reassurance. I half dozed for the rest of the night, until the gloom of night gradually lightened as the dawn approached.

I did check the trail for paw prints in the morning and there were definitely some fresh prints, but nothing as large as a bear paw mark. I had indeed heard some animal coming past during the night but there was no bear close encounter.

I had survived the night and got up when I heard some movement in the camp to light the fire. It was a short and easy paddle down through Raabe's Slough, named after the captain who had raced the SS Dawson at full speed down Thirty Mile River to rescue the survivors of the SS Columbian and who over wintered his boat here for several years running.

From some way up river, we could see a large domed hill called Tantalus Butte, named by Frederick Schwatka after the Greek mythological figure punished by having nourishment eternally just of his grasp as it can be seen from the river, from a long way off and the river winds considerably before finally reaching it. When George Dawson was mapping the Yukon in 1887, he had found seams of coal throughout the surrounding hills and there were to be several mines in the area.

Captain Miller started the first mine at this site, but later sold out to the Five Fingers Coal Co in 1903. The coal was sold to heat local residences and to fuel the sternwheelers. A tramway carried the coal from the mines to the wharfs to load onto the steamers. The coal was of an inferior quality with a high ash content so some sternwheelers reverted to wood which was plentiful and cheap. The mine was abandoned in 1908, in favour of the more productive Tantalus Butte coal mine which produced better quality coal. The original workings are largely flooded and have collapsed.

The new Tantalus Mine operated until 1922, when the main tunnel reached a fault line and the continuing coal seams could not be located. A forest fire set light to the coal seam running underground and even today smoke can sometimes be smelt rising from some of the mine openings. Production shifted to the opposite side of the river with another mine of the same name but this too was eventually closed in 1938. Mining was always difficult as the seams are at an angle of between 16–50 degrees so the standard tunnel and shafts method of mining (horizontal tunnels and vertical shafts) were not practical and mining had to use angled tunnels called minzes.

There were several subsequent re-openings and closings, depending on other mineral mines' economic prosperity in the area and their demand for fuel especially the Faro Mine. The Faro mine was the then largest open pit lead and zinc mine which also produced silver and other valuable minerals in small quantities. The ores were shipped out by truck to Whitehorse and from there via the WP&YR to Skagway until a period of temporary suspension of mining ended when the mine finally closed in 1982 which also meant that the WP&YR had no freight to carry and closed as well. Limited production resumed in 1986 under new management but ore was trucked directly to Skagway and ended any economic recovery prospects for the WP&YR.

We arrived at the Coal Mine Campground wharf just upstream from Carmacks where we were due to leave the river. There was a floating landing stage and it was low enough for us to get out from the river, straight onto the landing stage although it was a steep drag to get the canoes up the bank to get to flat ground.

The Coal Mine Campground was where we said goodbye to most of the group as only Bob and I were going on to Dawson. Therefore we had the rest of the day to fill until the next guide and group showed up. They were expected in the late afternoon but like a lot of things in the Yukon, time is not a deciding factor such are the vagaries of the roads, the flying conditions, weather, delays, breakdowns, bears etc.

Bob and I walked into town and followed the historical trail. It started near the bridge over the river and followed the water front and then cut inland across a small finger of land between the Yukon and the Nordenskiöld River (named by Frederick Schwatka who in typical form ignored the local name for the river and named it after Nils Adolf Erik Nordenskiöld, a Swedish nobleman and arctic explorer who was the first explorer to sail from Europe around the arctic coast of Asia and across the Bering's Straits to reach the Pacific Ocean) to cross the small tributary. It is a fascinating walk through history and there was an abundant supply of small wild strawberries to pick and eat, as you walked along the trail.

There was a First Nation seasonal settlement here and it was an important point used for trading goods. Well before the gold rush, George Carmacks built a trading post here in 1892 and started a small coal mining operation that was selling coal in 1894. The original centre of the settlement of Carmacks was nearer to the Nordenskiöld River as this was where a branch of the Dalton Trail emerged.

The Dalton Trail started at Pyramid Harbour near Haines at the top of the Lynn Canal in Alaska and worked its way up past Daltons Post, through Champagne and down the Nordenskiöld River. It was established by Jack (born John) Dalton, a rugged, ruthless and colourful entrepreneur, who developed the trail in the early 1890's to move freight and later livestock into the interior of the Yukon with branches reaching Carmacks and ultimately Fort Selkirk. It was also used by several prospectors to reach the gold fields and to move freight during the gold rush, although not a favoured option, as it is nearly 400kms long.

There are informative signs about many of the buildings such as the Telegraph Station and an example of a cache, a place to store goods off the ground. In 1902 the WP&YR had acquired the contract to build a road between Whitehorse and Dawson and carry mail along the road in winter and by sternwheeler during the summer. They had stables here to change horses until the early 1920's when alternative forms of travel were used.

There were several cabins from later than the gold rush, but also an example of a coal car from before the gold rush. But there was an example of a road house next to the river that had been meticulously restored. These were placed every 30kms to 50kms all along the trail to Dawson and provided food and somewhere to sleep for travellers.

At around 7pm, the transit arrived with the new guests. We were greeted by our guide, Martin, who was German by birth and had worked for a bank leasing company but had immigrated to Kamloops, Canada some years before.

Also there was Jürgen from Potsdam, a mechanical engineer and lecturer. The last two of the group, of just six to paddle from Carmacks to Dawson, were Rolf and Karen who I had first met a few years earlier. They had paddled with me for the first section of the Whitehorse to Carmacks part of the river. So it was time for reunions and exchange of paddling stories over an evening meal before retiring for the night.

CHAPTER 13

Five Finger Rapids

The route this morning was purposefully easy to ensure that any novice paddlers were able to learn and to practice their paddling skills, before we reached the most challenging section of the river. As it turned out, this wasn't necessary, as we had all paddled before. Consequently, it was a late breakfast but Martin and Karen had got up early to go fishing.

We put into the water at the Coal Mine Campground and with a gentle current, we were swept past the helicopter launching site next door and under the bridge that carries the Klondike Highway across the Yukon River and the last bridge over the Yukon in Canada. At Carmacks, the river meanders in several large bends that makes the river double back on itself and despite paddling several kilometres we were just a stone's throw from where we had put in.

I was paddling with Bob, Rolf and Karen shared a canoe and Jürgen was with Martin. We stopped at a First Nation fishing camp. It was not being used and hadn't been used the year before as the salmon run had been so poor. However the fishermen amongst the group still had a go and Martin caught a grayling. Whilst he fished, I panned but the site was a poor choice so it was no surprise when I didn't get anything and I soon stopped and just relaxed in the warmth of the afternoon sun.

We passed some hoodoos high up the cliff face and in mid-afternoon we arrived at our camp site for the night. This is where the coal had been mined by the Five Fingers Coal Mine Co. The coal was first mined here in 1894 but the ground was unstable and the shafts had steep gradients making mining challenging.

Coal production continued intermittently until 1908, when it was shut and never reopened.

Walking up the hillside above, where we pitched our tents, we found the old mine site. There were several piles of spoil, dug out of the hillside to reach the coal. The old openings of mine shafts were still there although they are merely hollows in the hillside, although one did have part of the tunnel beyond the opening that had not collapsed but it was filled with water.

At one bank that had been undercut by the river, was a fresh seam of coal. I dug out a handful of large lumps of coal. It wasn't dark shiny anthracite, steam coal or even bituminous coal that most people would recognise as coal. Instead, it was rather brown and crumbly, lignite, much lower in carbon content than anthracite.

I added them to the fire, on which we were cooking our evening meal. There were two grayling caught earlier during the day, which split between six people, doesn't go very far, hence it was to be a starter but nothing beats freshly caught and cooked fish. The campsite was not well frequented and so you didn't have to go far to gather wood. There was also the lumps of coal that I had gathered which were added to the fire and whilst they glowed red and gave off some heat, they burned fairly quickly and had a high ash content. Not surprising, therefore, that whilst some sternwheelers converted from wood to coal, many did not and some even reconverted back to more plentiful and cheaper wood.

Our next challenge on the river was the Five Fingers Rapids, not a big deal to experienced paddlers, but a major hazard to sternwheelers. Four tall columns of rock rise out of the river causing the river to split into five channels. The river speeds up to get through the constriction and there is plenty of white water as it rushes through. Only the far right hand channel is navigable. Boats going downstream must come out of the bend immediately above the rapids and keep hard to the right, and line up to run the rapids before the current takes them and hurls them against the rocks.

Several boats were lost until protruding rocks making passage difficult were blasted in 1902 to remove obstacles and widen the channel. Due to the speed of the river, boats going upstream needed additional help. A permanent cable was fixed to the bank and ships winched themselves up the rapids.

On the cliffs above the river, is a viewing platform reached by a short path from the Campbell Highway which follows the river for part of its route northwards. I knew it was there but from our position down on the water, we couldn't see the road or any traffic on it and I was concentrating too much on negotiating the rapids, to look up at the platform. We kept our distance, both from each other and from the rocks and rode the maelstrom of the turbulent white water and standing waves until we were through to the other side.

I had been apprehensive about shooting the rapids but having done it, it didn't seem so bad and my nagging doubts about going through were exaggerated. There wasn't much time for celebration as just seven kilometres further on are the Rink Rapids. These however are less difficult to shoot although there is still plenty of white water thrown up as the water rushes over the rocks and there are several standing waves.

We again kept to the right hand side of the river and other than getting splashed it was relatively easy. After negotiating the Five Fingers Rapids, these were almost a cake run. We rafted up and gently floated down steam, enjoying the calmness of the river and the countryside. Bob got out his penny whistle and played a tune to celebrate a safe passage through the two sets of rapids without incident.

In some of the banks, along the river's edge, can be seen a thin white layer of ash which occurs all over the area and is visible when some of the overlying sediments are removed. These are fondly referred to as Sam McGee's ashes, in reference to the poem written by Robert Service.

Their correct name but not so humorous, is White River Ash. It is a thin layer of tephra that originates from the eruption about 1,200 years ago of Mount Churchill and possibly its sister volcano, just 3kms away, Mount Bona. These are two large stratovolcanoes located in Wrangell St Elias National Park in south east Alaska. The ash layer is found across Alaska and the Yukon with traces in Greenland, Iceland and northern Europe. The layer is just a handful of centimetres thick in the Yukon, but in one bank it had collected in a dip in the ancient landscape and was over a metre thick, making a distinct white gash along the river bank.

At Merrice Island, we took the left hand channel which in retrospect, was a poor decision as we had to continue to paddle, whilst the right hand channel looked faster and we could have saved our strength and drifted in the stronger current.

Our next stop on shore was at Williams Creek. This is situated on a straight section of the river and was established as a telegraph office and mining village over a hundred years ago. The surviving cabins on site are still standing although degrading rapidly and it is a bit of a Mary Celeste environment. The words 'Williams Creek Copper Mining Co' in paint are still visible on a door made out of the company sign that once looked out over the river. There was a rich copper deposit here plus associated minerals including gold and silver which were prospected from at least 1908 intermittently until 1928.

There is still plenty of mineral ore here and just 8kms away, is an area owned by Glamis Gold Ltd who in turn, is now owned by Goldcorp which proposes to mine the area as soon as the economics of mining in this remote area move in their favour. (This location should not be confused with the William Creek gold mining area in British Columbia).

The scenery had changed markedly from that between Whitehorse and Carmacks. There were fewer high steep sandy and gravel river banks and the valley sides were set back from the river. There were fewer trees which now were a mixture of pine and aspen with stretches of open ground. There were more rock outcrops and the tops of local hills were devoid of trees.

The river was much wider and there were more islands that required decisions on which channel to take. River guide books were only partially helpful as the changing water levels and moving sand bars made any definitive permanent course impossible to predict and so you would be left in the hands of local river guides and pilots who may still be caught out by sudden changes.

We passed O'Brien's Murder Camp opposite Slackwater Crossing, so called as the spot where George O'Brien and Thomas Graves ambushed, killed and robbed three travellers on Christmas Day 1900. He was subsequently hanged for the offence but there is nothing to see at the site but the history of the spot makes an interesting story.

Next down the river was Minto, named after the Earl of Minto, the Governor General of Canada for 1895–1904 who visited the site in 1900. Its population has fluxed and waned over the years but now it is the site of a river crossing for the Minto Mine owned by the Capstone Mining Corp. There is a large open cast mining site on the left hand side of the river and ore is shipped across the river by ferry, to be taken by road down to the port in Skagway. In winter, the ore lorries can take the ore across the river ice, directly to Skagway.

When we passed, there were no ore ferries operating so we had a clear run down the river. We saw several of the ferries, held in reserve that had been beached on the shore. Just another ten kilometres downstream, we reached our planned campsite at Thoms' Location, named after Ernest Leslie Thoms. He had worked as a roadhouse keeper on the Indian River but moved here where he lived alone as a recluse. He was found dead in his cabin and was buried on the hillside behind the cabin.

The cabin is still standing and perfectly serviceable but we erected our tents on some flat ground in front of the cabin. It was a bit of a steep bank to climb and drag our canoes up the slope for safety, but it was a good location and set well above expected flood levels. It is well wooded and not too popular, so it was easy to find plenty of wood to burn, without having to go too far from the camp.

In the morning, getting the canoes from the top of the bank into the water was a lot easier than getting out. We had some mischievous fun but it wasn't exactly a seal launch off the top of the bank into the water. Someone would sit in the middle of the canoe and his paddling partner would give him a push and the canoe would slide down the muddy bank into the river. The paddler would then have to stabilise the canoe and keep it on the bank so that we could load all the gear into it. It's not good for the bottom of the canoe but it was wet and muddy and no tree roots or rocks to take gouges out of the hull, so no harm done.

Not only is the scenery different, but this section of the river is also noticeably different from the section between Whitehorse and Carmacks. There are numerous, uncounted and unnamed islands and as the gravel bars were always forming and reforming, it was always a challenge to sternwheelers and their captains to decide which route was the best route. The best channel might change from season to season. We were rafted up and kept to the main left hand channel.

Once the current took us off to the right, we were heading down a dangerous channel. It required some fast and furious paddling to get out of the current and down our preferred and calmer route. Near Mildred Island, one of the larger and permanent islands in the river, we passed One Pound Nugget Island with no prizes as to how this one got its name. We stopped and tried our luck at panning. Karen found a flake but that hoped for glistening of gold in the crease of my pan evaded me, so after an hour we moved on.

We passed the confluence of the Pelly River with the Yukon. For once, this was not named by Schwatka but by Hudson's Bay trader and explorer, Robert Campbell on 6th August 1840 after one of the company's governors, Sir John Henry Pelly. The Pelly is a smaller river but it carries more silt and therefore it is a different colour and the different coloured waters flow side by side until they become so mixed that they are indistinguishable. Karen wanted to try fishing here, so we slowed to keep the three canoes together as she cast from the front of the canoe as Rolf steered and paddled from the back. The river here has several bars and awkward cross currents, so we struggled to keep together whilst Karen fished and Rolf tried to keep position.

It was working well until we crossed a series of gravel banks where the current was stronger. We were tossed about in the current and became separated. As the water was very shallow, it made steering and paddling difficult, as the bottom of the blade of the paddle would dig into the gravel just inches below the surface. It was more like punting than paddling. Karen had to stop fishing and use her paddle to get back into the desired position. We were fast approaching Fort Selkirk on the left hand side and needed to get across the main current to enable us to land.

It was only a short paddle between Thom's Location and Fort Selkirk, perhaps 30kms. Around lunchtime, we arrived at Fort Selkirk named by Campbell after Thomas Douglas, Earl of Selkirk. This has been an important trading post for the First Nations for a long period. It had been first established by Robert Campbell of the Hudson Bay Company in 1854 but had been destroyed by the hostile Chilkat tribe in 1857 which was followed by the withdrawal of the company from the area.

All along the shore there were hoses leading down from pumps located on the top of the high bank above the river. These had been set up to protect the more than thirty historical wooden buildings from a forest fire that was raging just a few kilometres from the town. One area had a dozen tents already set up including a large mess tent to feed the couple of dozen firemen who were temporarily stationed here to control the fire and protect the settlement.

I spoke to Andrew, Keith, Chad and Francoise, who were all stationed normally in BC but other brigades help out as necessary, especially as the Yukon dry season starts before the BC dry season. There are a lot of fires in a season and too many to control all of them. Also although this is scenic forest, it is not valuable timber and there are few buildings or people up here. Their role is to control fires and keep an eye on developments, build fire breaks and to protect lives and economic assets (buildings) which are few and far between. No one lives here anymore, but it is a historical site hence their presence. There are some First Nation summer visitors, plus a few volunteers who look after the buildings.

There was a faint smell of smoke in the air, as we unloaded the canoes and carried everything up the steep bank. Then we dragged the canoes up the bank and left them at the top and set up camp, a short distance back from the top of the bank. Looking out across the river, from anywhere in the settlement, you can see a vertical basalt cliff on the far bank. This was formed from a lava flow that covered a large area of the far bank in ancient times. Only part of the Yukon was glaciated and it is thought that this was where a lava flow met the edge of the ice sheet thus creating this high cliff.

After pitching the tents, it was time to look around the historical buildings. They are set well back from the top of the steep bank and there is plenty of space between them. Many are open to visitors and some have been furnished as they would have been in their heyday. There are plenty of signs and information boards, many with pictures that recount the stories surrounding the settlement.

Fort Selkirk used to be a busy settlement but when roads were built to Mayo and Dawson, they bypassed Fort Selkirk. River traffic decreased so people gradually moved to other settlements such as Minto and Pelly Crossing so this whole settlement became abandoned in the 1950s.

Most of the buildings are well preserved and there are a number of stores, including a Hudson's Bay trading post when they returned in the 1930's and a Taylor and Drury store and warehouse. There are both well to do family homes and single room fur trapper cabins, a garage, a church, a NWMP post and several farms together with stables and a collection of out buildings and a number of caches built on a platform well above the ground level.

On the open ground, between the buildings and the bank of the river, was a large grassy area. A football pitch had been marked out and two goals fashioned out of round timber. However, it was serving another use as a landing spot for a fire helicopter used for fire spotting. There was a small aerial water bucket at the other end of the pitch that it could use for firefighting. It was Canada Day and the pilot fixed a flag and a weight to the end of a long cable and flew around the area for ten minutes. He said that he was flying the flag to raise their spirits as they were all assigned here for two weeks, at a time with nothing to do if they had any spare time.

At the far end are a collection of buildings built and occupied by the Yukon Field Force. This was a detachment of the Canadian army who were stationed here between 1898 and 1900. The NWMP force were happy to have these reinforcements as the number of prospectors swelled every settlements population as they made their way to the gold fields.

There were 203 troops armed with Lee Enfield rifles, 17 civilian employees and 870 tons of supplies that left Vancouver in May 1898, for Fort Selkirk, but it took them three months along the Teslin Trail, for the last of the contingent to reach their goal. It was always only a token force to protect Canadian sovereignty as they only had two Maxim machine guns and two seven pound field guns. But they were here as a token force especially as many of the miners were foreigners with a large proportion of Americans. And the border between the two countries had still not been determined.

As soon as the first soldiers arrived, they built store houses, barracks, mess halls and officers' quarters. It was these buildings at the southern end of the settlement that told the story of the army's presence in the Yukon. Later, fifty troops were dispatched to Dawson. They weren't just soldiers as their roles evolved to include assisting the NWMP in guarding bullion shipments, fighting forest fires and protecting government buildings.

There is a brass plaque in honour of the Yukon Field Force and a memorial to some of the soldiers who died in service, three in Fort Selkirk and one in Dawson but I wasn't able to establish how they died, whether it was fulfilling their roles as peace keepers or was it from accident or disease. There was also a sign pointing to a cemetery that was along a track that disappeared into the trees of the surrounding forest.

I followed the track, but with each step and turn, I was moving ever further away from the settlement. Ideas played on my mind about bears. If I saw one, I could always retreat back to the safety of the buildings. Of greater concern, was that no one knew where I was for certain, other than 'exploring the settlement' and should I see a bear on the return journey, it would be between me and safety. I whistled or sung a song to make some noise so that I didn't surprise one en route.

I reached the small cemetery with a handful of grey, weathered headstones. It was a dark, sombre and quiet place so after a quick look around, I safely retraced my steps and got back to the open grasslands around the settlement. A bit further back through the settlement and again set back in the forest, was the First Nations cemetery and this was a total contrast.

There were many more graves. Each had a fence or a balustrade around it. Some had a spirit house as well. But all were painted in bright colours. Dark blue or red were the most popular but there were also light blues with bright red, pinks and white.

On the way back to the camp, I met Bob, who had found a patch of wild gooseberries that were thriving in the open grass spaces between the wooden buildings. We filled every bag and our pockets with the small but sweet fruits. They have an abundance of sharp thorns so gathering the fruit was not without its hazards but we were pleased with ourselves as we got back to camp, loaded down with gooseberries for the whole group. We had a dessert that evening which was pancakes, gooseberries and maple syrup. We had also seen several raspberries that were setting, but they would not be ready to pick for a few weeks. I suspect that both had been brought here, but had gone wild and escaped from people's gardens and colonised this section of land, far removed from their natural range.

At around 3am, it had started to rain, a downpour of heavy, persistent rain. It was still raining at breakfast time and rather than try to cook in the open, we borrowed one of the buildings with a half an oil barrel that had been fashioned by some skilful blacksmith into a potbellied stove. We lit it and cooked on it, whilst it warmed the interior of the hut and we ate in comfort and warmth.

We moved slowly, all wishing and hoping that it might stop raining but no luck. It looked like it had set in, so we packed our wet tents away in the rain and this time, carried our canoes down the bank to the water's edge to load them. We said goodbye to the firemen. We had joked with the pilots the night before, saying that if the fire was too close to the river, could they helicopter us, the canoes and our gear around the fire and they said they would be delighted to do so. Now that it was raining, the helicopters were grounded.

The rain would slow the fire and if persistent it might even put it out so the firemen could carry out dousing operations over a large area and declare it safe. It was still an effort and despite the rain, they all seemed happier that they were winning the fight against the elements. We pushed off and gently paddled, letting the current do most of the work.

CHAPTER 14

Below Fort Selkirk

We followed the basalt cliff to our right, dark and menacing through the rain. Its height varies between 478m and 496m and stretches 18kms from the Pelly – Yukon confluence along the right bank. Just after the Ralston Woodyard, it suddenly stops and the banks revert to loose, light coloured material, easily undercut by the river and forested wherever the trees can put down roots. Confusingly, there is another Ralston Woodyard just round the bend, as he set up at one point and later moved his operation to a better location. Wood cutters would cut down so many trees that hauling them further and further to the river became move difficult as the cutters moved ever deeper into the forest, hence moving sites was common.

We were all looking out for wildlife and had grown accustomed to seeing shapes that looked like animals, but when you got closer, were just a tree root or a jumble of branches. I assumed that the canoe ahead of me would be the first to see anything and point it out to those behind.

I was in the front of the canoe and as we drew level I remarked to Bob behind me that one particular jumble really did look like antlers. With that, the antlers moved and up stood a mother moose and her two calves and turned and disappeared into the undergrowth. We had a superb view but no camera at the ready. Whilst we were in the canoe, the animal had only seen some tree trunk drifting past but as I spoke, it identified us as human and moved away.

We would stop for a morning break and there were plenty of low islands with easy landing places. It was still raining and there was no protection against the wind or the rain so we opted to carry on paddling. We rafted up for a while, but as we felt the chill, with the lack of activity, we split up and paddled again to keep warm.

There was a better spot for a break with some trees for shelter that Martin knew a bit further down the river. However, as we came round the bend, there were already three canoes moored there so we continued. Just 6kms further on, was a good spot and there was only one canoe moored there that we recognised so we turned into the shore and moored our boats. There was a tent already pitched and better still, an awning spread between some trees sheltering a picnic bench and chairs. This was the temporary camp that Stefan and Bolita had set up. They were in fact there but still asleep. They tended to get up late, then paddle until late, setting up camp in the evening. Not that time was important, as it was light throughout the night.

They eventually emerged from their tent and we greeted each other like long lost friends. We shared our lunch with them for their breakfast … only fair since we were using their awning. We got to comparing notes of our trip since we had last seen each other. One thing that Benny did each morning and after lunch that Martin didn't was to do some exercises to loosen up the body, especially the paddling arms and shoulders. Bob and I had discussed this and talked about doing something different … yoga or pilates.

The Swiss couple said that it was a good idea. They had seen us waving our paddles around at one stop and whilst agreeing that loosening up was important, it looked hilarious to see adults waving paddles around their heads. It turned out that Bob not only played the penny whistle but was a man of many talents and he also taught Irish dancing. Therefore, we learnt to do a number of Irish dance moves, in the rain, on an island in the middle of the Yukon. It must win a prize for being the most bizarre place to hold an impromptu dance class.

We had planned to stop for the night at a good high water camp site just after Menzies Location but just as earlier in the day, there were already three canoes moored there and I suspected, it was the same canoes that had occupied another site that morning. There is no point in joining them, as the nearest wood for fires would have been gathered and the best tent pitches taken, so we moved on. I was disappointed as a short walk below Menzies location, was Selwyn River, named by Schwatka after Dr A Selwyn, Director of the Geological and Natural History Survey of Canada, where gold had been discovered and over five years more than 500 ounces were removed.

The good thing about having a guide that knows the river is that he knows things that are not marked on the usual published river guides. We paddled on to an unmarked campsite on the right hand bank, just past Mascot Creek. There was a choice of flat pitches, either overlooking the river or set back in the trees plus a picnic table and benches. There was a hearth for a fire and plenty of wood near the camp which being under cover of the trees above was not too wet. This was supplemented by collecting driftwood which is my personal preferred wood, as it had been weathered and bleached and burns well.

Once we had set up the awning for the kitchen and pitched our own tents, we had some spare time. It had at last stopped raining, but it was still overcast and there was a damp in the air. Karen fished, Bob practiced on his penny whistle, Martin sorted through the provisions to decide what to cook for supper, Rolf went for a walk to collect more firewood, whilst Jürgen and I went for a wash in the river, far enough apart for privacy, but near enough in case help was needed, in the event of bears or moose.

Supper was pasta with salmon and broccoli sauce. We sat around the camp fire and roasted marshmallows for desert. Several canoes went past and as part of the comradery of the river, we waved at all of them. One canoe that went past was Stefan and Bolita and we exchanged shouted greetings over the water.

The rain had only eased off during the evening and it was raining again. The picnic table was soaked through and it wasn't worth even trying to light a fire, as it would take time and we would be gone by the time it was giving off any heat, so we huddled under the awning and ate breakfast standing up but at least we were out of the rain. Water had collected in puddles on top of the awning. Although there was a faint hint of smoke in the air, the rain had washed a lot of the soot from forest fires out of the air and the puddles had a thick layer of soot in the bottom of each one.

I had optimistically washed a tee shirt and shorts the night before and needless to say, they were still wet. I packed them away wet in a plastic bag and hoped that they wouldn't smell when they did eventually dry out.

The wind picked up, during the morning and was blowing straight up the river. Pieces of driftwood were being blown up stream, despite the current. There were white crests to the waves and paddling was slow and hard work. We stopped for an early lunch on a low flat island opposite Cottonwood Creek. I took time out to stand in the river in my rain gear panning the finer gravels for gold but found nothing. There were no reports of gold here but just five kilometres upstream at Britannia Creek, gold was discovered in 1911 that has sparked placer mining operations there ever since.

It is also home to a long line of mineralisation called the Tintina Trench that runs through the area that includes gold, silver, lead, copper, and a host of other metal ores such as tungsten and molybdenum but until the extraction costs dip below the market price of the metals they will stay in the ground and the pristine environment is safe.

We passed Excelsior Creek where Martha Black had met a group of New Zealand miners who wanted to call it Maori Creek, but she persuaded then to change it to Excelsior. Just a kilometre further on, is Ballarat Creek where gold was discovered in 1898 by W F Woodward and where intermittent mining continues today. It was named after an earlier gold rush of the same name in Australia where gold was discovered on 18th August 1854, which sparked the Victoria gold rush. That town is also the site of the only armed rebellion in Australian history. It was on 3rd December 1854 and lasted less than a day, but cost 27 lives, mostly rebellious miners complaining about the cost of mining licences.

We stopped again at Coffee Creek, nothing to do with Starbucks coffee, but named after the local Coffee Indian natives. Karen went fishing at the mouth of the creek, where it joined the main river. There is gold ore in the mountains, from which the river flows but there is no record of any placer gold being found here. There are plenty of gold ore bodies located with a local gold mining and exploration company waiting for the economics of recovery to move in their favour. It is interesting to note that the nine separate ore bodies already located have been given coffee related names to perpetuate the coffee theme such as Latte, Espresso and Cappuccino.

Bob and I paddled up Coffee Creek, as far as we could and we were stopped, not by running out of water, but by a big dam across the creek. Beavers had been busy building a dam ten metres across the creek that raised the water level behind the dam by one and a half metres. There were a series of dams above this and they effectively filtered out the silt so the water was a lot clearer below the dams but tinged brown from tannins in the runoff before mixing in with the silty waters of the main river. The dam was in good repair and we waited quietly but saw no sign of life.

Re-joining the others of the confluence, Karen had got lucky and was cleaning a large pike that she had caught, so it was going to be fresh fish for supper. Our camp for the evening was to be a large island near Langley Chute. The challenge was to get to our desired landing spot. A large pile of debris had piled up on the upstream side of the island which protected it from erosion. But, it had built up in such a way to channel water towards the right hand bank. There was a standing wave and a significant drop in the water as it speeded up to rush past the island which also eroded the river bed making the water deeper.

Our challenge was to get down the sudden drop and across the increase in current and make landfall just after the start of the island. Downside risks were capsizing, losing gear or being washed downstream, either upright or upside down, as the next good campsite was some way down river.

Luckily, we landed without mishap. True to Martin's guiding skills and knowledge it was a good site. Even landing at the end of the island was not a good option, as there were obstacles in the form of tree trunks and root balls that would have made lining our canoes up river, troublesome, tiring and slow. But just here there was flat soft sands and gravels. Lots of wood had been washed over and stranded on the island and had collected in great masses giving an endless supply of wood for the fire.

It was 4th July and we all wished Bob a Happy Independence Day when we got up. We threw the remains of the fire into the river and left no trace that we had been there, except for a lot of foot prints to add to the moose prints. Out first stop of the day was just seven kilometres downstream, at Linda's Bakery, named after its owner, Linda at Kirkman Creek. The Creek was named after Grant and Albert Kirkman from Tulare, California who discovered gold here in October 1898. It didn't pay initially and only saw intermittent mining for a number of years, but with varying degrees of success. But, there is definitely gold up this valley.

In winter, Linda lives in Dawson, but finds it too busy in the summer, so she retreats here to run a small coffee shop and bakery, for passing canoeists. The cabins and numerous outbuildings often dating back to the previous gold miners on the creek, rusting vehicles and ATVs, plus all sorts of other paraphernalia are set back from the river in a large area of freshly cut grass. It's a fascinating place to stop and wander around and the cakes are wonderful and worth a stop, just for a bite to eat. Just on the other side of the river is Independence Creek, a pure coincidence but apt for 4th July.

Then we had another great moose sighting opportunity. Firstly we saw a cow moose standing at the river's edge. It hesitated for a while and then moved off into the forest. Then, we saw two calves swimming to cross the river. They are good swimmers but the current was taking them downstream. When they reached the shore, they got out and looked back at us. They were a lot lower down the river than where we saw the cow moose, but they seemed unconcerned about us and nibbled at some vegetation and walked along the river bank, before disappearing into the forest in search of their mother.

O'Neill's Landing is where there is a straight section of river. It was named after Bill O'Neill, an engineer for Clear Creek Placers whose gold production peaked in 1950 but after a season of low water and poor returns the following year, eventually went into bankruptcy. Just below here and rising from the left hand bank, is a fresh man made scar that takes a gentle gradient up the bank and disappears into the forest beyond wide enough for two vehicles. It is a rough but fresh mine road for a new mine being developed somewhere in the interior which has yet to be marked on the maps and no sign on the landing stage to give any indication of its name, ownership or the ore that is being dug out.

On the left hand side is where the White River joins the Yukon. This drains from glaciers high up in the mountains and the fine glacial silt and volcanic ash is thick in the water and makes it seem milky and hence its name. We pulled in on the opposite side to climb up the opposite cliffs to get a view up the White River.

Just where we landed, is a little creek and at its mouth, are two claim posts. The first post is labelled Post No 2, dated 1st August, 2008 with the claimant's name, B McCann. There is a second post, labelled Post No 1, 9th September, 2009, McGarth. The first claimant didn't renew his claim so it lapsed so the second claimed the same area to try his luck. Both were obviously disappointed, as there was no evidence of any workings and had it been a good spot, they would have renewed their claims.

After struggling up the hill, there is a patch where the trees thin out and there is a great view up the White River. From this vantage point, you can see many islands at the mouth of the river, some plain gravel with a thin covering of grass, others longer established with trees. Between them, runs the milky river waters, flowing out of the White River to be carried down the side of the far bank and there is a distinct line in the water, between the milky White River waters and the darker Yukon waters. There was still a slight haze in the sky but we weren't sure whether it was water vapour or smoke, but by now, we had got so used to smoke in the air, we hardly noticed it.

A few kilometres after Frisco Creek, we landed on a gently shelving sandy beach and hauled the canoes out of the water to set up camp. Wood was becoming much easier to find, as there was a lot more of it washed down the river and collecting on the many islands, sometimes in great piles that towered above us. Karen went fishing whilst Bob struck it lucky and in just four pans found seven flakes of gold. I gave him a small plastic container with a snap on lid that I had bought for the express purpose of keeping gold flakes. Try as I might, I couldn't find any but that is just the luck of the draw.

I even asked him to fill my pan from the exact same spot that he had found gold but still I didn't find anything. Karen stopped fishing and joined in the hunt but she too was unlucky which made me feel better as it wasn't just me.

Bob had been saving some beer cans for this evening and we all toasted Independence Day with him. That evening, I was pleased with myself for being able to get into the tent without any mosquitoes following me in. However, I then realised that the beer had gone to my bladder and I needed to go for a wee. On my return, I wasn't so lucky and several mosquitoes followed me in so I must have spent twenty minutes trying to track them down and squash them. Every time I thought I had got the last one, I would hear that high pitched whine as one flew past an ear and I would have to get up again and look for it.

Light rain against the canvas of the tent woke me up early and I felt wide awake. I tiptoed across to the kitchen so as not to wake anyone and built up the fire and put some water on to boil so it was ready for breakfast and people could have a hot drink as soon as they got up. There was plenty of time before breakfast, so I went to have a pan. At long last I found some tiny flakes, more like micro dots, but they were gold. At last, I had found some on this section of the river but my haul was nothing compared to Bob's that he had found the night before.

I wasn't going to give up too easily, so I took some sand and gravel with me in the canoe. So all that morning, whenever we rafted up, I panned again from the edge of the canoe. If I ran out of gravel to pan, we just manoeuvred a bit closer to a sand bar and I would scoop up another panful and carry on panning. We passed the mouth of the Stewart River and immediately below it, Stewart Island and Henderson Slough, but I was too busy panning to take much notice.

I should have made the effort as the upstream island, immediately next to Stewart Island, is called Split-Up Island as it is alleged that some groups of miners would disagree whether to go up the Stewart River or down to Dawson and would divide up their goods including cutting things in half, so acrimonious could these disagreements become. It is claimed that there are cabins on Stewart Island, built by Russian traders long before the gold rush and so they must have encountered the hostile Chilkat tribe who burned Fort Selkirk in 1857. However, there is nothing there visible to substantiate the claims.

Robert Henderson had staked a town site on the left hand bank, opposite the island in 1897. It was a popular place, as in 1898, there was a community of over 1,000 people on the island but by June 1899, it was almost a ghost town with just a handful of people living there. It gets several mentions in the ongoing history of the area and gets a few reprieves but it eventually succumbs to the forces of nature as the river eats away at the island and now there is nothing to see on what is left of the island from the gold rush days.

At the end of Stewart Island is Henderson Creek and Henderson Slough which is where Robert Henderson found gold and staked a claim on 9th June 1897, naming them after himself. Jack London staked a claim here in 1897 and over wintered in 1898 but suffering from scurvy, he was hospitalised in Dawson.

His daughter Joan, wanted his cabin relocated to Jack London Square, in Oakland California but the US and Canadian governments couldn't initially agree, so they came to a compromise whereby, each would get half of the original logs and each would relocate a semi original, semi replica cabin, one in Oakland and the other in Dawson. The original site continued to produce placer gold with a large dredge operating from 1945 to 1956, when dredging ceased but artisan panning operations have worked the creek on and off for decades ever since.

At the end of Harland Slough, we pulled over to a sandy bank on the left hand side of the river for lunch. We had plenty of time and were ahead of schedule and at long last the sun was shining. I had been paddling and panning all morning and still had a go, but I'd had enough for one day. It was a good place to pan, as it was a sandy beach, but I relaxed for a post lunch dose in the sun. No one seemed eager to move on, so we spent another hour there.

Eventually, we had to get back into the canoes, if we were going to make our campsite for the night. This was a poor place for a campsite. Flat and sandy but no trees for shelter and no wood. We had only been on the water for a short while when we had a brush with the law.

A Conservation Officer, armed and in full uniform, accompanied by a dog in a launch with two powerful outboards motors, came up river and flagged us down. He introduced himself as Mark and his dog was Molly, an alert cocker spaniel and both eyed us over. We were asked several questions and he wanted to see some identification, the guide permits and fishing licences to ensure that everything was in order. We were asked where we were going, where we had come from, other traffic on the river and any bear sightings. His professional duties done he wished us good luck and with a thrust on the throttle the launch was soon speeding away from us to become a speck on the horizon although the sound of the motors stayed long after he was out of sight.

After Rosebute Creek, there are some hoodoos high on the bank above us. Just after this is a huge log pile that had reconnected Ogilvie Island with the shore, named after William Ogilvie, surveyor for the Dominion Land Survey on behalf of the Interior and Yukon's second commissioner. Even from our low point on the river, looking over the log pile, the water level behind it was noticeably lower and calm. The river has been diverted by the dam and rushes past the low river bank side of the island. The bank was at least a metre above the river level and there was little beach between the bank and the swirling rushing water. It was a challenge to land at just the right spot, but we had done similar challenges, enough times before, to know the drill, so not easy but not impossible.

We tied the canoes securely to the largest tree that we could find and went to explore. There were remains of several buildings, none with a roof but the walls were still standing. There were a couple of cabins, a barn, a stable complete with very weathered leather harnesses, bridles and reins plus other items that were not recognisable. Outside there was a metal harrow and a plough. Not anything can grow this far north but potatoes and rhubarb do well. Everything had just been left where it had last been put by the owner.

Arthur Harper and Joseph Ladue had set up a trading post here and Ladue built a small saw mill here before moving it to Dawson in September 1898. A NWMP post followed until it closed in 1905 and a telegraph office was established here as this was where the telegraph line crossed the river. Lewis Cruikshank applied for a homestead here in 1907 and had several wood permits by 1910. James Brown lived with Cruikshank and had started farming in 1914. When he left in 1919, Cruikshank took over the farm and became renowned for growing wheat, alfalfa, potatoes and rhubarb. The trees have long since started to reclaim the area as forest but the cabin remains, clearings for fields and plenty of rusting farm equipment are still discernible.

Opposite Ogilvie Island is Sixty Mile River, so named as it is sixty miles upriver from Fort Reliance which was just six miles downstream of the present location of Dawson which hadn't yet been built. Arthur Harper had discovered gold here in 1876 but additional discoveries were made further up its tributaries in 1891 and have been actively mined since. A road was made from Dawson to Boucher and Glacial Creeks and later Miller and Matson Creeks.

The gold bearing gravels were not rich enough for large dredges, but the area was actively mined up to the 1990s. This area forms the south west corner of the Dawson Mining District together with Fortymile, Klondike and Indian rivers. In 2010, 88 % of the total of 51,302 ounces of the gold mined in the Yukon, came from these four rivers. In total, 16.7 million ounces or 518 tons have been recovered from the Yukon.

Out on the river there was enough of a breeze to keep the insects away, but here in the dark damp of the forest, they are more active so we didn't stay long and were soon looking for the first large flat island after Ogilvie Island to set up camp. Just down river, was an island with a gently shelving beach of sand and gravel with plenty of flat areas for tents and plenty of driftwood. I chose a pitch on a sandy patch, overlooking the main river for the view. The others chose a stony area, set behind a log pile that would give some shelter from the predominant wind blowing up the river.

I tried a little panning, but the ground was too stony indicating that the current here in flood was quite strong and any gold that might have been washed down Sixty Mile River would have been washed straight over this bar. I saw Bolita and Stefan go past and exchanged greetings. Just a little later there was the roar of outboard motors as Mark and Molly returned to base. A large bird of prey flew over us but as there were no twitchers amongst us for a positive identification and none of us could agree what it had been. The light breeze kept the insects away whilst we ate our elk stew under a sunny clear sky which made a difference after the clouds and rain of the last few days. And my wet clothes had finally dried and didn't smell of damp.

I had had a great night's rest. It had been a clear sky all night and a three quarter moon. We had just set off into the current and we heard some loud animal noises on the far bank, just a little downstream. We did a ferry glide to the far bank and slowly drifted down with the current with all eyes peering intently into the forest. We didn't hear any more and saw no movement. We had all definitely heard those calls but were not able to identify them. We all had theories, such as a pair of cougars hunting together, baby moose calling to each other, foxes screaming, but nothing definitive.

We rafted up and drifted downstream, watching the scenery glide past us, over grown slopes, steep banks, low gravel bars, log piles and always watching for signs of wild life. After Reindeer Creek we crossed the central channel of the river to land for lunch at Mechem Creek. There was an unnamed wood camp here and had there been any gold, it would have been found.

We paddled back across the main channel to pass Indian River, just 29kms below Sixtymile River on the right hand bank. In 1894 Robert Henderson was grub staked (provided with supplies in return for a percentage of any future finds) by Joe Ladue on Ogilvie Island. He prospected for two years with poor results and crossed the King Solomon Dome which is the water divide between the Indian and the Klondike Rivers passing through Gold Bottom and Hunter Creeks.

He went back to Joe Ladue for more supplies and on his return, taking the same route up the Klondike, to cross over the Dome to get to his workings on Indian River, he met George Carmacks and had that fateful conversation before moving on. There were some rich finds made on the Indian River but either Henderson missed them or didn't recognise their potential.

Meanwhile, the extra paddling to cross the current had tired Rolf and Karen out and they were some distance behind, so we slowed down and rafted up. We had plenty of time so we didn't need to rush. It was a bright sunny afternoon and we took full advantage of it to lie back and enjoy the sun. Our next planned evening camp was on a small island immediately opposite Garner Creek. However the spring floods had been powerful and the island was considerably smaller than it had been last year and there was only a limited supply of wood; so we stopped on a gravel beach at the lower end of the island opposite Garner Creek on the other side of the river.

It wasn't such a good site as it was a gravel bank with no vegetation on it, with water on both sides between it and the two islands next to it. The spring floods had also altered this island which had cut it in two and we had landed on the gravel bank between them. There was a fast flowing wide channel to reach the upstream island. And whilst the downstream island was only three metres away, all its banks were steep and high, over three metres. There was a log jam, that if you were spritely with good balance, you could cross to the lower island but there was no point in attempting the crossing as there was no clear area to pitch a tent and little, if any, firewood. The gravel was fine for our individual tents but fixing the awning was a little more challenging, as the supports would sink into the loose gravel.

We rested the uprights on the paddles laid on the ground which worked but it's not a good solution, not good for the paddles which are essential for canoeing and it was too flimsy and rickety, if it was windy. We made do with drift wood for the fire but there would not be enough for other campers so Martin would have to investigate other sites for his next trip along this part of the river. A little disappointing for our last camp site on the river before reaching Dawson.

We set off for our final paddle into Dawson. There was no rush, as it is only 25kms to Dawson and there was little point in arriving too early. During the night the clouds had returned and it felt like rain. As we went down river there were more residences overlooking the river. There were fields and a golf course and it was obvious that there was a town nearby. Out of sight, behind a bend, was Dawson but we couldn't see it. But we knew it was there, as we could see Moosehide Slide, a great gash in the mountain behind Dawson, where the side of the mountain had slipped into the river. The bare rock is too steep and rocky to support any vegetation.

We stopped on a low gravel bar for a break and to fill in some time just outside Dawson City limits. The air was heavy with the smell of fire and ash, this time, being carried on the wind from fires burning in Alaska. Just as we tied up the canoes and walked to the centre of the gravel bar it started to rain. We looked at each other and decided to move on rather than get wet just minutes from our destination. After nearly three weeks of camping and paddling the Yukon we were finally at our destination in Dawson. After the last bend we reached the mouth of the Klondike River and crossed the river line, where the clear waters of the Klondike flow into the muddy waters of the Yukon.

We could see the town from the river, the Governors House just behind the levee that protects the town, the Canadian Bank of Commerce, built in 1901 in the Renaissance Revival style in decorative pressed metal where Robert Service worked and wrote the first few of his many popular poems. Next is the SS Keno, a lovingly restored sternwheeler and one of only three still in existence sitting high on the bank and lastly the Klondike Spirit, a replica sternwheeler that takes tourists along the river. Then we turned and landed at the town landing stage and we had reached our final destination. We unloaded the canoes, beached them on the side and gathered together for the inevitable group photo.

CHAPTER 15

Dawson City

Dawson City was created when Joe Ladue sought to make a profit from newly arriving prospectors to the Klondike. Joseph Ladue was born 28th July 1855 in New York State and had found employment in a gold mine, in South Dakota. He quit this job and went prospecting throughout America and finally, in 1882, he crossed the Chilkoot Pass and did some prospecting but also set up a trading post on Ogilvie Island.

It is certain that he had definitely traded with Robert Henderson and George Carmack. On discovery of the Klondike gold finds, he moved his base of operations from Ogilvie Island to a swampy flat area just below where the Klondike River joined the Yukon River. He staked out 72 hectares of the mud flats and laid out the grid plan for the new town. He established a store, the first saloon, and together with Harper, moved their sawmill to the new town. Hedging his bets for wealth creation, he also staked several claims.

There was a local settlement in the same area not far from the site. The local NWMP Superintendent Charles Constantine moved all of its native inhabitants nearly 5kms further away from their original site to the new location. The new white settlement was finally named Dawson City, after the director of Canada's Geographical Survey, Dr William Dawson by William Ogilvie himself.

Over winter, Dawson had a population of about 500 but by 1897, there were 5,000 and a NWMP post was established. Luxury items were available but at vastly inflated prices. There was often a food shortage, especially of fresh food and it is estimated that 2,000 people suffered from scurvy.

By the spring of 1898, the population had started to swell to more than an estimated 30,000, as prospectors continued to arrive from all over the world. There was no sewage system and no formal water supply and the roads were churned up mud. The area reeked of human effluent and in summer, it was plagued by flies, mosquitoes and typhoid.

Flat land was in short supply and the best plots changed hands for huge premiums, from which, Joe Ladue prospered. The town developed outlying communities as new arrivals looked for alternative locations away from the overcrowded infested downtown areas. Joe Ladue left Dawson and married Anna 'Kitty' Mason on 15th December 1897, but he was to eventually die of tuberculosis in Schuyler Falls in New York State 120kms south of Montreal on 27th June 1901.

Fire was a constant peril, from both natural causes and man-made causes. Buildings were heated by wood fired stoves and light was provided by oil fuelled lamps or candles. Several fires broke out and destroyed multiple buildings, especially as there was no formal fire brigade and at times, no water to fight the fire, as in winter the water was frozen solid.

However, unlike at Skagway, Dawson was generally a law abiding town and the NWMP made sure that law and order was maintained. In 1898, Colonel Sam Steele exercised control over the town and was known as a stern disciplinarian. In that year, there were only 150 arrests for serious offences, half for sexual offences. The officers were generally regarded as efficient and incorruptible law enforcers. The civilian authorities however were regarded with less enthusiasm on matters concerning claim management. This attitude was much improved after the summer of 1898, with the appointment of William Ogilvie, born 7th April 1846 and already aged 52 years old on this appointment.

He surveyed the town with an aim to establish some form of order, for the booming mining town. He had been a surveyor and had surveyed the area before the gold rush started. He had been on the same expedition as George Dawson to map the Yukon in the 1880s, surveying the Chilkoot Pass and the Porcupine River. He was part of the operation that established the border with Alaska as the 141st meridian west. He had hired George Carmack as a guide, for one of those surveying trips and Skookum Jim as a porter. He was the Yukon's second commissioner but retired due to ill health in 1901.

In the spring of 1898, the Bank of British North America opened operating from a tent but there was no assay equipment until the Bank of Commerce opened in the autumn. They later moved to a permanent structure up a road leading from the waterfront although the structure seen today is a replacement for the one that was burnt down in a fire that also destroyed several other buildings, including the post office in October 1898. The replacement post office had also been restored with period features and wonderfully maintained by the Parks Canada Service. Letters were intermittent, due to the difficulties of travel in the winter months but the NWMP did their best to keep the mail flowing.

There was no post office initially in Dawson, until the NWMP set up an office in October 1897 which was taken over by post office staff in 1899. Another problem, was the long distances involved and the absurd situation that post was sent through Dawson down to Circle City and then distributed back up the river to Dawson, so time delays stretched into months. Post had to be collected in person so people would have to queue for sometimes days to pick up their post, but this at least gave some people employment to stand in the queue for more wealthy miners, who could afford to pay someone else to queue, whilst they continued to mine their claim.

Letters were a form of news but there were also newspaper printers, eager to deliver news and some were never far behind the prospectors. Gene Kelly, the editor of the Klondike Nugget arrived first, but without his printing press, so it was the Midnight Sun who produced the first daily paper in Dawson. This was shortly followed by the third daily paper, the Dawson Miner and later, another paper opened.

By 1902, Dawson was a functioning city with government buildings, a library, courthouse, schools, four newspapers and several churches. A brewery had started up well before that in 1898 and there were numerous bars, shops and hotels.

There is plenty to see and do in Dawson and a trip along the water front is a must. The first sight going upriver, from our landing spot, is the SS Keno.

My guide was Marie Anne who showed me around in full period costume. It was built by the British Yukon Navigation Co in 1922 to transport silver, zinc and lead ore from the mines around Mayo 290kms along the narrow, winding and shallow Stewart River from its confluence with the Yukon River. It could carry 78 passengers and was specifically designed to navigate the difficult Stewart River conditions.

She is a bit less than 40m long by 9m wide with a draft of under a metre (the SS Klondike in contrast in Whitehorse was 64m x 12.5m and a draft of 1.5m). This was the sternwheeler that used the boiler and some other equipment from the SS Evelyn that I had seen at Hootalinqua. Operations ceased in 1951 when the Klondike Highway was completed and became the preferred transport option with all sternwheeler operations ending completely in 1955.

In 1959, the ship was donated to the government, it was repaired and sailed from Whitehorse to Dawson, under its own power on 25th August 1960, being the last stern wheeler to navigate the river under her own power. A new bridge had been completed at Carmacks but had not been made high enough to allow sternwheelers to navigate underneath it, so the wheelhouse and funnel had to be removed in order to allow the vessel to pass under the bridge. She arrived three days later and was winched up the bank to become a museum and tourist attraction.

The ore was transported in 57kg sacks and man handled on and off the ships. In 1938, she transported 8,165 tons of ore over the short summer steaming season. When the Keno reached the main river, the cargo of ore was unloaded to be transferred onto larger sternwheelers and she returned up the Stewart River with mining supplies and food to collect her next load of ore.

Upstream took three days but the journey down could be completed in just 12 hours. Following the destruction of the SS Whitehorse and SS Casca by fire in 1974 and the SS Tutshi in Carcross, also by fire in 1990, the Keno is only one of three of the more than 250 original sternwheelers operating in the gold rush era to survive in good condition.

Right next door is the sadly neglected frame of the building occupied by the Canadian Bank of Commerce, built in 1901 in the Renaissance Revival style in decorative pressed metal. It was here that Robert Service worked and wrote the first few of his many popular poems.

His cabin has been preserved and is on the edge of town. Robert William Service was born 16th January 1874 and was a British born Canadian poet and writer, often referred to as the poet of the Yukon and widely regarded. Some of his more notable and humorous poems such as 'The Shooting of Dan McGrew' or 'The Cremation of Sam McGee' made him seem to be a veteran of the gold rush and not a late arriving bank clerk that he actually was. He became widely known and associated with the Klondike. His poems didn't attain any literary credit from critics at the time, but they were popular with the public and many are still in print today.

Robert Service was born in Preston, Lancashire, and the eldest of ten children. His father, who was also named Robert Service, was a banker, originally from Kilwinning, Scotland. When the younger Robert Service was five years old, he was sent to live with three maiden aunts and his paternal grandfather, who was a post master in Kilwinning. It is claimed that his first poem was composed when he was six years old;

God bless the cakes and bless the jam
Bless the cheese and the cold boiled ham
Bless the scones that Aunt Jeannie makes
And save us all from bellyaches. Amen

Not exactly a masterpiece, but it shows that he had a talent from a young age. Aged nine he re-joined his parents who had since moved to Glasgow. On leaving school, he joined the Commerce Bank of Scotland which later would finally evolve into one of the constituent parts of the Royal Bank of Scotland. In 1895, when he was 21 years old, he travelled to Vancouver Island, British Colombia with dreams of becoming a cowboy. He drifted between California and British Colombia, doing a number of jobs and sometimes begging or borrowing from former neighbours who had emigrated from Scotland to Canada.

In 1899, whilst working as a store clerk in Cowichan Bay on the east coast of Vancouver Island, 40kms north of Victoria, he mentioned to a customer that he wrote poems. That customer was Charles Gibbons who was the editor of the Victoria Daily Colonist who eventually published six of Robert Service's poems by July 1900. In 1903 Robert Service was hired by the Canadian Bank of Commerce and was soon promoted to the Kamloops branch on the mainland. In the autumn of 1904, the bank posted him to Whitehorse and he followed the route of many prospectors, travelling up the coast by boat, then taking the WP&YR train to Whitehorse.

The initial gold rush was over, with many of the hopeful miners moving on to other areas in the hope of staking a claim. But there were still prospectors in the area and there was still traffic on the river. Whitehorse had grown into a small town and although smaller than at its heyday, with a mass of tents, the inhabitants still needed banking facilities.

He was active in the social life of the town and recited poems at gatherings such as 'Casey at the Bat' and 'Gunga Din', to entertain, so he was familiar with poems and public performances. One of his compatriots was Elmer J 'Stroller' White. He was born in 1859 and so was middle aged when he left Washington State to join the gold rush. He was a character and a lifelong and keen newspaper man. He had reported on the story of Soapy Smith, for the Skagway Times.

He had been in Dawson where he published 'The Stroller' and hence his nickname. By 1904 he had moved south to Whitehorse to be editor of the Whitehorse Star. It was he who suggested and encouraged Robert Service to write a poem for the paper on something about their lives in the north.

Robert Service was inspired one Saturday evening, whilst passing a saloon where there was some noisy revelry underway and the phrase 'A bunch of boys were whooping it up' sprang into his mind and he hurried back to the bank, nearly being shot by a guard in a case of mistaken identity as an intruder but by the next morning 'The Shooting of Sam McGee' was complete.

Just a month later, he heard a gold rush story of a prospector who cremated his fellow prospector. He spent the night walking in the forest and by morning, 'The Cremation of Sam McGee' was laid out in his head and he wrote it down the next day. The Miles Canyon inspired 'The Call of The Wild' and other poems followed, often inspired by stories he heard from prospectors and travellers, some of which may not have actually happened.

When he had enough poems, he sent them to his father, who had since immigrated to Canada and was living in Toronto, with a request to find a publisher together with a cheque to cover the cost of printing. His idea was to give the book away as presents but the publisher was so impressed with them that he returned the cheque and offered a 10 % royalty on all copies sold. There were multiple reprints and the 'Songs of a Sourdough' was reprinted seven times before its official release date and 15 reprints in total, in 1907 alone. Robert Service became a well-known name.

After three years in the Yukon, he was given three months compulsory paid leave and went to Vancouver, where he looked up an earlier old flame Constance MacLean. Now that he was a successful author, she agreed to his proposal of marriage. On his return northwards he was re-assigned to Dawson so it was 1908, a decade after the start of the gold rush that Robert Service finally arrived in the gold rush town of Dawson with which he is most associated with.

He listened to the sourdoughs and remembered many of their stories which inspired him to write more poems and these were published as 'Ballards of a Cheechako' in 1908 which was another instant success. A 'chechako' was a slang expression referring to newcomers to the Yukon similar to terms such as a tenderfoot or greenhorn. This was in contrast to the term 'sourdough' which was applied to people who had lived in the Yukon for several seasons. These were typically prospectors who knew that normal yeast would not survive the cold winters in the Yukon and hence baked sourdough bread, often starting from a mixture of dough kept on a leather thong around their necks next to their skin for warmth.

In 1909 the bank wanted Robert Service to return to Whitehorse as its branch manager. But he had fallen in love with the Yukon wilderness and the stories of its hardened peoples. Now that he was a successful author, rather than move south, he resigned from the bank. He rented a small two room cabin on the outskirts of town on Eighth Avenue, from Mrs Edna Clarke to start his new life as an author. As per his earlier midnight roaming, he would wander the forests at night, constructing characters and storylines, sleep in till late and sometimes not leave the cabin for days on end. After five months of writing, he took the manuscript of his novel to a New York publisher and his first novel was another instant success.

Robert Service was able to afford to travel to Paris, the French Riviera, Hollywood and a host of places in between and returned to Dawson to write his third book of poetry 'Rhymes of a Rolling Stone' published in 1912. It is not known what happened between Robert Service and his lover Constance MacLean, as there are few records of this period but having a potential spouse who walks alone at night and sleeps during the day, is not a widely accepted practise of couples but it is known that she later married a surveyor and railway engineer, named Leroy Grant, in 1912 based in Prince Rupert on the northern coast of British Columbia.

Robert Service left Dawson forever in 1912 and became a correspondent for the Toronto Star during the Balkan Wars 1912–13 and moved to Paris until 1938, marrying Germaine Bourgoin. He joined up at the outbreak of the First World War, but was declined due to bad health. He served as an ambulance driver until his health deteriorated and he convalesced, writing a book of war poetry in memory of his brother, killed at the front. During the Second World War, he lived in California until after the war and moved back to France to live in Brittany. He died in Lancieux on the north shores of Brittany, not far to the west of Dinard near St Malo, on 11th September 1958 and is immortalised with a road named after him.

His cabin has been preserved by Parks Canada since 1971 and although it is small it is an interesting visit, especially if you know some of the background of the story behind the simple two room cabin. You are unable to enter but you can get a good view of the interior through the open windows and doors of the cabin. There is a stove, several period pots, kettles, snow shoes, a writing desk, a bed all under the roughhewn logs for walls and a turf roof. Tours of the cabin include some local history, some recitals and a walk in the forest along the same paths that he had walked to finish at a lookout above the town with views of the river.

Along the river front, behind the levee is the Commissioner's Residence mansion which was a large building that originally looked out over the river which is now partly obscured by the levee which protects the town from flooding. I met Marie Anne outside the building, wearing another period costume. I asked her about the costume and the staff are encouraged to dress in costume, to enhance the visitors experience but they have to provide the clothes themselves. They are not alone as there are volunteers who source clothes and dressmakers to adjust them. And to be true to the authenticity, the undergarments are also period. She was attractive and I was tempted to ask her to prove it but I didn't want a slap in the face.

The Commissioner's Residence was built in 1901, as proudly proclaimed under the apex of the roof, by which time the initial gold rush had nearly finished and civilisation was coming to the initially unruly prospectors tented encampment. The house is a typical example of late Victorian tastes and inside is a time capsule of furniture, objects d'art, carpets, tapestries and the like from the era.

Set back from the river is the Grand Palace Theatre, a superbly restored period theatre which from the outside looks great and on a guided tour you can enter and see inside. With another guide, Gabriella again in full period costume, I was ushered into the foyer and later into the stalls to be told stories of how the local prospectors would swap gold for tickets and favours to be lavishly entertained. There are flags of Great Britain and the United States and plenty of bunting to decorate the insides.

After the performance, the chairs could be stacked to one side and the premises turned into a dance hall. There were private boxes around the perimeter walls with a better view of the stage for the more discerning and bottles of champagne were available at astronomical prices. It is all set out as it would have been more than a hundred years ago.

There are plenty of anecdotes associated with the dance halls. Sam Bonnifield was a saloon owner and gambler, who made a fortune and was known as 'Square Sam', as he treated people fairly. He went on to follow the gold rush fever to Fairbanks and established the National Bank of Fairbanks, but disaster struck and he suffered a serious mental breakdown and was looked after by his family in Kansas.

Another story surrounds Kate Rothwell or 'Klondike Kate'. Born in 1873, she was a rebellious character and fetched up in Whitehorse as a dancer. She moved to Dawson, working for the Savoy Theatrical Co. Her act was very popular with the prospectors and she gained fame. She also met her lover, Alexander Pantages, but they went their separate ways and he was to go on to make his name in theatres and movies. With the decline of the gold rush, Kate moved away from the goldfields to British Columbia.

The large amounts of gold being dug up, encouraged conspicuous consumption amongst the prospectors, who felt that they had plenty more where the original few flakes, colours or flour of gold had come from. Saloons were open 24 hours a day, whisky was the standard drink and gambling was endemic. The saloons had their own gambling dens in private rooms and there were plenty of enthusiastic prospectors, out for a good time and equally willing card sharps and the like, to milk them of their gold. It was the custom to scrape and coerce the gold out of the gravel and alluvial deposits and spend it lavishly on entertainment. And all the saloons and dance halls were lavishly decorated, to justify the high prices that they charged.

At the top of the Grand Palace theatre, is the bedroom and make up room for the chief artiste performing on the stage which was a long way below. Sometimes, they were attracted by the outlandish wages on offer to entertain the prospectors but several of them came in the remote hope of meeting a rich man who had made it big.

Next door to the Grand Palace, was a non-descript and unassuming wooden building but on its side was painted a verse from Robert Service's poem 'The Spell of the Yukon' which is one of his most quoted. It read;

I wanted the gold and I sought it:
I scrabbled and mucked like a slave.
Was it famine or scurvy – I fought it:
I hurled my youth into a grave.
I wanted the gold and I got it–
Came out with a fortune last fall:
Yet somehow life's not what I thought
And somehow the gold isn't all.

Some distance away, is the Red Feather Saloon, another well preserved relic from the gold rush era, restored to exactly how it would have looked, more than a hundred years ago. There are bottles behind the bar, a long polished mahogany bar top and you could just imagine shots of whisky being slid down the length of the bar, to waiting customers at the far end as in all the best western films.

There were other stories of entrepreneurs making money from both new arrivals and those who struck it rich. The price of supplies rocketed, due to shortage of supply and rising demand. Even in late 1897, the NWMP evacuated some prospectors to Fort Yukon in Alaska and others moved out of Dawson in search of supplies and shelter for the winter. Prices rocketed over the winter and the rush for fresh produce in the spring, kept prices high as prospectors who had money or gold, could bid ever higher prices for the few goods available for sale.

Whilst walking through town and some of the less visited areas, there are some of the older buildings listing at a crazy angle, whilst some of those that were level had been raised up on blocks at the corners. The ground is permafrost and melts in the summer and so its load bearing qualities vary with the speed of thawing and re-freezing at different times of the year. Therefore, the astute Yukon homeowner, needs to constantly readjust the blocks on which his house stands in order to keep it level. Those buildings not in continual habitation or under the Parks Canada auspices therefore suffer from this freeze-thaw annual event and end up cantering at unusual angles without remedial action being taken.

That evening, I had a special outing to Diamond Tooth Gerties Gambling Hall. This was a large building without windows set well back from the river frontage. Not much happens during the day but it livens up in the evening and it gives a sense of what was happening in countless bars and back room gambling dens a century ago. There is a cabaret show that has several sessions throughout the evening, each one differently themed and on this particular evening, the building was heaving.

I had not seen many people around town but this was a special evening. There was a poker competition under way and many of the participants most have been relaxing during the day in their rooms awaiting the big event. This evening they were all in Diamond Gerties playing their games to try and win the accolade that was on offer.

The cabaret came on and the poker players continued playing. I was so overly enthusiastic in my whooping and clapping for the high kicking can-can showgirls and comedians that I was pulled up on stage to pose for photos and as part of the audience participation. I reflected that I must have been over enthusiastic, as it was out of character for me to be the willing participant to play the part of the willing spectator, to get up on stage and be made a fool of. I would not be doing so much clapping and whooping next time, at any pantomime or whatever the occasion may be.

The poker players were quietly playing on throughout the acts with stern expressionless faces. Some were gaming for huge pots and bidding for ever higher stakes and others had to throw their cards in as that night was not their night. There were house watchers to make sure that none of the players were getting help from stooges in the audience or in the balconies. Meanwhile we were enjoying ourselves, the show and the spectacle of people betting high stakes in games of poker, bluffing and double bluffing.

In a lull in the cabaret, we each got a text from the hotel. If you want to see the northern lights, you can leave your details with the hotel reception and if you are asleep or otherwise busy, they can text you that the lights are visible. That evening, the conditions were just right and the eerie glow of green light which was pulsating across the sky was visible. We left Diamond Tooth Gerties Gambling Hall to find a darker area away from the rare street light or other light from bars and hotels cascading into the street to get a better view of the northern lights.

We walked to the river's edge and lay down on the grass, to stare up at the sky to observe the dancing coloured spectacle of the northern lights, pulsating across the sky. The lights are called the aurora borealis and are caused by the collision of energetic charged particles from the solar wind that is ejected from the sun by coronial ejections. These particles are directed by the earth's magnetic field into the atmosphere at the poles and are named after the Roman goddess of dawn Aurora and the Greek name for the north wind Boreas (in the southern hemisphere the lights are called the aurora australis or southern lights).

The lights we saw were green, dancing across the sky. I had seen them as a nineteen year old in northern Norway, but in my naivety as a teenager I had not realised their significance nor their rarity but it took more than another two decades to see them again and appreciate their uniqueness. We watched for ages until the cold seeped into our bones and having taken some photos we retired to the hotel. The photos that we had taken did no justice to the spectacle that we had just witnessed, but would live on in our memories as a spectacular natural light show. And I never did find out the result of the poker competition.

CHAPTER 16

Gold Panning

Go up the Yukon River just a short distance and you reach the mouth of the Klondike River, where it flows into the main river. A road follows the river valley up the first section of the river and ultimately to Whitehorse. Branching off to the right is a dirt track and this leads to Hunter Creek and the Gold Bottom Mine and an area that Robert Henderson is known to have travelled through. I had had a share in a gold claim outside Dawson, but it was not a commercial success and the claim had lapsed. The mine I was visiting today had been set up by Len Miller, decades ago but it is still a family owned and operated mine, now being worked by his grandson and they have a total of seventy claims in the area.

Today this is a quiet wooded little valley with just one building which was a wooden roadhouse and where a lot of artefacts are stored. In its heyday there were 5,000 people living and working here. From pictures on the walls there was a mass of tents to live in and some that provided basic services, stores, bars and the like and it even boasted a hospital and two doctors. Noticeably, there were no trees as they were all cut down for fire wood or stripped off to give access to the gold bearing gravels.

The room was set up as if the owners had just left, but with the living area given over to displays of a few of the more important items. These included gold scales, bullets, lanterns, cutlery and other metal items recovered from the area. There was a telegraph machine and mastodon teeth, bones and ivory … one of the few legal sources of ivory. These are found in the permafrost and are owned by the government and when they are found they are carefully put to one side. A palaeologist periodically comes and inspects them and takes the more interesting pieces but the rest stay on site.

The permafrost starts about a metre below the surface and can extend more than sixty metres down to bedrock. It has stayed frozen since the last ice age but once defrosted, it never refreezes and only the surface thaws and refreezes each season. This was a serious impediment to the early miners.

Originally, mining knowledge allowed two options for miners to get to the gold bearing gravels. One was hydraulic mining, where water under pressure washed the soil and gravel into sluices and to separators to capture the heavier gold particles as it passes over riffles or slots across the line of flow. The Romans had used low pressure water and in the 1849 California gold rush, prospectors had used high pressures water jets, so this was simple and familiar technology.

The other option was using a dredge to dig up the soils and gravels and process them in a similar manner to capture the gold. Dams were built with a mass of pipes to provide water and this method was effective but needed lots of water and could only be used near the valley bottom as large pumps and a lot of energy would be needed to get water higher up the hill and these weren't available. Also, this method only worked in summer, as the water froze in winter. Prospectors on claims higher up the hill used a slower process using rockers. This was a box suspended from a frame and with the help of just a little water, to assist separation, and shaken to get the gold to settle to the bottom. But these water based operations were only on a small scale.

The problem was, that both methods required heavy equipment and power which the early prospectors didn't have and neither got over the problem of permafrost. Instead, the first prospectors were eager to get to their gold built fires to melt the permafrost down to perhaps 30cms. Then the gravels could be dug out and another fire built, until the required depth was reached.

This wasn't very successful as it used a lot of wood and the radiated heat melted the sides of the pit which collapsed. The marsh gas formed from rotten vegetation and frozen in the ground would either be released and spread noxious fumes or suddenly burn or explode. In the very cold winter weather the wet gravels would freeze again and couldn't be processed until they thawed out in the warmer summer weather allowed them to be processed.

Claims were standardised at an early stage. The centre line is fixed along the river and a claim can be 1,000 feet long and 250 feet to either side of the centre line. A discovery claim can be twice the size, if you are the first to lodge a claim. A bench claim up the side of a valley is 1,000 by 500 feet. Claimants only receive title to the mineral rights but the ground is still government owned. For instance they could insist on you moving a cabin for a road.

Claimants can stake their claim as already mentioned and have ten days (it has been longer in the past) to register their claim. They need to check the Mining Record map which is on public view and if no other valid claim has been registered, they pay Canadian $10 to register and also a Canadian $2,000 fee for a permit to mine. In return, the claimant gets two metal plates that details their claim to fix to a post to confirm a valid claim. Claimants must be over eighteen years old but can be any nationality.

Before an area was properly surveyed, claims would be made and recorded. When the area was properly surveyed, there were often inexactitudes between the reality and the theoretical location of claims. Hence, there could be disputes of over lapping claims and equally bits of unclaimed land resulting in a bonanza for lawyers, but usually the theoretical post survey claim was the recognised legal claim.

There was also a trade in claims for various reasons. One saying that came to be used was never buy a claim from a Chinaman. Even worked claims may have missed some gold or the gold bearing gravels were too deep to access, without heavy equipment. But the Chinese had a reputation for being hard working and thorough and had usually stripped every ounce of gold from a claim, hence there was no value in buying one of their worked claims.

There is an annual fee of Canadian $200 per claim, if the claimant works his claim otherwise it is classed as abandoned and can be claimed by someone else. There is an upper cap of Canadian $2,000, thus an encouragement to amalgamate claims for economy. Needless to say, there are rules on what counts as 'work' on a claim. This is based on the amount of dirt moved which is 300cu yds. With modern machinery, this is relatively easy using a bulldozer pulling a ripping tooth to loosen the ground, ready to be dug up and carted away. Early panners had to put in a lot of effort to move this amount of dirt by hand but have to only meet a lower volume equivalent to a pile 6 x 6 x 4 ft but that is still a lot of gravel to pan your way through.

Early miners used a variety of methods against the permafrost, including lighting fires and later more sophisticated methods of using boilers to produce steam. But this all involved extra time and cost in cutting down yet more trees to cart them long distances to where the mine was located.

The gold bearing gravels lie beneath an overburden of other material locally called muck. At this spot there is four metres of muck before you reach the pay dirt or the gold bearing gravels. Bulldozers are expensive so a cheaper method is often employed. The face being mined is exposed and allowed to defrost. Then it is removed by using jets of water to wash it away. This exposes a stretch of gravel at the base of the frozen muck above. The gravels are removed and the frozen face of the muck left to defrost naturally to repeat the process.

The gold bearing gravels are poured into a trommel, a modern sluice box. It has a central channel with lateral angle iron riffles and either side is expanded metal, under which, traditional miners used coconut matting but Astroturf is just as good. All that is required, is copious amounts of water, gravity and agitation. The water rushes across the trommel taking the gravels with it. The agitation assists the separation with the lighter material being washed over and the heavier gold falling into and being caught in the Astroturf.

The process works as gold is nineteen times heavier than water. The other heavy material caught is magnetite which is eleven times heavier than water, plus the inevitable bits of other rock. The mats are periodically taken off and the captured material is removed and dried.

The dried material is then sieved through fine and ever finer meshes. The first sieve captures the nuggets, the second coarse flakes, the third fine flakes and left at the bottom is dust. The magnetite can be removed by using a magnet. The last part of the process uses a gold wheel. This is a wheel with a spiral groove running from the outside, into the centre. It is rotated at an angle and water gently poured over it, to assist separation. The lighter material is washed away and the heavier gold tumbles around in the groove until it reaches the centre and has had all the other pieces of rock removed.

The gold found here is not pure gold but is about 80 % gold with 18 % silver and 2 % of other heavy metals. The gold is heated up with borax to remove impurities and cast into ingots. Then these are taken to the gold buyer and assayed for purity. A small sample is retained, as proof of purity, of the host in case of future disagreement over the purity.

For early miners, selling the gold was the end of the mining process but modern miners have additional responsibilities. They have a responsibility to reclaim the land that they have just extracted their gold from. They must rebuild the contours of the land and put back any roads. Planting is not necessary, as the forest will regenerate naturally.

Water used to strip the muck, must go through settling ponds, to filter out the mud and silts. This is used to mix with the top layer of processed gravels to give plants a chance to grow in some soil. Most rivers downstream are also spawning grounds for fish so there is an additional reason to capture mud and silt and it is relatively successful as fish still spawn below working mines.

Then it was my turn to pan after a demonstration from an expert. To ensure my technique was just right, I took my boots and socks off and stood barefoot in the cold water in the middle of the stream. I loaded the pan by scooping handfuls of gravel from the river bed. After washing and removing the larger rocks and after a lot of agitation, the heavier gold sinks to the bottom and the waste gravel can be swirled off the edge of the pan. In the crease at the bottom of the pan, the heavier material collects and can be inspected by eye.

Amongst the fine material in the bottom of the pan, were just four tiny specks. I filled a glass vial with water, and with a wet finger, picked up each speck and carefully placed the speck on the end of my finger over the glass vial and by inverting it, the water washed the speck from my finger into the bottom of the glass vial.

I filled up the pan again and repeated the process. From then on, I didn't notice the rough riverbed on the soles of my naked feet nor the cold water. I just loaded my pan again and again for those few tiny specks of gold in the bottom of the pan. I was lost in my own little world for the rest of the afternoon. Eventually, it was it was time to go. Panning real gold bearing gravels is so much more rewarding than the hap hazard prospecting that I had carried out on my canoe trip to reach Dawson.

I realised that it was time to go. Most reluctantly, I had to get out of the stream and put the pan down. I dried my numbed feet and put my walking boots on. I was delighted with my success and my biggest flake was the size of a pinhead … almost a nugget! My few grams of gold would not make me a millionaire, but with a gold price peaking at over $1,700 an ounce, in 2011, I had nearly $80 of gold in just an afternoon, but it was hard back breaking work.

At the other end of the mining scale are monster machines. After 1905, the easiest gold had been extracted by the artisan miners and with an increase in the gold price, big business started taking over, buying up claims or more often forcing people to sell. With wealthy backers such as the Rothschild and Guggenheim families and access to finance they were able to invest in heavy equipment and finally the dredgers moved in. One of these stands some distance out of town and up Bonanza Creek is Dredge Number 4. This is a bucket line dredge standing eight storeys high with a long bucket line at the front and a long conveyor belt boom at the back. I was met by Gabriella who on this day wasn't wearing period costume but a smart Parks Canada uniform.

This particular dredge was built in 1912. It was designed and built in Ohio and then stripped down and the parts freighted to Vancouver, up the coast and using the WP&YR over the pass to Whitehorse and down the Yukon by sternwheeler. Some parts were too large for the tunnels and deep winding cuttings on the pass and were freighted to St Michael on the mouth of the Yukon and carried up the river.

Together with many other dredges, these monsters changed the way that gold was extracted. Gone were the individual prospector with gold pans and sluices and in came big business with big investments. These big dredges were more cost efficient than traditional mining methods at moving huge amounts of gravel and extracting the gold and could dig deeper than artisan miners could easily achieve. More gold could be extracted and some earlier tailings could be economically reprocessed. It started at the bottom of the creek and worked its way up.

The dredge would sit in its own lake, formed by digging out the river bottom and building a dam across the river behind itself. It needed just four feet of water, under 1.5m. The bucket line could dredge up the gravels and process the gravels in the same way as a prospectors sluice box with the gravels rinsed with lots of water and the heavier gold particles being caught in riffles and coconut matting but only on a much more massive scale. The waste rock was taken by the conveyor and dumped on the dam behind the dredge.

There were two spuds or long legs that were lowered onto the bed of the lake to increase stability and two anchors fixed to the ground upstream of the dredge that held it hard against the gravels. By readjusting the spuds and pulling and slackening the lines between the anchors and the dredge, the bucket line could be moved across the face of the gravel. As the gravel is processed, the dredge moves slowly forward upstream and the tailings dumped out of the back, continually build up the dam behind the dredge.

The dredges would operate 24 hours a day for the season that would start in late April or May and continue perhaps up to November, when the ground would become too frozen to continue. Progress was slow and it might move just one kilometre up the valley in a season.

When operating, there was a tremendous amount of noise and the dredges could be heard operating all the way back to the centre of town. By now the town had its own electricity supply, generated by water from a dam 80kms up the Klondike River and the first city to have hydroelectric power.

This also provided the power to operate the dredges. Despite its size and weight, it needed just half a dozen people on board to operate. There was a temporary increase when the coconut matting needed to be replaced, but this was done quickly by teams of twelve working on one section at a time so as not to interrupt operations. There were many more people working on land to clear the forest upstream of the dredge ready for processing and to move the anchors when needed.

Recorded thefts were few and we may never know whether any were successful. The twelve man team to change the coconut matting had two over seers and guards to ensure no misappropriation. The processing the coconut matting and storage of the gold flakes before melting were where two incidences occurred.

One theft attempt was made by a worker who filled his bicycle tyres with gold dust. Suspicions were aroused when it was too heavy to cycle and he had a problem holding it upright. Another man had worked all season, but decided to leave work the week before the end of the season and therefore, miss out on his terminal bonus. He had packed the internal linings of his fridge with gold and when he came to remove all his possessions it took four men to lift the fridge even though it appeared to be empty.

CHAPTER 17

Sourtoe cocktails

Whilst walking around the town I wandered down the road to one of the two small corner shops in Dawson. I was interested in checking the prices and whilst prices in Whitehorse were higher than Vancouver, up in Dawson, they were even higher and the vegetables and fruit looked a little tired, old and very expensive. I made do with a bar of chocolate.

I met up with some of my fellow paddlers and we walked up the road to one of the few restaurants that hadn't shut for the season called Klondike Kate's named after Kate Rothwell. Several of the items on the menu, were not available so I ended up having chicken quesadilla although like many things in the Yukon, everything seemed expensive. We were the only people in the restaurant and after we left, they closed for the evening.

We went back to the bar in the Downtown Hotel. They have a Dawson tradition and a challenge of drinking a Sourtoe Cocktail. The Sourtoe is a real human toe that has been dehydrated and preserved in salt. The original Sourtoe Cocktail was established in 1973.The original rule was for the toe to be placed in a beer glass full of champagne but that rule has been relaxed and any drink can be substituted for the champagne, but there has been no relaxation of the requirement that the toe must touch the drinker's lips.

The drinker must sign the book with his name and address. The toe is taken out of its box of salt behind the bar and any surplus salt brushed off. The challenger must wear a river captain's hat (also now relaxed) and before drinking his choice of drink, with the toe in the bottom, the on lookers chant;

"You can drink it fast
You can drink it slow
But the lips
Must touch the toe."

My chosen beverage was whisky. I was the last of the three men in the group willing to have a go to try the challenge and by this time, the toe was sticky and had stuck to the bottom of the glass. I had to tap the bottom to get the toe to touch my lips. It made no difference to the taste of the drink, except that it is a bit gross when you think about it and a bit salty. So if you are going to have a go, I suggest that you don't think about it. My first certificate to show that I had met the challenge is numbered 43,554.

The origin is said to have been a dare between two river captains. One particular Captain Dick or 'Captain River Rat', was always bragging. Another captain knew a prospector that had got frostbite on his toe and as it became gangrenous, he had to cut it off and he pickled it in a jar. It was this toe that was dropped in the River Rats' drink and he was challenged to drink it, which of course he did and the Sourtoe Cocktail was born. There have been several different toes over the years, as some were lost or kept as keepsakes but there are several toes to act as reserves from donors who wish to keep the tradition alive. There is now a hefty fine of Canadian $2,500, if the toe is swallowed.

The next morning, we were to leave Dawson, so it was going to be an early start. We packed our bags, loaded up the pickup with our luggage and hooked up the trailer with the canoes. Our first stop was the garage to get petrol and check the tyre pressures. Pumping the air in was easy but the tyre pressure gauge was broken, so we had to guess the correct pressure.

Our guide drove out of town, along the Klondike Highway up the Klondike River past the tailings and the airport and soon we were in forest without any other sign of humans. We had only driven a short distance, when we had a flat and we pulled over to the side of the road. We tried the spare but that was also flat, so we drove slowly to a garage on the corner of The Klondike and the Dempster Highways, with a sign that said that this was the last garage until Whitehorse over 500kms away.

We waited whilst the mechanics got the tyre repaired. There was a small cafe but that was all. A large lorry pulling a trailer passed the garage and turned onto the Dempster Highway throwing up great clouds of dust from the unpaved road. There was no other traffic, as we waited for the half hour or so for the repair to be made. We checked the pressures of all the tyres, including the spare with an air pressure gauge that appeared to work and then we set off again. It was a long drive but making an unscheduled stop also cost us time, so it was going to be an even longer day.

After an hour, the scenery was unchanging with rolling hills, some darker green pine trees contrasting against the leaves of the deciduous trees, mostly birch, which were turning an array of browns and yellows of autumn. Late morning we stopped at a road side cafe at Moose Creek consisting of a few log cabins on the side of the road run by a Swiss couple. It was a beautiful sunny day but we all wore fleeces against the chill. Inside, there was a log fire that made the cafe very snug.

A river crossing makes a change from the endless forest. We crossed a bridge over the Stewart River at a place unimaginatively named Stewart Crossing and soon we were back in the forest. Next, we crossed another bridge over the Pelly River at a place equally unimaginatively named Pelly Crossing and after another hour or so we were soon back alongside the Yukon River. We stopped for lunch, overlooking the Five Fingers Rapids to gaze at the rapids that we had run many days earlier. A little later, we crossed the Yukon River at Carmacks and pulled into a supermarket, to stretch our legs. At the Coalmine campground we stopped to have some hot food.

Finally, we made it to Whitehorse. I took a flight to Calgary and from there I would transfer to another flight back home. As I sat on the plane, I reflected on the trip and however much fun you might have, after a long time away from home, it was nice to be getting back home.

I had at last completed my journey, following in the footsteps of those early prospectors, the Klondikers, to their goal at Dawson to pan for gold. In my top pocket was my own little souvenir of my gold panning experience and a number of gold flakes, in a small glass vial. That small amount would never make me rich but it was a great experience and rich in memories.

CHAPTER 18

What happened to ...?

The fate of Soapy Smith has already been revealed, as it was such an integral part of the story of Skagway. He had never actually been a prospector or panned for gold but made his money by swindling hopeful prospectors as they made their way to the goldfields.

Robert Henderson was the prospector who had suggested to George Carmack to pan Rabbit Creek. He was born in 1857, so he was already middle aged by the time of the gold rush. His refusal to trade tobacco cost him very dearly. He had staked several claims but the law had changed whilst he was out prospecting.

When he came to record his three staked claims, his application was refused. Only one claim could be registered and there was a strict time deadline between staking and registering a claim of 60 days. The registrar refused to accept the claims and Robert Henderson was out of luck. After all his hard work, he had nothing to show. By the end of the gold rush, he was working as an assistant to the government mining engineer and died poor in 1933, probably very embittered.

Frederick Schwatka, was the bold young man that happily and irrepressibly renamed a whole host of Canadian landmarks. He ignored local names and named places after people he admired. There were so many people that he admired I wonder whether he had brought along a book of famous people for he seemed to know a large number of assorted dignitaries. He died on 2nd November 1892 nine years after completing his journey down the Yukon and long before the gold rush. He was still young, he died at age 43 years old, in Portland, Oregon. He died from an overdose of morphine but it is not clear whether it was accidental or whether suicide was intended.

And what happened to the original discoverers of those gold flakes in Rabbit Creek on 16th August 1896? George Carmack and Kate left the Yukon and settled in California. Kate had been with George for 12 years in her native forest in the Yukon and had trouble adjusting to her new westernised regimented life and developed an alcohol addiction.

George deserted his native wife Kate in 1900 and moved to Seattle where he married Marguerite Laimee. They had a twelve room, white frame house and Marguerite was quite an astute business woman, she invested her husband's money in real estate, apartments, offices and hotels. But George never lost his thirst for gold and continued to prospect with claims in Sierra Nevada and the Cascade Mountains. He died in 1922, aged 62, whilst he was working on a new claim.

George's native wife Kate attempted to gain alimony but was unsuccessful. She was disheartened by the slow process and her lack of money to pay legal fees, to pursue the claim. In 1901, she returned north to live in Carcross in a cabin built by her brother, Skookum Jim. She lived in obscurity there, helping out in the mission and residential school run by Bishop Bompas and died there 29th March, 1920 in a flu epidemic aged around 58 (there is some doubt regarding her exact birthday as this was not recorded but native stories suggest sometime in 1862).

Skookum Jim, had first worked as a packer working on the Chilkoot Pass where he obtained his nickname 'Skookum' meaning strong or reliable, in the local language. With his wealth, he built a grand house in Carcross but he struggled with alcohol addiction and in 1905, set up a trust to guard himself against wasting his wealth and to provide an income for himself, his family and his local community.

He continued to prospect for gold in summer and returned to a more native life of hunting and fishing. He suffered in later life, from poor health and after a long illness, he died in Carcross, 11th July 1916, aged about 61 years old (again there is uncertainty over his birthday but I have chosen 1855 but some non-contemporary records suggest 1859 or 1860).

Dawson Charlie was born sometime in the 1860's and there is even less certainty about his actual birthday. In contemporary accounts, he is referred to as Tagish Charlie, but there was another Tagish Charlie and so to differentiate between the two, he is called Dawson Charlie after his association with the gold find in Rabbit Creek, near the town that was to become Dawson. With some of his wealth, he bought the Caribou Hotel in Carcross. He married and had two children but his wife couldn't adjust to the new life style and Charlie's alcohol addiction. He died on 26th December 1908, when probably under the influence of alcohol, he was walking across the WP&YR railway bridge and fell off into the Nares River and drowned.

The lure of gold was never satiated and even some of those that were rich did not hang onto their wealth and died in poverty. Alex McDonald was one of the early arrivals. He had tried prospecting unsuccessfully in Colorado and Juneau before in his forties he arrived in the Yukon and bought up land for the Alaska Commercial Co at Forty Mile where gold was eventually discovered there in 1897. He bought a share of Claim 30 on Eldorado Creek from a Russian named Zarnowsky for a side of bacon and a sack of flour.

This turned out to be a great gold bearing mine and he leased it to two other miners for half of the proceeds. With his initial success, he bought up other claims and mines and became very wealthy. He was the largest land owner and employer and donated to worthy causes such as a hospital and a church. He had several nicknames, Big Alex, Big Mac and King of the Klondike. Despite the gold rush moving on to other areas, he continued to buy up land ever hopeful of cashing in on the next find there but squandered his money. On his death in 1909, from a heart attack at the age of 50, his debts exceeded his assets.

Another early arrival was Antoine Stander, who also had a share of one of the most productive claims on Eldorado Creek. He also made and lost a fortune, he drunk and dissipated his fortune and ended up working in a ship's galley, to make a living.

Swiftwater Bill Gates didn't marry Gussie Lamore whom he had tried to tempt by offering her the equivalent of her weight in gold. Besides which, she was already married. Several other wives followed and he was still married when he married again, so he continued to be a multiple bigamist. He ended up in Peru, still searching for gold but was murdered there on 21st February 1937, no doubt over an argument about a woman.

William Ogilvie, the surveyor, became the second commissioner for the Yukon 1898–1901 until retiring due to ill health. He left the Yukon shortly afterwards and on the journey home down the Yukon, met Miss O P Richardson. The small boat they were using to transfer to the ocean going ship capsized and he saved her from drowning. They were married on 15th April 1903 in Texas. He returned to the Yukon annually, for the summer dredging seasons 1908–1912 as president of the Yukon Gold Dredging Company on its Stewart River leases.

The Ogilvie Mountains, the Ogilvie River, the Ogilvie valley and the Ogilvie aerodrome are all named after him in his honour and several were named after him during his lifetime. Amongst his several publications, his last book, 'Early Days of the Yukon' was published in 1913, but he never saw it in print as he died 13th November 1912, in Winnipeg, aged 66.

Jack London, the author who coined the phrase the 'Dead Horse Trail' to describe the Chilkoot Trail, reached the goldfields but suffered from scurvy, giving him constant pain in his hip and leg muscles, losing his four front teeth and leaving a facial disfigurement. He returned to San Francisco in 1898 and started his writing career with books, short stories and articles in magazines.

He was married for a short time and had two daughters before being a war correspondent during the Russo Japanese war in 1904. On his return, he married again and bought a ranch which was not a commercial success. He had become an alcoholic, he had dysentery and uremia, a kidney disease and took morphine to relieve his constant pain. He died on his ranch on 22nd November 1916, possibly of an accidental overdose.

The newspaperman Elmer J 'Stroller' White ended up in Whitehorse in 1904 as editor of the Whitehorse Star having worked on the Klondike Nugget in Dawson City, before publishing his own paper, 'The Stroller'. He was around to record all the goings on of its inhabitants and had given Robert Service encouragement and a platform for his poems to be aired to the public. He owned newspapers in Whitehorse, plus Douglas and Juneau but sold the paper in 1916 and died in 1930, at the age of 71 years old, still writing articles for newspapers on his reflections of the gold rush.

Kate Rothwell or Klondike Kate had left for British Columbia and finally settled in Seattle where she died in 1957. The restaurant in Dawson, still called Klondike Kates, has expanded into renting out cabins. It claims to have been in business since 1904 which I have no reason to doubt, but given that running a restaurant is hard work and she was looking for adventure, I doubt that she had anything to do with its establishment and running, other than an enterprising business-man, borrowing a popular name to promote his business.

Martha Louise Munger made a success of her sawmill and ore crushing plant businesses in Dawson. In 1904, she married her second husband, George Black, originally a prospector but becoming a politician in later life, acting as the Commissioner of the Yukon 1912–16. In 1935 she campaigned for the federal election often campaigning on foot, throughout the Yukon and was elected as an Independent Conservative.

She was the second woman ever to be elected to the Canadian Parliament. She was made a Fellow of the Royal Geographical Society following a series of lectures on the Yukon and in 1946 she was made an Officer of the Order of the British Empire for her services to the Yukon. She published her autobiography 'My Seventy Years' in 1938, which was updated and re-published in 1998 as 'Martha Black; Her Story from the Dawson Gold Fields to the House of Commons of Canada'. She died on 31st October 1957, aged 89 years old, in Whitehorse.

Dawson at the height of the gold rush had a population of over 30,000 crammed into the main town site and the surrounding tent camps. Unlike Soapy Smith's fake telegraph in Skagway, the real thing arrived in Dawson stretching from Skagway in 1899. The WP&YR finally opened in 1900 making the journey much easier to reach Whitehorse and the Chilkoot Pass trail, the aerial ropeways and tramways were all made redundant.

Many people were unable to make a living, after arriving in Dawson and soon left. The surplus of labour depressed prices for those that stayed on. Dawson became a more conservative run of the mill town albeit still miles from anywhere else. Discoveries of gold elsewhere, attracted many prospectors and hopefuls who were still keen for adventure and to stake their claim and become rich. There were plenty of alternatives nearby, such as finds as at Atlin Lake, in August 1898, or at Nome at the mouth of the Yukon the following year.

By 1907 the population had shrunk and some areas of the town were deserted away from Front Street facing the river. There were piles of rubbish and abandoned mining equipment littering the deserted areas. By 1912, there were only 2,000 people left and even today the population is put at about 1,300 but with the proviso that many leave to avoid the harsh winters and the actual permanent population over winter may be half that.

Dawson today survives on tourism, attracting over 60,000 visitors annually and despite producing over 570 tons of gold, since the initial discovery, there is still a small gold mining industry, for those brave diehard prospectors who still work their claims.

Author's note

The trip as described was not undertaken as a single trip but was in fact, the amalgamation of several trips, taken several seasons apart. Also, the story as told was not experienced as told and some sections were travelled in reverse order. The astute reader will note that I didn't explain how I got from Vancouver to Juneau and that is partly because these were separate trips at different times.

I reached Juneau by flying to Whitehorse and on to Carcross by bus, then taking the heritage train from Carcross over the White Pass to Skagway. I took the Fjordland Express catamaran from Skagway to Juneau where the narrative journey to the goldfields continues from Juneau back to Skagway. In the interests of trying to make the story follow the journey, as faithfully as possible to what the Klondiker hopeful prospector might have experienced, I had to tell that part of the story in reverse order.

In order to get from Skagway back to Whitehorse, I had to take a coach along the Klondike Highway, that doesn't follow the route that the Klondikers would have followed as it diverts east past the shore line of part of Tutshi Lake before crossing a watershed and following the shoreline of Nares Lake, before reaching Carcross.

Equally, in reality, I had descended the Yukon River by canoe and had then met up with a contact in the hotel in Whitehorse for the trek over the Chilkoot Pass. In the interest of the storyline, I decided to insert the trek across the pass before the descent of the Yukon River to Dawson in order to maintain the rhythm of the story of the Klondikers.

There were many other people in the groups that I travelled with on my various trips. But in the interests of keeping the number of names to a manageable number, I have had to exclude some names and characters and I would like to express my thanks to them for their contribution and apologise that they may not have got their names in to print.

Similarly, some of the events attributed to individuals were actually properly attributable to other unnamed individuals that wouldn't appear in any other part of the narrative. Again, in order to avoid too many names I have attributed them to one of the names that do appear in the narrative or are mentioned but without a specific name. But the event was so memorable that I couldn't not use the story. My apologies for both inaccurate naming and to omissions of people who were with the group but do not appear by name.

Anecdotes

People who spend the whole year in the Yukon are hardy souls and have a certain notoriety. They have a certain characteristic that can be summarised as typically male, unshaven with a love of the outdoors, hunting and self-reliance. There are women who enjoy the lifestyle, but the work is mainly hard graft around panning for gold, hunting caribou and moose, cutting wood for fuel for the long winters or paddling along rivers for hours, just to get to see a neighbour for a chat over coffee.

Outside the main towns there is no mains electricity, no mains water, no public sewage system and the only gas available is from a gas tank. The winters are long and harsh with extreme temperatures and biting winds with the weather so bad that there is nothing that you can do outside for weeks on end. You have just your own company with possibly no internet, no television and no telephone.

You really are alone. There are bears and wolves in the woods and none of the usual support structures nearby of doctors, pharmacists, police, local councillors, pub or local corner shop and in such a remote environment you need to be self-reliant, adaptable, capable, have an ability to be independent come what may and to be confident in yourself. And in order to keep your sanity you also need a certain sense of eternal optimism.

During the summer season, there are direct flights from Frankfurt to Whitehorse in order to service the great demand from German tourists, who long for a taste of the wild which is the country of origin of the largest number of non-North American tourists.

I heard several jokes, whilst I was in the Yukon and here are a few one liners;

You know you're a Yukoner when …
- … your snow plough has more miles on it than your car
- … you owe more on your snow plough than on your car
- … you know what square tyres are
- … you have fallen off the roof trying to remove snow
- … you have spent two hours putting out Christmas lights on your house when it is minus 30°C
- … your car battery has a blanket
- … the temperature is minus 30°C and you can say it was warmer on the same day last year
- … minus 10°C in winter is a warm day
- … you put more chlorine in your water supply when you see what's melting out of the snow
- … there are four seasons, summer, hunting, winter and dog poo
- … there are four seasons, nearly winter, winter, still winter and construction
- … you think that your host is inconsiderate if he doesn't have a Styrofoam toilet seat in the outhouse
- … driving in winter is better than the summer as the snow fills in the potholes
- … you put your coat on to go to the toilet
- … it is socially acceptable to have shotguns mounted on your walls provided they are not loaded
- … it is normal to find shotguns cartridges in your jeans before putting them in the wash
- … you are not sure whether to load a slug for bears or 40 gauge buckshot for mosquitoes
- … you take a shotgun with you to go to the shops
- … you kitchen doubles as an abattoir several times a year for moose meat
- … you have forgotten how to use a razor
- … you faint at the cheapness of goods in Vancouver
- … you faint at the sight of so much bare skin on the beaches in Acapulco
- … you always clean the barbeque after every use so as not to attract bears

- … you are surprised to discover that the start of the hunting season is not a bank holiday
- … you are delighted to be able to grow something other than fireweed in your garden
- … you can greet everyone you meet in the street by their first name
- … the mayor greets you using your first name
- … when canoeing you are greeted with 'Guten tag'
- … there are piles of bear rugs and antlers around the house
- … the children always wear snowsuits under their Hallowe'en outfits
- … the local paper has one page of international news and ten on local news and sport
- … you can play ice hockey outside your front door for six months of the year
- … the back seat of the car is covered with jump leads, shotgun cartridges and extra coats

The author

Norman Handy was born in 1957 in Beckenham, Kent in the South East of England. He went to school in Beckenham and later went to boarding school in Cranbrook, Kent. He studied Business Economics and Accountancy plus Law for Accountants at Southampton University.

During his studies, he also travelled and after finishing university travelled and worked abroad. He returned to the United Kingdom and after some time working in a riding school, followed a career for thirty years in the financial services sector in London, including periods working overseas.

He has two children and is a keen horse rider, walker and skier and of course writer! He spends his time between his home in West Sussex and travelling.

novum 📕 PUBLISHER FOR NEW AUTHORS

The publisher

> *He who stops being better stops being good.*

This is the motto of novum publishing, and our focus is on finding new manuscripts, publishing them and offering long-term support to the authors.
Our publishing house was founded in 1997, and since then it has become THE expert for new authors and has won numerous awards.

Our editorial team will peruse each manuscript within a few weeks free of charge and without obligation.

You will find more information about
novum publishing and our books on the internet:

w w w . n o v u m - p u b l i s h i n g . c o . u k

Norman Handy

Overlanding the Silk Road

ISBN 978-3-99048-708-2
354 Pages

Overlanding the Silk Road is a real page turner, taking you on journeys you never thought you'd go on! From London to places like Kyrgyzstan, known as Asia's little Switzerland. Sit back and enjoy the beautiful scenery and experiences this book will take you on.

novum PUBLISHER FOR NEW AUTHORS

Norman Handy
K2, The Savage Mountain

ISBN 978-3-99048-716-7
262 Pages

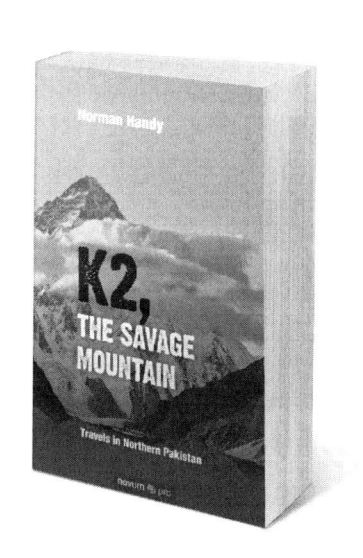

Strap yourself in for this one as you're in for quite a ride! This is the story of one man's travels in northern Pakistan. The final challenge comes for the ascent to the base camp of K2, the world's most deadly of mountains. A definite must read!

Rate this book on our website!

www.novum-publishing.co.uk